MIMESIS
INTERNATIONAL

CINEMA
n. 2

I0018473

INTERACTIVE FICTION IN CINEMATIC VIRTUAL REALITY

Towards the Interactive Immersive Movie

by
María Cecilia Reyes

MIMESIS
INTERNATIONAL

This book is published with the support of the School of Humanities of the University of Genoa.

TABLE OF CONTENTS

To those who have left their prints in the labyrinth, to show us the way.

LIST OF ILLUSTRATIONS

LIST OF TABLES

LIST OF ABBREVIATIONS

AI	Artificial Intelligence
ANS	Autonomous Nervous System
AR	Augmented Reality
BCI	Brain Computer Interface
cVR	Cinematic Virtual Reality
CG	Computer Graphics
CVE	Cinematic Virtual Environment
DoF	Degrees of Freedom
DOP	Director of Photography
ECG	Electrocardiography
EEG	Electroencephalography
EDA	Electrodermal Activity
EMG	Electromyography
HCI	Human-Computer Interface
HF	Hypertext Fiction
HCD	Human-centred design
HMD	Head Mounted Display
HRV	Heart Rate Variability
KAS	Capacitive Sensors
IDN	Interactive Digital Narrative
IDS	Interactive Digital Storytelling
ID	Interactive Drama
IF	Interactive Fiction
IFcVR	Interactive Fiction in Cinematic Virtual Reality
IMU	Inertial Measurement Unit
IR	Infrared
IV	Interactive Video
LED	Light Emitting Diode
MR	Mixed Reality

NG	Narrative Games
NLP	Natural Language Processing
NU	Narrative Unit
NT	Narrator Type
PPG	Photoplethysmography
SKT	Skin Temperature
UCD	User-centred Design
UI	User Interface
UX	User Experience
VE	Virtual Environment
VR	Virtual Reality
Webdoc	Web Documentary

ACKNOWLEDGMENTS

My professional and artistic career has unfolded across various domains, including journalism, radio, writing, video production, and web-based projects. Among these pursuits, filmmaking has been the most challenging and rewarding. What captivates me about this medium is its innate ability to convey a narrative in a way that aligns seamlessly with human cognition, as Christian Metz argued films are, in essence, stories that we "read" almost instinctively. It was this fascination with the cinematic experience that led me to delve into the realm of Virtual Reality (VR) and explore the convergence of hyper textuality, virtual reality, and fictional storytelling in a mediatic graft: Interactive Fiction in Cinematic VR (IFcVR).

Both Jenkins and Manovich expressed a shared sentiment regarding the early days of cinema—a desire for more systematic documentation of the advancements that shaped cinema as we know it today. This sentiment resonates with VR (and extended reality in general) media scholars and practitioners today, as we navigate an ever-evolving landscape where changes in mass communication theory and research occur at a rapid and often unpredictable pace (Bryant & Miron, 2004). In this context, my objective aligns with the aspiration voiced by Jenkins and Manovich: to document the process of crafting a cinematic experience that transcends the traditional notion of a movie as a fixed, unchangeable entity, transforming it into a dynamic process that extends beyond the author to involve the audience.

When I embarked on the exploration of IFcVR, my initial vision was to create an immersive experience where participants were not merely passive observers in a live-action virtual environment but active participants in the narrative. At first, it appeared to be an evolution of cinema itself. However, after delving deeper into this research, it became clear that IFcVR represents an independent artistic and narrative form, distinct from traditional cinema. Despite this uniqueness, traces of the cinematic experience endure, albeit in a transformed state, prompting us to reconsider the very essence of what it means for a work to be "cinematic."

This book is the culmination of my doctoral research[1], conducted in a double-degree program between Digital Humanities at the University of Genoa in Italy and Communication at Universidad del Norte in Barranquilla, Colombia, and its publication was granted by the School of Humanities of the University of Genova. The convergence of these disciplines allowed me to approach Interactive Fiction in Cinematic Virtual Reality from a kaleidoscopic perspective, as Janet Murray emphasized in her keynote presentation at ICIDS 2018. My work was further enriched during my residency at Akademie Schloss Solitude in Stuttgart, Germany, and gained further momentum during my study period at the Future Media Theatre Lab residency at the University of Skövde in Sweden.

During my time in Skövde, I had the opportunity of sharing my research with filmmakers at the Gothenburg Film Studios. This experience revealed a pressing need for disseminating knowledge about interactive immersive filmmaking. Filmmakers from traditional backgrounds are looking for guidance on how to enter this new realm, while technologists working with immersive technologies need insights from the humanities and earlier art forms to infuse depth into their immersive experiences.

While words can never fully express my gratitude, I wish to extend my heartfelt appreciation to those who contributed to my journey in creating this book. I owe a debt of gratitude to Giuliana Dettori, a researcher par excellence in the field of narrative learning, who has guided me with care from the early stages of my career, offering support and assisting with the editing of this book. My professors at the University of Genoa, Sergio Poli, Giovanni Adorni, Maurizia Migliorini, Fabrizio Bracco, have been constant pillars of support, especially Elisa Bricco. At Universidad del

---

1   As the result of a doctoral research, some of the concepts here presented have been published in journal articles and conference papers.

Norte, my advisor Toby Miller provided invaluable insights into media, culture, and life, while professors Jesús Arroyave, Alfredo Sabbagh, and Alejandro Navia ignited my passion for communication studies. The insights, support, and constructive criticism from my academic community have been instrumental in my growth as a scholar. I extend my thanks to Rebecca Rouse, Hartmut Koenitz, Claudia Silva, Jim Pope, Chris Hales, Agnes Bakk, Alejandro Angel Torres, Christian Roth, Valeria Piras, Andrew David Miller my student Clara Machacon Rodelo, and Josh Fisher who honors me with the foreword of this volume.

I would also like to extend my appreciation to the team of friends and artists who collaborated on the production of ZENA, the first immersive interactive film shot in Genoa. Especially, Serena Zampolli, Lorenzo Caviglia, Eduardo Lozada Cabruja, Massimo Frattarolo, and Maestro Piero Ponzo, who played essential roles in bringing this project to life.

JOSHUA A. FISHER
FOREWORD

Since 2015, Virtual Reality's resurgence has rekindled our fascination with immersive media. Interactive VR, constructed from 3D models and game development engines, captivated human-computer interaction specialists and the digital narrative community. Trailblazers like Oculus Story Studio and Baobab Studios ventured into this realm, offering glimpses into the transformative potential of VR interactive fiction. Simultaneously, cinematic Virtual Reality (cVR) or 360° video attracted many film enthusiasts, from scholars to students. Collectively, we could imagine escaping the confines of a rectangular frame to embrace the entirety of a sphere. The Lumiere brothers' train no longer remains static on a screen; viewers can perceive its movement, turning to watch it zoom past. This spatial and dimensional freedom amplifies the immersive magic of cVR.

Yet, challenges arose. cVR advocates grappled with arguments about the medium's interactivity, especially compared to VR's game engine counterparts. Further, they had to contend with the essential relationship between interactivity, immersion, and sense of presence. Audiences yearned for more—a desire to influence the narrative, to perhaps change the train's direction. In this landscape without guidelines, media pioneers eagerly experimented, seeking to combine the interactivity of VR fiction with cinematic languages and forms to develop grammars and direction. Among them stands María Cecilia Reyes—an international artist and scholar who teaches at the Universidad del Norte in Colombia. In this book, María equips readers with a comprehensive guide to Interactive Fiction in Cinematic Virtual Reality (IFcVR), synthesizing theory and practice to give form to the discipline.

At the 10th International Conference of Interactive Digital Storytelling in Madeira, 2017, I had the privilege of meeting María. With her presentation on ZENA—a case study discussed in this book—she sparked the intellectual curiosity of attendees. At the time, I held reservations about cVR, often doubting its proponents' claims of the medium's ability to foster empathy and understanding. It was the early days for cVR, and hyperbolic showpeople and cynical critics were everywhere. However, María's approach was compelling.

Avoiding the conventional stance—held by many, myself included—that merely deciding one's focus in a 360-degree environment constituted interactivity, María envisioned something more complex. She proposed a system where interactors could navigate 360° videos through the same systems as interactive fiction. She suggested that viewers could traverse pathways between these scenes through active or passive interactions to forge a genuine dialogue between the narrative world and the interactor. This perspective, to me, epitomized interactivity in cVR. María's idea underscored how dramatic agency could evolve cVR into the IFcVR format.

The domain of cVR is rich and accessible, drawing in diverse audiences, from practitioners to scholars and eager students. While plenty of industry manuals, blogs, and articles delve into individual experiments with the medium, no definitive guide exists on conceiving, crafting, and circulating IFcVR experiences. This gap can be attributed to the form's novelty and intricate nature, drawing from vast fields such as cinema, performance, perceptual psychology, game design and development, narrative, interactive digital narrative, user experience design, and human-computer interaction. It requires the perspective of someone like María, who has worked across and through multiple media, to draw together the necessary insights to lay out the challenges, in both theory and practice, for IFcVR.

María offers readers a robust foundation in this book, equipping them with the historical and theoretical knowledge required to navigate the IFcVR landscape, from the nuances of development, where cinematic professionals will learn the mechanics of interactive systems, to the production intricacies where María expertly navigates challenges in scripting and storyboarding. When discussing post-production, she doesn't just discuss editing for cVR but delves into the art of editing for true interactivity. This harmonious blend of traditional cinematic methods with emergent interactive narrative practices is groundbreaking. Such a synthesis is rare and invaluable to anyone entering the space. Critically, the book ends by providing us with tools for evaluation. As IFcVR develops, such tools validate scholars' and practitioners' insights. Further, they help us understand audience reactions and will help the emergent IFcVR grammars mature.

The history of immersive cinema is both vast and complex. It's a confluence of disciplines, technologies, and rich media legacies that have converged over millennia. Begin at the dimly lit caverns of France, where the ancient cave paintings resonate as the earliest form of immersive storytelling, akin to the awe-inspiring grandeur of cathedrals. These primeval art forms, the definition of immersive for their epoch, bridge to innovations like Robert Baker's 18th-century Panorama—a landmark in spherical imagery. As time progressed, even the Lumiere brothers, in the 1930s, unveiled panoramic projection screens, setting the stage for cinematic innovations like the 1950s Cinerama and the iconic IMAX. By 1967, Radúz Činčera's *Kinoautomat* (1967) heralded the age of interactive cinema.

The advent of accessible computing widened horizons: visionaries like Gunpei Yoko, Hideo Kojima, and Bob Bejan melded cinematic fiction with interactivity. By the 90s, the medium evolved, with adventure games employing filmic cut scenes. The new millennium saw a cinematic renaissance, from the innovative *Switching* (2003) and complex *Late Fragment* (2007) to the layers of *Her Story* (2015) and *Bandersnatch* (2019). In 2015, the Oculus Story Studio began experimenting with linear, non-interactive cVR as did practitioners such as Chris Milk and Gabo Arora. Since then, practitioners and scholars like María have been seeking to synthesize the theory and practices of interactive cinema to those of interactive VR.

Interactive narrative, cinema, and storytelling perpetually evolve to take advantage of new technological and media affordances. As a result, traditional narrative structures undergo metamorphosis, urging the birth of new languages and practices. Scholars like Janet Murray, Marie-Laure Ryan, Scott Rettberg, and Hartmut Koenitz have brilliantly illuminated how interactivity and new media recalibrate our narrative compass. María's work seeks to do the same at a new crossroads of VR, cinema, and IDN to prepare scholars and practitioners to create and discuss IFcVR. In this domain, filmmakers must master the art of guiding a viewer's gaze in a vast, frameless expanse. Scriptwriters face the exhilarating challenge of engaging interactors who might pivot from the central narrative, forging unique storylines. Cinematographers and set designers, meanwhile, must craft visually and aurally rich environments that ignite curiosity, prompting moments for dramatic agency.

As María points out in the first chapter, cinema practitioners are no longer creating work for an audience sitting and watching; they are designing for an active human in the center of everything. Practitioners can no longer rely on authorial control—they must be open to multiplicity and opportunity. The pressing and exciting challenge for today's practitioners isn't just about crafting fiction in VR cinema—it's about orchestrating spatial cinematic experiences where every interaction propels the fiction. And therein lies the transformative and immersive power of IFcVR.

Scholars and practitioners can explore this representative power to tell stories in new and exciting ways with this book. Using focalization, point of view, narrative density, and other mechanics discussed by María, practitioners can create opportunities for interactors better to understand a subject, space, or identity. Kaleidoscopic narratives offering fluid perspectives become more achievable when an interactor can move between positionalities.

The integration of IDN systems and game mechanics further transforms the cVR landscape. No longer just passive recipients of a story, interactors can now steer its direction. A lingering gaze at an artifact, a hotspot, might seamlessly transition the viewer to a new narrative unit, amplifying the depth of their experience. The potential infusion of generative AI extends this dynamic, fostering an evolving interplay between the interactor and the IFcVR storyworld. Beyond these technical innovations lies an uncharted terrain of creative potential. From reimagining classical cinematic tools like montage within the realm of IFcVR to crafting novel transition methods through hotspots, a canvas of creativity beckons. Storytellers now find themselves on the cusp of a narrative frontier teeming with opportunities and challenges.

The realization of IFcVR signifies more than just a leap in cinematic storytelling; it heralds a transformative wave across various domains. María's work, exemplified by ZENA, unveils the potential of urban landscapes as narrative labyrinths, and one can envision adventures unfurling in cities worldwide, each weaving unique grammars and interactive patterns. Beyond cinematic narratives, the techniques elucidated in this book hold immense promise for realms like education, therapy, and documentary. Especially for institutions on a tighter budget, the allure of 360° cinema presents a cost-effective alternative to intricate virtual environment development.

I urge readers to immerse themselves deeply in the rich insights of this book. In doing so, you equip yourself with the tools for the future of IFcVR and position yourself as a pioneer in this emerging domain. The horizon is vast, and the promise is genuinely exhilarating.

Lastly, I would like to thank María for giving me this opportunity to write this foreword. The book is the culmination of many years of work and is truly impressive. I have no doubt that it is the beginning of an exciting new chapter in the world of storytelling.

INTRODUCTION

Since its inception, the emergence of the digital environment has seduced artists and writers to tell stories and transmit their perceptions of the world through a medium whose coding allows the convergence of different types of languages and artistic forms under a single content that needs the interaction of the receiver to be decoded. This interaction of the receiver with the artwork changes the logic of the fixed output (Koenitz, 2017), putting such a process at the core of the aesthetic experience. Hypertext, hypermedia, multimedia, or cyber art are some terms that refer to digital artistic content that exposes its components for the interactor to organize into a linear experience, forced by the linearity of time itself. This authorial desire to expose ideas, narratives, and perceptions of the world in small pieces, explicitly and without apparent organization, is not new. Although digital coding opened the doors for both author and receiver to access the artistic work through the same interface, already in literature, theatre, and film some authors created interactive narratives in analogical ways. In each medium, these interactive narratives have different structures, different ways of interacting and arranging the components of the artistic text, and different levels of interaction for the user. All, however, share the same spirit: to free the narrative from the single read.

For authors, extracting from our minds what we want to express is not an easy task. Inside us, the message is present as a chaos of words, images, colors, shapes, and signs that need a syntax and a code to be transmitted, and only when we are seated in front of paper, canvas, or a blank screen we can begin the hard process of expressing the content conjoining substance and form. The advent of the computer allows authors to centralize in a single device, yet separately, their digitally encoded ideas in different formats. Rapidly, the computer acquired two facets in the artistic act: creating and manifesting. The creation process or the assembly of the components is done through the computer, then the computer itself performs the artwork, and finally, the narrative is re-created by the interactors when tracing their path in the multimodal textual forest that reflects the mind of the author.

The author creates an apparently chaotic and unordered universe, whose components are connected, and it is in these connections, especially in their multiplicity, that meaning resides: the experience lies in the navigation alternatives. In contrast, the generation of meaning rises from the connections that we find between apparently disconnected contents. "Great narrative is an invitation to problem finding, not a lesson in problem-solving. It is deeply about the plight, about the road rather than about the inn to which it leads." (Bruner, 2003, p. 20). Ted Nelson, in his book Literary Machines, warns us that the hypertext is not "another type" of dark structure, but the reunification and reorganization of various types of electronic texts. Nowadays the internet has allowed this reunification to be decoded by a user sitting in front of a terminal in any part of the world, then re-coded by himself, this time as an author, and uploaded to the cloud so that the cycle reoccurs countless times.

The hypertext, which can be easily implemented by means of electronic tools, allows a nonsequential organizational structure of the content (Nelson, 1987, p. 15). This content can be narrative or non-narrative, fictional or not. This is how Hyperfiction or Interactive Fiction (IF) was born. In the same way, the digital medium allows the development and proliferation of interactive audiovisual narratives, such as Interactive Video (IV), the Web Documentary (Webdoc), or Narrative Games (NG). More complex narrative systems have also emerged, such as Interactive Drama (ID) (Szilas, 1999). These interactive digital narratives are run by Artificial Intelligence (AI) based systems and transmitted by a wide variety of interfaces. This type of narrative is known as Intelligent Narrative Technologies (INT) (Riedl & Bulitko, 2012). Computer-mediated narratives have been known as Interactive Digital Storytelling (IDS) or simply Interactive Storytelling (IS) for many years. However, as Nick Montfort notes in his introduction of the volume Interactive Digital Narrative: History, Theory and Practice (Koenitz et al, 2017), the most important theorists in the field have opted, in recent years, to coin the term Interactive Digital Narratives (IDN) to embrace a vast spectrum of art forms and technologies.

One of the technologies that, during the last century, has tried to achieve the human dream of creating and living new realities is Virtual Reality (VR). VR takes human cognition away from the materiality of physical reality to transfer it to a computer-mediated time-space that does not replace physical reality but is a reality of its own, by connecting the user's senses to a digital environment. VR, as a medium, offers new possibilities to all types of human activities (social, educational, artistic, communicative) within a *neo-reality* (Diodato, 2005) that concerns the experiential dimension of the human being. In March 2015, Chris Milk defined VR as "the ultimate medium, since, while in other media the consciousness interprets the medium, in VR the consciousness is the medium. As a primarily audiovisual medium, VR takes a step further in the rupture of the fourth wall, by totally encapsulating the cognitive capacity of the interactor through sound and image, while technological development works in connecting user's emotions and movements to the *neoreality*.

In this way, VR, unlike other media, looks for a type of communication that goes from conscience to conscience, in Jaron Lanier's words "a post-symbolic communication" (2010). We are no longer talking about telling stories or transmitting speeches, but about creating multisensory experiences. We are getting closer, from the creation point of view to the construction of artificial experiences which are real in appearance. Until now, only through altered states of consciousness and sleep (not a coincidence that Google named one of its VR companies "Daydream") we have been able to attenuate, almost until it's fading, the line between physical reality and cognitive reality. However, through VR this could change fading to merging between both realities is a fact: the more time we spend in a virtual environment (VE) proposed by a creator, the more organic and natural it gets to our brain; the more realistic its interface, the greater the immersion and smaller the disbelief; the more advanced the technology, the better the graphic and auditory representation, the faster and smarter will be the interaction with the VE and its agents, as possible the full-body immersion (Sra & Schmandt, 2015).

From its very beginning, VR has aroused a strong inter and transdisciplinary interest that looks for the understanding of the medium, its language, its forms of production and reproduction, and its applications in various fields. However, unlike radio, film, television, or the internet, the general public has not been able to adopt and manipulate the medium, even though VR has been just around the corner for more than 60 years, thus what we know about users' uses and gratifications of VR is truly very little. Since 2010, with the decrease in the cost of VR tools for production and reproduction, the mass market has been able to access a technology that was exclusively available to a few laboratories in the world.

The hype is largely due to all these facilities that we have today to create and enjoy VR experiences, but it is noteworthy that already in the 80's a good segment of researchers and computer scientists predicted the scope of VR as the next Information Technology (IT) platform that would replace sitting in front of a screen and a keyboard, in other words, a reality shift (Heim, 1993). It is undeniable that VR proposes an important paradigm shift, as within it the interface completely encloses our vision and hearing to the point that "we do not realize when we are trapped in our minds and cyber systems" (Heim, 1993, p. 80). For the authors of VR artifacts, this means transmitting not only their discourses but also their physical perception of reality. This transmission of reality needs a comprehension of the VR semiotic sign that transcends the complexity of the audiovisual sign, that is constituted by the combination of two types of discourse, visual and auditory (Hall, 1980), and opens to spatial perception, haptic stimulation, and interaction with the storyworld through different types of, conscious and unconscious, user's inputs in real-time. For the interactors, VR opens a door to other dimensions asking them to fully trust the author with their cognitive and perceptive sense of reality.

Accessing a medium with these characteristics brings us closer to the creation of artificial experiences that are woven by the oldest immersion form we know: storytelling. Artists, architects, writers, musicians, caricaturists, programmers, filmmakers, etc. have turned to experimenting with the plasticity of VR. In his book *Metaphysics of Virtual Reality* (1993), Michael Heim quotes Jim

Morrison to describe the scope to which a computer interface can reach on its way to truthfulness: "There may be a time when we will attend the Weather Theatre to recall the sensation of rain" (p. 82). Currently, the race for the XR market is moving into experimental territories with large doses of uncertainty. The entry of a colossus like Apple with a mixed reality headset, Meta's new developments in the construction of hyperrealistic avatars, and the promise of Microsoft Mesh, suggest a future that opts for mixed reality rather than virtual reality. However, knowing that the technology is in development and these limits will likely be soon overcome, the exploration of the medium capabilities should not be stopped, to further expand the frontiers of art and storytelling.

At the current rate of VR technology, the number of visual artists who experiment with the medium is steadily increasing. From the artistic creation point of view, a first crossroads arises in the creation of VEs through 3D or 2D CG or using "real images" through the acquisition of 2D or 3D 360º videos, also called Live Action. Naturally, the acquisition of 360º video has attracted special attention from those who come from the field of filmmaking. Switching from traditional video capture to 360º video involves a series of changes in all the stages of the production of a video/film project. From development to distribution, through pre-production and production, the filmmaker faces different challenges that arise mainly from the elimination of the frame. The frameless image seems to remove a relevant part of the author's control over the audiovisual work because the what-to-see and when-to-see are conceded to the interactor, threatening the traditional conception of the Director's role.

In the presence of a new medium, relying on known methodologies seems fair, borrowing concepts, dynamics, and structures that have been used in other artistic forms or consolidated media. Sergei Eisenstein (1977) points out that "cinema is not altogether without parents and without pedigree, without a past, without the traditions and rich cultural heritage of past epochs" (p. 232). In the same way, we cannot look at a new media or artistic form as an unrelated artifact. Cinema has its roots in literature, photography and theatre, television in film, and radio in theatre; during the twentieth century, the innovative structures proposed by cinema and new media managed to be re-mediated (Bolter & Grusin,

2000) on artistic forms with secular existences. The challenges and novelties that a new artistic text proposes need to be understood by defragmenting its nature, identifying the intermediations that are generated between the different ways of transmitting a story and the different ways of representing it (Chatman, 1980). The question of how to transmit and represent the story in an immersive and interactive medium as virtual reality arises.

Currently, on the different online video distribution platforms and VR stores, it is possible to find a high number of narrative projects made with 360º video, both documentary and fictional. While VR develops also as a field for research, various terms have been used to refer to recorded 360º video: Live Action VR, Surround Video, Immersive Video, Spatial Video, or 360º Video, among others. Although, the appearance of the 360º video as a tool to create VR experiences has generated controversy within the VR field. On one hand, VR purists maintain that 360º video is not properly VR, since the VE does not react to the user's interaction and it does not change while running the experience, emphasizing the limits of video as a fixed element. On the other hand, some claim that the capture of reality in 360º allows interactors to stand in existing places, increasing their level of immersion due to the naturalistic realism of the image. To address this issue, the term Cinematic Virtual Reality was coined to denominate VEs created with 360º live action video. By using this term, the 360º video is validated as a tool for the creation of VR experiences, and VR, in turn, upholds a connection with its cinematic roots, as contemporary VR can be seen as "still an experiment in a cinematic point of view" (Bolter & Grusin, 2000, p. 4).

cVR projects are mainly audiovisual contents whose duration does not generally exceed eight minutes. Although interactors have a certain level of autonomy within the cinematic VE (cVE) by choosing what they want to observe within the visual sphere, there are no other mechanisms that allow them a greater level of interaction with the cVE and therefore with the narrative text. The experience is limited to the sensation of immersion and to the possibility of visually exploring the cVE, yet interactors do not have interactive elements that enhance the experience or decisional power over the development of the story. The feeling of being immersed in the cVE contrasts then with the inability of the user to interact with the storyworld. The addition of interactive elements within a 360º video allows users to have a greater degree of interaction with the virtual experience and move the narrative forward (Vosmeer et al, 2015), although the virtual environment is still not modifiable. The creation, however, of an interactive structure, with links that connect different narrative units or story beats, and the incorporation of diverse multimedia materials inside the storyworld, can generate experiences with multiple navigation alternatives besides a high degree of realism, due to the recorded reality. The final output of an Interactive cVR (IcVR) experience relies on the user's individual process of choosing to *what-to-see* and *when-to-see* and having decisional power upon the development of the story within a storyworld rich in content and expression stimuli.

The fields of application of cVR experiences can be very varied, from journalism (Hopkins, 2017) to military applications (Lele, 2013; Rizzo, 2005). However, an important niche for Interactive cVR can also be found in documentaries or nonfiction (museum installations, interactive documentaries, guided visits to places of interest, and immersive learning, among others). Even though most of what is presented in this book can be applied to non-fictional experiences, this research focuses on the creation of fictional audiovisual narratives that are both immersive and interactive: the convergence between Interactive Fiction and Cinematic Virtual Reality (IFcVR) or in other words, Interactive Immersive Movies.

Towards the Interactive Immersive Movie

This book analyses the theory and practice behind the creation of an immersive and interactive film experience, comprising the aesthetics of cVR as well as the study of the narrative and interactive elements of IFcVR, approaching the IFcVR as an Interactive Digital Narrative (IDN). As far as practice is concerned, the production process and the evaluation of IFcVR have been analyzed through the realization of an immersive interactive film prototype called "ZENA".

The epistemological approach analyses the nature of IFcVR as a hybrid art form in which several components are noticed: the

aesthetics of the VR medium, the remediation of narratology into
the cinematic VR environment, and interactivity as an agent for
immersion, on both the narrative and Perceptual levels. The object of study then focuses on the fictional narrative. The analysis is based on two conceptual assumptions: (1) Interactive Cinematic Virtual Reality is an Interactive Digital Narrative (IDN) art form, and therefore can find a theoretical ground for its creation, practice, and assessment in IDN ontology, taxonomy, and frameworks; (2) IFcVR as a specific IDN art form must develop a medium-conscious narratology with its methods, techniques, and instruments. The epistemological approach is based on three theoretical axes: aesthetics, narratology, and interactivity.

Chapter 1 "The Human at the Centre of the Story World" regards the first theoretical axis: the change of aesthetic paradigm that VR proposes. The ultimate medium is the first macro area to be deconstructed, identifying its evolution and its current state, its characteristics as a medium and the changes that it generates in the communication process, wondering about the role of the author and the role of the user.

Chapter 2 "The Narrative Form of Cinematic Virtual Reality", comprises the narratological elements that characterise Cinematic VR. Through this macro area, the connection that exists between VR and its cinematographic aspect is developed, analyzing the processes of remediation that take place between VR and cinema, and in which underlie, simultaneously, concepts of classical narratology as Focalization, Point of View, and Narrative Density. In this chapter, the study focuses especially on the study of fiction narration, considering aspects such as dramatic progression and the creation of a Storyworld. This axis provides the theoretical basis for a screenwriting that is aware of the nature of the VR, taking into consideration the change of paradigms for the director, crew, actors, and scene management.

Chapter 3 "Interactive Fiction in Cinematic Virtual Reality" regards Interactivity. It seeks for the convergence between Cinematic VR, deconstructed and defined in the two preceding chapters, with Interactive Fiction. To achieve this theoretical convergence between narrative and media forms, the study starts from the evolution of the IF and its current state, differentiating it from other forms of IDN. Different narrative structures are studied, and some problems related to interactive storytelling are addressed, the consistency of the dramatic tension independent of user's choices, joining the discussion of the narrative structures on IDN and the need for a climax or several climaxes. As a hybrid genre, IFcVR generates a juxtaposition of various media and narrative forms: cinema is contained in virtual reality, and cVR is contained in interactive fiction. This juxtaposition generates various intersections that can be found in the convergence between the components of Interactivity, Cinema, Fiction, and VR. By analyzing these intersections, it is possible to set a methodological basis for the creation and assessment of Interactive VR Fiction Films.

- Interactivity + Fiction = Interactive Fiction
- Interactivity + Cinema = Interactive Cinema
- Interactivity + VR = Interactive VR Experiences
- Cinema + VR = Cinematic VR
- Fiction + Cinema = Fiction Film
- Fiction + VR = Fiction VR Storytelling

Chapters 4 and 5 explore the creative workflow of producing an IFcVR, from development to post-production. The computer-mediated nature of the IFcVR prototype is presented and uses as a basis the Protostory model for the design of an IDN. Regarding the IFcVR narrative design, I propose a specific framework for the screenwriting of the interactive script, based on Syd Field's (Field, 2005) cinematographic paradigm and the interactivization of a traditional narrative structure, such as the Hero's Journey (Campbell, 2009), as a model to diversify scenes and navigation paths. Guidelines for shooting and editing are suggested.

Chapter 6 addresses the evaluation of this kind of experience. The main questions of this research are approached: Can IFcVR be considered an entertaining experience able to deliver coherent stories? Is the IFcVR experience comparable to watching a movie as opposed to playing a video game? To answer these questions, a methodology is presented to evaluate the IFcVR user experience (UX). As a hybrid product, the assessment methodology merges two theoretical aspects to evaluate the Interactive Fiction and the Cinematic Virtual Reality axes:

- Virtual Reality Assessment
- Interactive Digital Narrative Assessment

ZENA, an Interactive VR Film

ZENA, an interactive VR fiction film, was developed and executed as an IFcVR prototype to steer the progress of the project and examine the viability of this kind of artifact. Before delving into its content, let me briefly introduce the Italian city of Genoa, which served as the primary source of inspiration for the storyline.

With a rich history of more than 1000 years, Genoa was once an independent republic known as the *Repubblica Marinara*, respected throughout Europe, the Mediterranean, and the Black Sea. The UNESCO world heritage historical center of Genoa comprises a complex network of narrow streets called *vicoli*, contributing to its unique urban design that has retained its authenticity over the years, making it a vibrant city today. As a foreigner, my early days in Genoa were challenging, as I had to learn to navigate the labyrinthine streets. However, as I explored, I discovered new vicoli and gained knowledge of the various paths, whether commercial or residential, and the different cultural backgrounds of the people who lived there, from Africa, Asia, or Latin America. As a port city, Genoa is a melting pot of cultures, full of old and new stories.

As a filmmaker, I was immediately struck by the cinematic potential of Genoa's unique location. René Clément's *Le Mura di Malapaga* (France-Italy, 1949) and Michael Winterbottom's *Genoa* (UK, 2008) are two notable films that have taken advantage of the city's characteristics, particularly the twisting streets that often lead characters to get lost in the labyrinth. The twining streets move among very tall buildings, forcing visitors and walkers to look up to discover a narrow line of the sky or the ancient frescoes that decorate the buildings. This peculiarity is very appropriate for 360º video or photo because it invites the viewer to look up and around. It is quite common for people who live in the historical center to wake up in the morning, poke their head out of the window and look up to see how the weather is. At the same time, filming in Genoa is very difficult because the camera exposure must be adjusted for the darkness of the ground level and the sunlight that enters through the narrow space between the buildings.

Genoa stands out from other Italian cities with meticulously preserved historical centers designed primarily for tourism. Unlike these cities, Genoa's historical centre is home to a diverse population, encompassing all social classes and nationalities in the same building. The streets can be dark and dingy which gives a mixed sense of security and insecurity at the same time. The industrial port makes Genoa a very lively city, full of commerce, tourism, students, and very particular situations, such as sex workers offering their services during the day near the most frequented streets of the centre. These factors contribute to a strong sense of communal living, where people from different backgrounds and cultures share the same space.

When I started to get interested in interactive narratives, Genoa offered me -in real life- an interactive immersive narrative experience every day. ZENA, which means Genoa in the Genovese dialect, does not pretend to look like a commercial production but to show the feasibility and effectiveness of the proposed theoretical approaches to create interactive immersive experiences, even for independent video makers with a low budget. ZENA was produced with a filmic rather than a videogame approach, hence the production stages have been ruled by the workflow of film production.

ZENA's story unfolds in a 360º environment created through Live Action 360° high-definition video capture. The interactive structure was created with a software that was not updated to newer headsets. As I write this book, I am in the process of bringing ZENA back to life by employing software that will be compatible with both current and future VR headsets. Access to playthrough footage and various scenes of the interactive fiction film is available. In the story, participants assume an active role in shaping the narrative by engaging directly with the plot. They will be able to make decisions about where to go, follow or disregard a character's advice, and access supplementary information that enhances their comprehension of the story. The scenes unfold in the narrow alleyways and several notable palaces in the Old Town, immersing viewers in these settings for the first time in Virtual Reality.

The creation process of ZENA will be described and the most relevant outcomes of this process will be shared. Lessons are drawn from the achievements, mistakes, and shortcomings that I found during the realization of this prototype. Therefore, the stages and practices described here do not try to become a canonical procedure, but rather guidelines, which can also serve as inspiration for the future creation of IFcVR experiences.

1.
THE HUMAN AT THE CENTRE OF
THE STORY WORLD

1.1. *The Frameless View*

The beginning of our journey toward the creation of immersive interactive movies involves devising an aesthetic paradigm that presupposes the frameless vision. This understanding leads us to discover the plasticity of the Virtual Reality (VR) medium to build an understanding of how communication process works in this new mediatic space. This first chapter is focused on the epistemological study of Interactive Fiction in Cinematic Virtual Reality (IFcVR), proposing a reflection that starts from the current state of VR, to look towards the past. This sort of archaeology of the VR will look not only at the medium in its material state but at the evolution of the human, as both sender and receiver of messages, about this new extension of its nature.

On the reality continuum (Milgram, 1994), Virtual Reality represents the opposite end to the Real World. Reality is principally represented by what is visible and audible; technology is what transforms the Virtual into Reality. Technology is to be intended not only as a set of hardware and software tools but in a broader sense as the *disposition* (Agamben, 2006) that Cyberspace (Heim, 2012) represents in the current socio-cultural landscape. Technology mediates the human relationship with the world, while art appears as the visual metaphors that allow humans to interact and live in Cyberspace. Virtual Reality opens a new chapter "in the relationship between art and technology" (Ryan, 2015, p. 50), locating itself at the core of the relationship of the human being with images (Grau, 2003), and the human vision is located at the center of the (digital) image. The challenge that VR is posing to us goes beyond the mere reception of the digital 360° image, it imposes us to coordinate different sensory languages within a virtual environment that completely encloses our perceptual cognition. In other words, we need to learn how to 'live' in other realities.

Archaeology of Virtual Reality as a visual medium, with anthropology as a constant, takes us to the first paintings in the caves of Altamira or Lascaux, passing through the Egyptian and Etruscan tombs, up to the medieval cathedrals and Renaissance villas, where man recreated non-digital virtual environments that enclose sight and body in a spherical artistic representation telling a story: the story of those who lived there, biblical stories, or representations of the daily life. In these environments, people can move around and make a stop in those areas of the wall that called their attention. People can read the images in any order and can analyze a single detail if they want. There is a special feeling when crossing the entrance to the church of Santa Maria del Fiore in Florence or the tomb of Tutankhamun since we are aware that we are entering a story space. This human desire to create new environments for the human body and cognition was concretized very slowly until reaching the creation of special devices designed for this purpose.

In his book *Panorama: History of a mass medium*, Stephan Oettermann (1997) makes archaeology of visual media with a cylindrical or spherical form. In particular, he refers to the Panorama, an innovation patented in 1787 by Robert Baker, initially called *La nature a coup d'oeil*. The panorama was a spherical landscape painting in which the viewer was placed in the center of space and could walk observing the painting around him. During the same period, the Panopticon was born, a prison where, using light effects, the prisoners could be constantly observed from a control tower located in the centre of the construction. These two inventions were born during the industrial revolution, at a time when there was also a kind of 'evolution of the eye': the first binoculars and microscopes appeared, and with the creation of hot air balloons, the concept of horizon, much appreciated by Goethe, begun to be elaborated by the common man (Oettermann, 1997). At the time, Goethe was very interested in studying vision and especially 'subjective observation'. According to his studies, the subjective observation was not an 'interior space or a theatre of representations' but it was an increasingly exteriorized process; his objects and the body of the observer begin to constitute a single field in which interior and exterior are merged (Crary, 2013, p. 77). How humanity observed the world around changed radically, especially during the period between the 18th and 19th centuries when the conception of the *viewer* changed (Manovich, 2009; Crary, 2013). The observer was no longer a physiological observer, but an active and autonomous producer of her/his own experience.

At the beginning of the 19th century, the panorama became an indispensable instrument for geography, becoming even more popular than maps themselves: 'While reading a map was a technique that had to be learned, anyone with some years of instruction could understand a panorama' (Oettermann, 1997, p. 57). What finally gave a kind of victory to the panorama upon the map was the possibility that it offered to 'live' the experience of being at the top of a mountain. Today, two centuries later, VR still backs up this concept, considering that Virtual Reality itself is above all, an 'image-object ' (Diodato, 2005), and what is striking of this concept is precisely the possibility of seeing a representation of reality in the same way we see reality. Soon, several photographers began to make panoramic photographs, and even geographical maps tried to add this all-encompassing view.

During the first decade of film history, the Lumière brothers also flirted with panoramic projection screens, that they called the *Photorama* (IJsselsteijn, 2005). In the late 1930s, the *Vitarama* was developed, another system of hemispheric projection that was later adapted into a gunnery simulation machine during the Second World War. These first panoramic projection experiments evolved into the *Cinerama* in the '50s, what we know today as IMAX and Omnimax, in their 2D or 3D formats, systems that offer the larger and sharper resolution frame ever seen (IJsselsteijn, 2005, p. 11-13).

During the 20th century, along with the evolution of audiovisual media, other inventions were born with the intention of trapping user's cognition by creating hardware and software that not only enhance vision but also allow the connection of different human senses to one experience, going beyond the audiovisual narrative to perform simulations. Such experiments can be considered the first forms of VR. An early one is Morton Heilig's *Experience Theater* (1959). Its aim was to 'say goodbye to the rectangular picture frame, the two-dimensional images, the horizontal audiences, and the limited senses of sight and hearing, and reach out for everything and anything that would enhance the illusion of reality' (as cited in Schreer, 2005, p. 13). It was Heilig who, after the *Experience Theater*, created the *Sensorama*[1] in 1962 and then the *Telesphere Mask*, one of the first Head Mounted Displays (HMD), a game-changer in the evolution of vision, by recreating the stereoscopic vision and the natural Field of View (FOV) of the human eye. With this attempt, Heilig went further and tried to connect other senses to the experience by giving inputs like movement, aromas, wind, etc. Afterward, with the massification of computers, some software tools for panoramic view were created such as the *Encarta Encyclopedia* or web applications like *Google Street View*, systems that allow the navigation in a 360º environment (Nite, 2015). This type of exploration taking place on the two-dimensional window of the computer rapidly became well known by the public at large.

All the experiments mentioned above have in common a particular characteristic: the release of the image from the frame. It is important to note that all these technological processes have always been accompanied, and in most cases led, by artistic creation. The engineering of media apparatus guided by the creative impulse takes us into a field in which it is difficult to determine if the Lumière brothers, George Méliès, Morton Heilig, Jaron Lanier, or Robert Baker, as many others, were artists or engineers (Grau, 2003, p. 3):

> Media artists represent a new type of artist, who not only highlights and extracts the aesthetic potential of these advanced methods of image creation, posing new options for perception and artistic position in this media revolution, but also researches innovative forms of interaction and interface design, thus contributing to the development of the environment in key areas, both as an artist and as a scientist.

A frameless image leads to a frameless view. The frameless view has one relevant characteristic: human perception is located at the centre of the world. Wladyslaw Tatarkiewicz and Jaworska begin their book *A History of Six [aesthetic] Ideas* (1980), phrasing

---

1   http://www.mortonheilig.com/SensoramaPatent.pdf

Giovanni Pico della Mirandola's *Discourse on the Dignity of Man* from 1486:

> *Ti ho posto al centro del mondo, affinché con maggiore facilità tu possa guardarti intorno e vedere ciò che è* (p. 11). [I have placed you in the centre of the world, so that you can more easily look around and see what exists].

Pico della Mirandola is one of the first thinkers placing human cognition at the center of a 360º metaphorical vision of world knowledge, followed by Giulio Camillo Delminio, who, in 1550 designed the *Teatro della Memoria*, a system that organizes and categorises human knowledge through mnemonic images from mythology, so as from the center of a theatre's stage the viewer had visual access to the information (Bolzoni, 1984). This system of organization of world knowledge is frequently compared to the semantic web, which connects web digital material through metadata that relates its meaning(s). Following the path of his predecessors, Giordano Bruno in 1582 presented the *Ars Memoriae*, 'a mnemonic structure that bridges human awareness with raw data' (Heim, 2012, p. 1). The conceptual switch consists in placing the human not before the 'iconic interface' through which we access the knowledge of the world, but at the center of it. This switch is subtly evidenced using the term 'panorama', which initially designated a pictorial-circular expression, as a metaphor that denotes a holistic understanding of a phenomenon or situation. Both the artistic object and the metaphor, however, enclose the same idea: a human is placed at the center of the vision so they are is in the position to receive and process the information from the outside without any type of disturbance or margin.

The panoramic or panoptic vision, with all its applications and derivations in different media, laid the foundations of the optical simulation by forcing the viewer to view the world through its imitation. Paradoxically, over time, the frameless view not only released image and vision but also became a prison for the eye, as the HMDs evidence. The frameless view sets a clear separation between the reality that is contained inside the experience theatre or HMD and the real reality; there is no escape, the viewer must choose between one or the other. This is one of the main obstacles that VR has been facing from its beginnings, people are not sure about whether to enter the different reality. A problem already faced by the *Panorama*, initially introduced as a new art form, but 'conceived to create a market for mediated realities and (seemingly) emancipated gazes' (Huhtamo, 2013, p. 5).

If the content of a new medium is an old medium (McLuhan, 1964), the content of VR is the frameless/omnidirectional image. As an evolutionary process and not as a finished product, the panorama is the code that sets the foundations for the evolution of VR as a visual medium, whose hardware differs from other visual media where the viewer is placed in front of an apparatus (cinema, television, computer, radio, smartphone, tablet, newspaper, etc.) that has a defined range of visual and/or auditory transmission. When a medium becomes the content of another medium, it sets up the symbolic form or the aesthetic style used to create messages (Strate, 2008). This new aesthetic paradigm has consequences on the transmission of messages for both sides of the communication process, posing a challenge for both sender and receiver, both must place themselves at the center of the world to *see* what the other *sees*.

1.2. *Experience in Artificial Worlds*

It was the French poet and playwright Antonin Artaud who for the first time used the expression *Realitè Virtuelle* in his book *Le Théâtre et Son Double* published in 1938, referring to the kind of storyworld brought on stage by theatre. The fact that the same term is used today for a computational system that generates a realistic VE, highlights the link between the artistic creation and the technology that allows us to access other universes that are real in effect. This link transcends VR's visual nature to dive into a metaphysical nature. For example, when we remember a past event, we abstract ourselves from physical reality so as to 'visit' a reality that no longer exists as an external event. We see and live our memories as a narrative (Bruner, 2003 p. 65). We narrate our life experiences, our dreams; we become the stories we create. However, narrative needs symbols to be transmitted.

Analogously, since the beginning of the artistic expression, humanity has sought to isolate cognition from the real world to create alternative spaces that mimic the sensation of reality, trying to live 'artificial experiences'. Some situations in which we experience different realities can be achieved by altered states of consciousness, such as sleep, hallucinations, hypnosis, or meditation. All these examples share two conditions with VR: (1) the individual sensory perception is positioned at the centre of the experience, and (2) the implicit decision to separate ourselves from our physical reality to enter a different cognitive dimension. Although artistic discourse constitutes an access point towards a peculiar dimension created by some author, in Virtual Reality this pact goes even further, compromising our physicality and our senses into the digital materiality of that other reality.

It seems that there is an intrinsic human desire to live in alternative realities in which it is possible to experiment the life of others or unknown spaces. In 1954, Aldous Huxley wrote in his book *The Doors of Perception, Hell, and Heaven:*

> Thus, it seems virtually unquestionable that I will never know how it feels to be Sir John Falstaff or Joe Louis [...] sensations, feelings, intuitions, insights, or fantasies are private and, except for symbols and at second-hand, incommunicable [...] Words are pronounced, but they do not illustrate. The things and events to which the symbols refer belong to fields of experience that are mutually exclusive (Huxley, 1954, p. 3).

The core of this plight seems to be our inability to transmit our experience of the world, not what we think about it. VR could be the answer to this desire. In April of 2018, during his TED talk 'How we need to remake Internet', Jaron Lanier, pioneer[2] of what we know today as VR, compares the existential moment of VR in the context of the evolution of humanity, with the first stages of the appearance of language. In this sense, Lanier points out the birth of a new era in the history of human communication, inadvertently replying to to Huxley's plight:

> With language came new adventures, new depth, new meaning,

---

2   https://www.wired.com/1993/02/jaron/

new ways to connect, new ways to coordinate, new ways to imagine, new ways to raise children, and I imagined, with VR, we'd have this new thing that would be like a conversation but also like waking-state intentional dreaming. We called it post-symbolic communication because it would be like just directly making the thing you experienced instead of indirectly making symbols to refer to things.

The post-symbolic communication, according to Lanier, can be described as 'a shared, waking state, intentional dream... Instead of the word 'house', you will express a particular house and be able to walk into it... It will be a fluid form of experiential concreteness providing similar but divergent expressive power to that of abstraction' (2018). A similar definition is given by William Gibson (1986) who called Cyberspace 'a consensual hallucination'. VR as a *Sprachmaschine*[3], no longer refers to a word-processing application. Rather, it reimagines the act of communication, as it moves beyond the transmission of a message from one point to another, to a fleeting moment of telepresence in the digital void where virtual entities and realities come to life (Heim, 2012). This new form of communication moves away from symbols and gets closer to pure perception, but as a computer-mediated process, it must accommodate inputs and outputs to what Kant called the human 'sensory-schemata' (Heim, 2012).

What we call VR refers specifically to a computational system that generates events and entities that are real in effect but not in fact. Through this computational system, artistic creation can play a decisive role in the creation of meaningful experiences in a medium 'that awakens fundamental questions of philosophy such as: What is real? and What is existence?' (Heim, 1993, p. 3). Artists now have the material possibility of creating artificial experiences that explore, to a certain degree, those metaphysical questions that Huxley or Lanier expressed. During this study, something

---

3   The literary translation for Heidegger's terminology would be 'Language Machine'. Michael Heim in his essay *Heidegger and Computers* (1990) relates the difficulty that he found translating this concept: 'As scholarly translators often do, we ended up taking the cautious route of literal translation, putting *Sprachmachine* into the vague English 'language machine' But a subsequent experience made me realise that Heidegger's reference to the language machine was in fact a prescient insight into what was to become computerised word-processing technology'.

that always captured my attention was the acceptance, *a priori* and without questions, of the existence of other realities. This thought arises multiple questions that are beyond the scope of this investigation: Is it possible to talk about a physical reality that is the real reality and separate it from the cognitive reality that is the virtual reality? Is the real reality an objective or subjective reality?

It is coherent that most of the names of VR companies are related to that other reality: 'Meta', 'Vive', 'Within', 'Daydream', 'Spaces', or 'Alt' are some examples. It is also very common that when talking about VR, terms like metaverse, cyberspace, matrix, among others, are suggested to refer to that other space. As Michael Heim notes, Cyberspace is a spatial metaphor where human perception meets digital data (Heim, 2012), but in VR, when the human senses interact with a VE, the metaphor is no longer needed, the human-computer interface refines the sensation of truthfulness of the VE and reaffirms it in its *real* condition. With the improvement of technology some issues about the distinction between real reality and virtual reality arise. How to recognize 'the real' when there is nothing but the surface? How to recognize 'the real' in virtual reality when the surface is a data representation? In an interview published by *The Atlantic*[4] on April 25th, 2016, Donald Hoffman, professor of cognitive science at the University of California, discusses human perception and translates this philosophical issue into the technological field:

> There's a metaphor that's only been available to us in the past 30 or 40 years, and that's the desktop interface. Suppose there's a blue rectangular icon on the lower right corner of your computer's desktop — does that mean that the file itself is blue and rectangular and lives in the lower right corner of your computer? Of course not. But those are the only things that can be asserted about anything on the desktop — it has colour, position, and shape.

In 1980, during an interview, Stuart Hall - arguing Baudrillard's conceptions about meaning - states that there can be two assertions when trying to recognize the real. The assertion that 'there is no absolute meaning or ultimate signified, just a chain of signifi-

---

4   https://www.theatlantic.com/science/archive/2016/04/the-illusion-of-reality/479559/

cations' and the assertion that meaning does not exist at all (Hall, 2006). Prescinding from vision, post-symbolic communication, as an immediate and transparent exchange of perceptions, looks for the transmission of that ultimate signified, and technological development on brain interfaces (Lécuyer et al, 2008; Aranyi et al, 2016) that meet in a VE, concretizes this search. Referring to Chardin's strawberry basket, Jonathan Crary locates the immediacy of the experience of sense into a scenic space in which the relation between one object and the other, does not concern only optical appearances but rather the knowledge of isomorphisms and positions in a unified terrain (Crary, 2013, p. 66). Since the experience of space is a cerebral function[5], brain-computer interfaces will be able to communicate diverse types of messages, through audiovisual-spatial perceptions that can only take place in a virtual environment.brain interfaces will communicate diverse types of messages, through visual-spatial perceptions that can only take place in a VE where human sensory imagination can project and be experienced.

When speaking about VR content, we are no longer talking about films, shows, games, or simulations; the VR content is called Experience, and inside this umbrella term one can find different types of experiences, as those mentioned before. We start to talk about creating and living 'artificial experiences', but what is artificial is the human-made space, not the human-lived narrative. The creation of meaning in VR experiences passes through what Eugene Gendlin called the felt meaning, a concept that describes how our bodies process information with as much, if not more speed and accuracy than our minds' (cited in De Kerckhove, 2016), a conception that Horst Ruthrof called 'The Corporeal Turn'(Ruthrof, 1997):

> Rather, verbal meaning occurs when linguistic expressions are activated by non-verbal signs, such as tactile, olfactory, gustatory, thermal, haptic, aural, and other perceptual readings. As such, meaning is an intersemiotic and heterosemiotic event, a linkage among distinct sign systems [...] I have termed the semiotic corroboration

---

5   A. Schopenhauer *The world as will and representation (p.763)* cited by Jonathan Crary in *Techniques of the Observer* (2013)

thesis, according to which the reality force of meaning increases in proportion to the number of sign systems activated in any meaning event. (p. 254)

The previous stage of the symbolic communication on the development of language by the child is strictly related to our perceptive nature. Jean Piaget called this stage the *pre-symbolic communication*, in which symbolic language conventions have not been adopted yet (Piaget, 1997). Post-symbolic communication looks for the transmission of elaborated thoughts as primary perceptions without the support of symbolic representations. Following Ruthrof thought, it seems that post-symbolic communication looks for the transmission of *Vorstellung* or 'mental representations'[6] aided by computer interfaces. A simple but abstract desire that requires a rather complex technological apparatus. VR is symbolic as it transmits perceptual stimuli.

1.2.1. *Virtual Reality: The Medium*

In 2015, Chris Milk, founder of the company Within, coined one of the most used definitions of VR in his TED talk *How Virtual Reality can create the ultimate empathy machine*. During the talk, he states that 'VR is the ultimate medium, because while in other media consciousness interprets the medium, in VR the consciousness is the medium'. This phrase recalls Marshall McLuhan's famous statement 'The medium is the message' (McLuhan, 1964). However, Milk's thought is already contained in McLuhan's conception of technology, what he saw as a human extension. According to McLuhan, technology creates new environments and becomes itself the artefact of which the user is the content (Heim, 1993). 'This applies to electric lights, any language whatever, and, of course, housing, engine cars, and even tools of any sort. The user or con-

---

6   'The standard English translation of *Vorstellung* as 'idea' is as convenient for formal semantics as it is misleading. A more accurate translation would be 'mental representation.' In this sense Vorstellung is at the heart of corporeal semantics. Without the fantasising acts of quasi-tactile, quasi-visual, and other representations the schema of linguistic expressions could not be made to mean. More radically one could say that without Vorstellung we could not even walk'. (Ruthrof, 1997, p. 257)

tent of any medium is completely conformed to the character of this man-made environment' (McLuhan, 2008, p.27). Users interpret the messages they receive, process sensory data, generate meaning from their environments, from the artifacts within them, and from the events that take place there (Strate, 2008, p.132). McLuhan saw the medium as the environment that surrounds the individual: 'the environment we inhabit, where we move, where we produce meaning, where our myths acquire significance: the medium is the message' (Roncallo-Dow, 2014). In this sense, VR represents the apex of the medium/space pair, and it does not need to have a direct relationship of dependence with *real* reality (Riegler et al, 2000). As a three-dimensional digital environment with a vast spectrum of possibilities, VR becomes the metaphysical laboratory of reality (Heim, 1993), a function that until now belonged to the sphere of the human mind.

The concept of medium is polysemous and covers a wide spectrum of significance and signifiers. Each area of study, according to its context and applications, relies on a particular meaning of medium, which in some cases can hinder interdisciplinary dialogue, but converging into a single meaning of medium could improve exchanges between the arts, the humanities, philosophy, technology, cognitive sciences, etc., yet opening the doors to the risk of losing different meanings of the concept (Ryan, 2014). The continuous evolution of technology offers more and better supports for the articulation of different media. Ryan (2014) suggests a definition of medium based on a narrative approach because the choice of the medium determines which 'stories can be told, how they are told, and why they are told [...] Through the form that is given to the narrative, the medium is also shaped and therefore the human experience' (p.25). On the other hand, Rebecca Rouse (2016) points out that an overly literary approach of the medium can skew our idea of what constitutes progress for the field, for example to keep waiting for the 'Citizen Kane of VR' (Rouse, 2016).

The current media landscape lets us think that we will continue to articulate, mix, and adapt the traditional limits of each medium, also blurring the limits between creator and user. For both researchers and artists, I feel that the invitation is to look beyond the formats from legacy old media, to identify and assimilate the native properties of the new medium itself (Murray, 1998), since different uncertainties arise from the unique characteristics of each medium; each medium produces distinct and exclusive narrative effects that set it apart from other media (Chatman, 1989). The narrative vision of the medium applied to VR allows us to approach this new environment, in a first instance, through what it looks for: the creation of worlds that allow the viewer to experience possible realities, a notion already accepted in narratology (Wolf, 2011). In VR, the artificial experience is the narrative that the user creates, while the VE is the storyworld created by the author and in which communication between author(s) and user(s) takes place.

Each text finds its mechanism to be transmitted, and the creation process becomes a kind of struggle between what the author needs to express and the materiality that will support and transmit it. The creation of interactive experiences challenges both author and receivers, and this challenge passes at first, through the knowledge of the materiality and the different functionalities of the object-medium that will instantiate the experience during the fruition process. "It is emblematic that the distorting power of a medium (a lens, the air, or a liquid) is considered neutralizable, and that this can be done by intellectually mastering the properties of the medium, so it becomes effectively transparent through an exercise of reason" (Crary, 2013, p. 66-67). Every form of communication or language operates through codes within the syntagmatic chain of a discourse. If the audiovisual sign is complex - constituted by the combination of two types of speech, visual and auditory (1980) - how can we define the sign of VR, which is constituted by a combination that goes far beyond the visual and auditory stimulation?

As Rebecca Rouse writes in her paper *Media of Attraction: A Media Approach to Panoramas, Kinetography, Mixed Reality and Beyond* (2016, p. 97), the evolution of a medium should not be interpreted under a media-centred approach in which a medium is a sort of 'final result' or is accepted as 'serious art'. Instead, she proposes to consider every medium experiment as an autonomous art form that contributed to its evolution. This suggestion is also effective to understand the historical moment of VR. For more than 60 years, VR has been around the corner, waiting for its great moment. Several devices have had brief but exciting moments of hype in the 70s, 80s, and 90s, moments in which the arrival of VR to the mainstream seemed imminent. Nonetheless, among the common consumer, VR never had a massive reception. Something similar happened in 2016, the year in which VR left a beta state of more than sixty years to seek to reach the mass market. This leap to everyday life is still waiting to take place and we still do not know if this will ever happen. This may be because, from a macro-social point of view, media are the spaces in which we build our social realities (Strate, 2008, p. 133) and VR is still far from that stage.

However, the image of Mark Zuckerberg, CEO of Meta (Facebook at the time) walking in the middle of a crowd wearing HMDs, during the Mobile World Congress in Barcelona in 2016, kicked off a year of competition between the big technological companies that are betting on this new medium: from the manuacturers of devices for reproduction and creation, software developers and producers, through to the various platforms for distribution. Processors and screens of today are much more powerful than those of twenty years ago, and the current technological environment with all its possibilities is undoubtedly more conducive to the creation of mixed reality experiences. But, still, in 2023, VR is almost in its 'natal condition', and despite its 'abject crudeness' it keeps to 'convey an amazing new kind of experience in a way that no other media ever had' (Lanier, 2010).

Something curious is happening with VR that has not occurred with other audiovisual media: it exists, it fascinates everyone, it fills conferences, and it is in constant development for different applications, but, without the common user's feedback, nobody really knows what to do with it. We still do not know why someone would use VR. However, VR has managed to gain a space in the global collective imagination, since its inception as pure science-fiction, and later as technology, it has always aroused interest, but even now it remains something for the few. Palmer Luckey, the founder of Oculus Rift, said it this way in an interview with the BBC: 'VR got featured in movies, TV shows, games, and books as a kind of holy grail technology about to change the world.' It is common to find in Information Technologies (IT) researchers and developers born in the 50s and 60s, total and sad scepticism about VR precisely because they lived the ups and downs of the VR hype.

There has been a strong economic investment in VR technological and artistic development in recent years. Everything indicated that during the pandemic, VR would have reached social systems and not just some individuals. Despite all efforts, VR did not have the reception that had been expected. Probably, due to the novelty of VR and the change of paradigm that it supposes, people do not feel ready to evade reality completely. The introduction of technological innovations creates uncertainty in individuals, leading them to seek information to evaluate the technology and reduce uncertainty. The technology adoption rate is influenced by how the social system perceives its characteristics, such as its benefits, compatibility with existing practices, complexity, and observability. (Rogers, 2010)

The difficulty of predicting the adoption of VR in the past five years confirms that it is not possible to guarantee that a technology will be adopted. It is not reliable to predict technology diffusion since the methods of social sciences for behavior-related data analysis are based on the 'here and now' and not on the 'there and then' (Rogers, 2010). The adoption of innovation also conditions the evolution of the technology itself, knowing what interactors do with the technology, leading to a better understanding of the use and scope that this can have. This could be the blind spot where VR is today: until the technology is adopted within a social system, we cannot decipher the way forward in its evolution of hardware and software levels.

VR has generated a dreaded uncertainty, as it has an evident potential to isolate us from physical reality (to justify this claim, it is enough just to observe a person using an HMD). Moreover, technology has always generated fear in society; this was the case with computers, for example, even today, some people see it as an opponent of human intelligence, although in practice it is just a component (Heim, 1993). McLuhan, from a sociological context, warns us that it is the medium that has an impact on the human being and its social systems, and not the messages we send or receive, 'what counts is the nature of the medium and its structure, not its intentions' (Strate, 2008, p. 132). Our romance with computers, as indicated by Michael Heim in his book *Metaphysics of Virtuality* (1993), goes far beyond mere aesthetic fascination, 'we are searching for a home for the mind and heart' (p. 85). As computational logic is inspired by human reasoning but does not reproduce it, in the same way, VR as an electronic space should not try to lucidly reproduce reality, but only be inspired by the perceptual processes through which we perceive reality.

There is still rejection and disbelief towards VR. One of the main obstacles that it has faced in reaching the mass market is the quality of the visual experience: we still see the pixels on the HMDs. However, despite the uncertain path that VR will take soon, computer science is living quite a prolific moment for academic and artistic research, as well as for the industry, in terms of innovation and profitability. This technological context opens the doors to many experiences (simulations, video games, social networks, narrations, etc.) in different areas of application: education, entertainment, training, telecommunications, psychological and medical help, among others.

We produce media content and do research in media knowing that 'like volatile stormy weather, at some level changes in mass communication theory and research occur almost too rapidly and unpredictably for even the best-intentioned reporters to chronicle and explain accurately' (Bryant & Miron, 2004). However, if we look back to mass media history, we can find common patterns. For example, we could use the same words written by Oettermann (1997) referring to the evolution of panorama, to describe the current moment of the historical evolution of VR:

> Neither the Panorama nor the Panopticon was ever at the forefront of their times: both phenomena, each in its own way, was the reflection of the most progressive and liberal thought of its time. From these circumstances, the paradox emerges that the panorama has become obsolete on the day of its presentation. At the same time, he sought to hide his anachronism by reproducing in himself new apparently different variations of the themes of fashion. In this way, it continued for a century trying to understand the needs of a large public that had not even had a small role in its creation. (p. 47)

1.3. *To be at the Centre of the World*

Recognizing the human being at the centre of perceptual experience was a true revolution. It started with the new conception of the observer as an active subject and then quickly extended to the overall view of the human being about the environment. Maine de Biran proposes the term *Coenésthèse* to describe the immediate perception of the body's presence, the contemporary feeling of the whole and the composite awareness of all vital impressions inherent in the organism (Crary, 2013, p. 76). VR, that is at the same time image-object and image-event (Diodato, 2005), can be conceived as an experiential topography of electronic data (Heim, 2012). Within its scenic space, the embodied subjectivity of the observer becomes the place where the observer status itself is made possible (Crary, 2013, p. 72), as it happens.

VR looks not only for a verisimilar representation of a certain environment that augments the feeling of immersion but for the possibility of physically interact with the VE. The possibility for the user to interact with the environment is equally important as the images in building the effect of realism (Manovich, 2009, p. 225). As a spatial medium, there are some requirements for the creation and enjoyment of a meaningful VR experience. Even though these requirements can be fully accomplished through high technical quality, there are three terms related to the user experience that constantly appear when speaking about VR and IDN in general: (1) Immersion, (2) Presence and (3) Agency.

1.3.1. *Immersion*

Probably this is the most problematic term since the appearance of the VR HMD, as VR doubles the meaning of the term. Narratology provides an initial definition of immersion, associating it with an aesthetic illusion that involves a sensation, varying in intensity, of being mentally and emotionally engrossed in a depicted world and experiencing it in a manner akin (though not identical) to real life (Wolf, 2009). As noted in the *Encyclopedia of Narrative Theory* (Herman et al, 2008), immersion is related to the human ability to enter in a state of absorption. Its nature is a simulative process, a specific form of the pervasive phenomenon of mental simulation. It is vehiculated by props or mimetic primers, which may be verbal, visual, visual-acoustic, or even visual-acoustic-tactile; being its target domain is a mentally projected world, i.e., a holistic set of cognitive representations that emphasises the subjective experience and spatial qualities, arranged from different perspectives. Monika Fludernik in *Towards a Natural Narratology* (1996), introduces a term especially pertinent when applied to VR: Experientiality. She defines it as 'the quasi-mimetic evocation of real-life experience' (p. 12). She introduces the notion of experiencing, just like telling, viewing, or thinking, as a holistic schemata acquired from real life that can be used as building stones for the mimetic evocation of a fictional world, and as it happens on film and drama, also in VR, "the visual experience works on a reflector mode in which we appear to experience reality from within another's psyche" (p. 20).

Janet Murray in *Hamlet on the Holodeck: The Future of Narrative in Cyberspace* (1997) presents her definition of immersion remembering the origins of the word, which is the psychological feeling of being submerged in water, a different element from air in our normal environment. Immersion in computer-generated environments, as it happens when we are submerged in water, requires that we learn how to digitally swim and enjoy immersion as a participatory activity (p. 211). At the beginning, the term VR was used also to refer to CG environments, even though they were reproduced on a 2D computer window. When these VEs started to be reproduced on HDMs or CAVEs, then it began to be called 'Immersive VR'. Today, however, we call VR only omnidirectional VEs. The term immersion, afterward, took a new role in the development of VR as a medium. Immersion became the lighthouse of the technical development of VR. The finest and most common is the connection of the human perceptive nature within the virtual environment, the higher the level of immersion. This translates into more senses connected to the VE and more interactor feedback (movements, emotions, speech, etc.) interacting in real-time with the VE and its agents. In this sense, VR development points to immersion in its perceptive nature.

Both definitions of immersion, however, are collected by Roth and Koenitz in the paper *Evaluating User Experience in Interactive Digital Narrative* (2016). To evaluate user experience in IDNs they propose to take into consideration both Perceptive Immersion and Narrative Immersion. Each definition comprises a series of factors that generate both types of immersion. These factors can be summarized in the following concepts:

1.3.2. (Tele) Presence

Following the definition of Immersion given by Roth and Koenitz when describing the user experience dimensions on IDN, *Presence* is a component located inside perceptual Immersion together with *Flow*. Even though presence is considered a sub-factor of perceptual immersion, it represents an important characteristic when referring specifically to VR. Presence is defined as the subjective sensation of being in one place or environment while physically located in another. It is an awareness phenomenon that is based on the interaction of sensory stimulation and environmental factors that generates involvement and immersion (Singer and Witmer, 1998). The sensation of presence is reached through the degree of realism of the proposed world, where the interactor accepts the nature of that other reality that does not necessarily coincide with the real nature.

The concepts of Presence[7] and Telepresence have been one of the main objects of research in the past decades, since the appearance of Cyberspace. Telepresence was defined by M.L. Ryan (1999) as the conjunction of immersion and interactivity, claiming that telepresence relates to presence as virtual reality relates to reality. This approach considers Telepresence as the overall feeling that VR looks for, a sense in which interactors are immersed -perceptively and narratively- but without leaving behind the fact that at the same time, they have agency to interact and modify the VE or a physical space from remote. This second conception is often neglected as Lev Manovich points out in *Language of New Media* (2009). He starts from Brenda Laurel's definition of telepresence as a remote presence, to then draw a definition in which Telepresence means 'to be present in a virtual environment or to be present in a real environment from another location through the transmission of images in real-time, telepresence allows the subject to control not only the VEs but also the reality' (p. 210-211).

In the book *Immersed in Media: Telepresence theory, Measurement and Technology* (Lombardi et al, 2015), it is noticed that Presence Theory is highly interdisciplinary and includes different points of view for the understanding of this phenomenon: non-mediated

---

7   The term 'presence' will be used as a component of perceptive immersion.

presence, social presence, self-presence, co-presence, etc. Although, the prevalent discussion in the technological context focuses on *spatial presence*, the presence of feeling within a human-made mediated space. This concept implies 'that an individual perceives and experiences media stimuli almost in such a way as if they were real, even though they are not' (p. 117), 'a subjective experience, conviction or state of consciousness, when perceivers feel bodily or physically situated in a mediated environment' (p. 118). The level of presence has an impact on different fields of application: medical training, video games, and VR-Learning (Bottino et al, 2016), including cinematic and interactive cinematic experiences proposed in this work.

VR authors are especially committed to the feeling of presence, which, as a perceptual condition, requires the digital creation of a predominantly visual and auditory scenic space that, although fantastic, should be perceived as real. This challenge goes through the understanding of the nature of human perception. In this sense there are two components for the generation of presence in VR: on the one hand, the manufacture of the devices for generating and reproducing virtual realities, and on the other hand the creation of a storyworld that needs to make the interactor feel physically comfortable inside the audiovisual experience. This search reminds the famous phrase of the architect and futurist Buckminster Fuller: 'I'm not trying to copy Nature. I'm trying to find the principles she's using' (cited in Vogler, 2008).

1.3.3. *Agency, Interactivity, and the Illusion of Freedom*

'The essence of telepresence is in its anti-presence' (Manovich, 2009, p. 213). Telepresence allows a subject to experience a certain reality (virtual or remote) without being physically present in that place. *Agency* in the context of VR materializes this essence. One of the great challenges for a creator is offering the feeling and pleasure of Agency for the user. This capacity is often called 'freedom', although in digital environments, in general, there is no such thing as freedom. In its broader conception, freedom is the capacity of individuals to think and act according to their will. Janet Murray (1997) defines agency as 'the satisfying power to take meaningful action and see the results of our decisions and choices' (p. 125). In

VEs, the agency on one side by the technical capacity of the VR generator system to be modified depending on the decisions of the interactors in real time, and, on the other side by the creativity of the creator to foresee all possible actions and reactions of the interactors within the VE. These agency factors are summarised as: system usability, autonomy, and affectance (Roth & Koenitz, 2016).

Agency is related to the concept of *Interactivity,* and interactivity is a very controversial topic (Mason, 2013), particularly in the context of IDN. True interactivity requires that both agents of the communicative act elaborate coherent answers based on the input of their interlocutor. What we know today as interactivity with computer systems continues to be more reactive than active responses (Crawford, 2005) preconfigured in a database of possibilities. A film, for example, "is just one possible path in a database of recorded moving images" (Manovich, 2009, p. 283), and a linear VR experience is the alignment of all the visual areas of the sphere that interactors put together one after the other. According to Crawford (2005), this is not real interactivity but an illusion of interactivity. Following this claim, other IDN theorists, like Koenitz (2016a), prefer to use the term *interactivization* of traditional media (film, literature, etc.) rather than interactive storytelling. From a narrative point of view, the convergence between story and interactivity leads to the 'narrative paradox' (Louchart & Aylett, 2004): the higher the level of interactivity the less control the author has upon the story unfolding. 'The contradiction between authorship and participation is an important element of the narrative paradox previously mentioned. Conventionally, an author seeks control over the direction of a narrative to give it a satisfying structure. Although, a participating interactor demands autonomy to act and react without explicit authorial constraints' (Aylett & Louchart, 2004). Marie-Laure Ryan in her chapter *The Interactive Onion: Layer of User Participation in Digital Narrative Texts* (2011) points out that 'the major obstacle to the development of truly interactive narratives is not technological but logical and artistic. How can the user's freedom be reconciled with the need to produce a well-formed, aesthetically satisfactory story?' (p. 48).

Real interactive storytelling, intended in Chris Crawford's terms, will possibly be reached with future developments in Artificial Intelligence (AI) and Machine Learning (ML), fields of study intrinsically related to narratology and neuroscience (Morson in Schank, 2000, p. xiii). With the aid of AI, it is believed that an IDN system will be capable of running real-time story generation, achieving a true interactive narrative, in which interactivity penetrates the core of the story (Ryan, 2011). What we have now are increasing levels of interactivity that slightly *touch* the surface of a storyworld. Ryan (2011) has identified 4 levels of interactivity: (1) Peripheral Interactivity, (2) Interactivity Affecting Narrative Discourse and the Presentation of the Story, (3) Interactivity Creating Variations in a Predefined Story, and (4) Real-Time Story Generation. The Interactive Fiction in Cinematic Virtual Reality corresponds to Level 3: Interactivity Creating Variations in a Predefined Story.

2.
THE NARRATIVE FORM OF
CINEMATIC VIRTUAL REALITY

2.1. *Cinematic Virtual Reality*

For creators, VR poses interesting challenges from the narrative point of view. A first approach to the virtual environment, even with the simple use of an HMD, opens a wide spectrum of issues regarding technique, narrative, and creativity, in the same way as it opens enormous possibilities related to the creation of story-worlds and interaction modalities. At this point, a conceptual base for creation is offered by earlier media and artistic forms, comprising literature, theatre, cinema, architecture, and videogames. Cinema and videogames -as interdisciplinary audiovisual art forms- offer a more complex understanding of audiovisual and interactivity techniques. However, the spatial nature of VR requires insights from the theatre on managing how performer, spectator, and space come together, while architecture offers insight into both the design of the scenic space (Carlson, 1993) and the application of way-finding theory (Blades, 1991).

In principle, Cinematic Virtual Reality (cVR) can be considered a branch of VR, in which the VE is created by capturing real environments with a 360° video camera (also called Live Action), differing from Computer Graphics (CG) generated environments. The cVR category also includes 360º 2D and 3D animations, as well as 360º 3D video and volumetric video. These categories in their 'flat'[1] version have also been recognized by the cinema industry, which is even including VR experiences into film festivals: Cannes, Venice, Sundance, Tribeca, are just some of the most important

---

1   In Cinematic VR jargon, traditional videos are called 'Flatties'. This term was coined by Google VR artist and theorist Jessica Brillhart https://vimeo.com/jessicabrillhart

worldwide film festivals that have created a special space for VR. This door has been opened in a very organic way despite the low reception of VR in the mass market. It is become more common to call CGI VR narratives "cinematic virtual reality" due to its narrative nature.

It is natural to wonder about the immediate relationship between VR and cinema. The question is not new. Cinema itself faced this issue at its beginnings when it was constantly compared to established arts. Rudolf Arnheim in *Film as Art* (1957) points out that in its birth period cinema was considered nothing but the mechanical reproduction of nature and therefore not art (p.127). Somehow, the same position is implied when speaking of VR as art. In her chapter about film editing in *A Companion to Film Theory* (Miller & Stam, 1999, p. 64-83), Lucy Fischer identifies the issue from two points of view:

> On one level, this impulse speaks an aesthetic curiosity: How does a new medium extend or revamp our understanding of earlier artistic forms? On another plane, however, such diatribes are meant to 'legitimize' the cinema by heralding its ancestry and origins in more respectable forms (Fischer, 2007, p. 69).

This is the same logic of McLuhan (1964), who invites us to think of the media as extensions of our senses. As in every field, each medium carries a genetic load from its predecessors. In each new branch that grows on the big tree of media, we look for the similarities with well-known media, as well as for those differentiating elements that move a little further from the centre. In this landscape, cinematic VR is the section of VR closest to the cinema branch. The way in which cinema articulates all the elements that reproduce the story is called the Film Form. In the broadest sense, the film form is the total system that the viewer perceives in a movie. The form is the global system of relationships that interactors can perceive among the elements of the whole of a film (Bordwell & Thompson, 2010). It is possible to start the analysis of the form of cVR by applying the same words that Eisenstein (1977, p. 3) used to describe the two main features of cinema:

Primo: photo-fragments of nature are recorded.
Secondo: these fragments are combined in various ways.

Both actions are perfectly applicable to cVR, however for each of them there are differences implied by the spatial nature of cVR. The fragments (*primo*) and its relationships (*secondo*) is a two-fold process "enhanced in cinema in the deepest and strongest ways in comparison with other arts" (Eisenstein, 1949, p.4). In linear cVR, this process keeps its character even though it acquires a new dimension: the omnidirectional image and sound. The photo-fragments compose a visual sphere in which the vision will be enclosed, while spatial audio creates an auditory landscape; placed one behind the other, these elements create a living space. The framed shot, which is the minimal narrative unit of cinema, in cVR disappears, while the continuos spatial shot becomes the minimal narrative unit. The scenic space can be designed by the creator, who choreographs various spatial *audio-visual counterpoints* (Eisenstein, 1949). Although the scenic space is frameless, human vision naturally frames space: the linear montage of each fragment of the sphere is a task for the interactor to do.

The audiovisual counterpoints designed by the creator goes beyond the 'storytelling process involving agents and actions, establishing a dialogue with iconographic traditions, ancient and modern' (Xavier, 2007, p. 337). Ismail Xavier recognizes two creation-reading axes for the *Primo* status of cinema that can be perfectly applied to the omnidirectional scenic-space, as the minimal narrative unit of cVR: (1) The horizontal narratological succession of shots to create specific space-time structures of action and (2) The vertical relationships created by the interaction of image and sound, or by the intertextual connections between the film's pictorial composition and cultural codes deriving from painting and photography. Both horizontal and vertical organizations of the semiotic nature of film can be applied to the cVR montage.

The concept of montage in cVR shall not be intended just as a post-production event but as an activity that unfolds during screenwriting, production, and post. In this sense, we can understand montage in cVR on three levels:

1. Creator's montage of what happens within the scenic space, that is, the choreography of all the sensory stimuli.

2. Interactor's montage of the *frame-after-frame* within the frameless image.

3. Creator's montage of the *space-after-space*.

By making the typical comparisons between cVR and its predecessors, we can wonder if a new interpretation of montage could be the basis for understanding the cVR language, as it happened with cinema. In cinema, montage was not only the meeting point of the inheritance and tradition of other arts, but the element that later would have created its language. In VR, the cinematographic montage, carrier of the genes of the theatrical montage and of certain literary structures, is undoubtedly an important gene of VR genealogical tree. Eisenstein (cited in Fischer, 2007, p. 75) locates the issue of the meaning-creation in cinema in his 'conflictive' interpretation of montage:

> By what, then, is montage characterized and, consequently, its cell: the shot?
> By collision. By the conflict of two pieces in opposition to each other.
> By conflict.
> By collision.

It is worth wondering how these collisions occur within the cVR scenic space. Fischer quotes Eisenstein *Film Form: Essays in Film Theory* when he spots the legacy of theatre and literature in cinema. Both ancestors of cinema are reflected in the differentiator feature of the emerging art: *montage*. Eisenstein describes in *Dickens, Griffith and the Film Today* (Fischer, 1977, p. 195-255) the legacy of Dickens 'parallel action writing method in Griffith's montage practice, which would then lay one of the main foundations of current film montage. The artisanal craft of cutting and pasting images one after the other was the cinema's 'plastic sharpness' that 'very soon became sensed as some sort of a "language" [...] Attention was gradually shifted from curiosity concerning excesses towards an interest in the nature of this language itself [...] Thus the secret of the structure of montage was gradually revealed as a secret of the structure of emotional speech.' (p. 248-249).

Today, VR lives in the same period that Eisenstein described. The attitude of the world towards VR is closer to what Eisenstein called a "curiosity concerning excesses". The efforts of most VR researchers somehow ignore the generalized scepticism and continue to deepen in the gear of this new language. 'If the art of cinema consists in everything that plastics and montage can add to a given reality' (Bazin, 2004, p. 26), the art of VR consists in the reality that human perception and computers can build together. This time, the montage of the perceptual stimuli keeps unrevealed the structure of the emotional speech, perhaps not in the form of discourse, but of pure, immediate emotion. In this abrupt change of paradigm that asks us to disconnect from the known reality, skepticism is understandable. Despite it, Manovich (2009) points out that there is nothing to be afraid of because 'the relationship that exists between the structure of the digital image and the language of the contemporary visual culture is characterized by the same dynamics' (p.285) and that even in the new media narrations persist. This study approaches the epistemology of Cinematic Virtual Reality as a conceptual and aesthetic bridge toward this - probably imminent - immersive future.

2.2. *Space vs Time: Vertical and Horizontal Montage*

There are two abstract components that represent the spacetime dichotomy posed by VR nature: the spherical digital 'image-object' (Diodato, 2005) in its quality of frameless visual medium and the indisputable linearity of time. Within the image-object, a multiplicity of events coexists simultaneously, while each event unfolds a change of state in its own independent temporal sequence. This is the same paradox of Borges' *Aleph*[2]:

> "What my eyes beheld was simultaneous, | but what I shall now write down will be successive, | because language is successive. Nonetheless, I'll try to recollect what I can".

From the point of view of a human who observes the sphere, the idea of missing something is already a preconceived agreement.

---

2   El Aleph, 1945. Translation by Norman Thomas Di Giovanni in collaboration with the author. http://web.mit.edu/allanmc/www/borgesaleph.pdf

In our experience of agency, we choose what to pay attention to; within the sphere, we select a visual area to focus on, even though we choose based on mostly unconscious selection mechanisms. 'Choices are actions, and they are often determined by processes of which we are unaware' (Holton, 2006). In the meanwhile, other multiple events are happening; the term 'Image-event' was coined to name this quality of the visual sphere (Diodato, 2005).

This multiplicity of visual events created some controversy among filmmakers and videomakers entering VR in the early 2010's. They felt that they are losing control of their story by losing the frame. This generalized feeling agrees with André Bazin's thoughts when referring to the power of cinema upon the spectator: 'Through the contents of the image and the resources of montage, cinema has at its disposal a whole arsenal of means whereby to impose its interpretation of an event on the spectator' (Bazin, 2004, p. 24). However, this is an attitude that needs to be abandoned. In VR, the concept of authorial narrative control acquires a whole new interpretation. Through its spatial audiovisual sign, VR arsenal of means does not try to impose a visual interpretation, but on the contrary, it releases multiple possibilities. This authorial narrative control travels along different dimensions and the first step in enlightening this new interpretation passes through the unraveling of the aleph paradox. To do this, it is possible to apply Eisenstein's theorization of Vertical and Horizontal montage.

According to Eisenstein, 'Vertical' montage corresponds to the 'inner synchronicity between picture and music' (cited in Afra, 2015), while 'Horizontal' montage is the temporal juxtaposition of images, and the relationships produced by them. The Vertical Axis (Y) crosses the sphere, while the Horizontal Axes (X) represents the linearity of time. Christian Metz, in his aim to develop a *Semiotics of Cinema* (2007), distinguishes between Syntagmatic and Paradigmatic categories to specify the relationships that emerge among signs. A 'syntagma' is a unit of actual relationship, while a 'paradigm' is a unit of potential relationship. *La Grande Syntagmatique,* or *The Large Syntagmatic Category,* 'is the organisation of the major actual relationships among units of relation in a given semiological system (these relations may be potential ones, but they are not paradigmatic, because they are actualized in analysis)' (Metz, 2007, p. xiv). These concepts can be applied to linear cinematic VR, because multiple visual and auditory signs can be arranged in a shot by vertical montage, that constitutes a syntagma, while the large syntagmatic category considers what unfolds shot after shot, and space after space, along the horizontal axis. Paradigm, on the other hand, finds an actual representation in interactive fiction structure of an immersive interactive movie.

2.2.1. *Space (Y)*

The vertical axis montage corresponds to the composition of the scenic space. In cinema, this is the first form of cinematic articulation, which creates the very basis of the cinematic process and permits the presentation, in continuity on the screen, of successive photographic frames (Gaudreault & Jost, 2007). This montage comprises the cinematic audio-visual counterpoint enhanced by the spatiality of omnidirectional image and spatial audio. The VE can be accessed from a HMD in sight-only mode, or full body through a CAVE (Cruz-Neira et al, 1993). In *Aesthetics of Virtuality* (2005) Roberto Diodato explains the virtual image by sorting out its materiality until it can be defined as an environment. In cVR, space is a visual sphere constituted by an image-object, the equirectangular[3] frame. As a moving image, when wrapped up as a sphere, the equirectangular video becomes an image-event. However, when the video becomes a narrative space, which is a theatrical stage due to its sense of spatiality, it becomes a 'corpo-ambiente' [environment-body], with an 'irreducible alterity', that is, it is an external body that exists beyond use and the sensation of being-there (Diodato, 2005, p. 110). The corpo-ambiente is the scenario in which interactors' and creator's perceptive stimuli come into dialogue. Entering the VE for the first time raises some questions: Who am I? Where am I? And what is my purpose here? Regardless of the aim of the experience, such philosophical questions will find an answer within the storyworld itself, confirming narrative as an intrinsic characteristic of human experience.

The main feature of a storyworld is its *evenementielle* capacity (Genette, 1972), that is, the capacity of convening a multiplicity of situations, whether as developing actions and events or as po-

---

3   Equirectangular

tential storylines that can emerge from the combination of these actions and events. Inside the spherical space, although all the evenementielle information is happening simultaneously, what interactors see are fragments of the sphere, which is the natural frame for human vision. This natural frame corresponds to the human Field of View (FOV). It is measured from a fixed point and slightly varies by facial anatomy. Typically, the binocular visual field is 135° vertical and 190° horizontal (Howard & Rogers, 1996). When humans visually explore a space, they build a sort of string of pearls, with each frame they choose to watch, in other words, a narrative. Within the FOV, human vision chooses what to focus on, closing again the range of space to put the attention on.

This fragmentation that humans do during the visual exploration of a space will determine the design of the scenic space and the placement of events and elements within it. These events and elements to which people pay attention to are called Points of Interest (POI). This is a concept proposed by Jessica Brillhart[4], first cVR creator of Google JUMP. She suggests identifying the areas of the video in which the author wants to call interactors' attention. POIs are closely related with interactors' motivation to find human (or human-like) figures. During a scene, the points of interest can move through space forcing interactors to move around to follow characters' actions. With spatial audio a POI can also be auditory and located in space in correspondence with the sound source. Multiple POIs can be arranged within the same scenic space and change location or alternate. In this way, the narrative becomes a choreography of sensory inputs where time and rhythm define the flow of the story.

Looking for POIs and following character actions within the scene space requires the interactors to move their head around. The interactive feature of HMDs is to allow interactors to visually explore the 360º space. This mechanism is realised by tracking head movements. HMDs can vary depending on how much they allow interactors to explore the space by moving their heads. There are three basic types of visual movements that allow 6 DOFs

---

4   In the essay *From screenwriting to space-writing* (Reyes, 2022), I present a
     more detailed anaylis of Brillhart and other creators on the beginnings VR
     storyboarding.

(degrees of freedom): pitch, yaw, and roll, which plots your head in terms of your X, Y, and Z axis to measure movements forward and backwards (pitch), side to side (yaw) and shoulder to shoulder (roll).

However, in VR and cVR, a very old concept comes alive again, and stronger: the horizon. Human experience needs to recognize the physics we live in to feel a new VE as real. At a visual level, the first element that we perceive to recognize space is the horizon line. From a physical point of view, the awareness of the horizon gives us stability and the reference to recognize distances, giving a sense of perspective. The construction of any VE starts from the setting of the horizon, and according to it the location of POIs and their movements. The lack of horizon causes motion sickness and spatial disorientation and should be avoided unless it is a desired effect within the narrative.

Once the horizon has been set, POIs and actions can be composed within the scene-space in relation to the eye of the interactor. Distances from the eye of the interactor can give a different meaning or importance to the POI. E.g.: a POI located 5m -or less- from the interactor's eye will be easy for the interactor to observe in detail, while a POI located 20m away will be seen less clearly. The distance of POIs' locations can therefore correspond to what in cinema are the different types of shots.

2.2.2. *Time (X)*

The horizontal axis (X) represents Time. 'We know less about time than anything else', wrote Tarkovsky (cited in Skakov, 2013, p. 1) engaged in complex philosophical and physical thoughts about the fourth dimension. Time in cVR exercises the same function that it has in cinema, as cinema is positioned between still image and performance. According to Arnheim (1957), 'Film is given a middle position between photography and theatre [...] film gives us images only, whereas a play unfolds in real-time and real space' (p.12). As in cinema, temporality differentiates cVR and from 3D model.

Time in narrative has always been a complex issue, and it is not different when creating virtual reality worlds. Time is the factor that distinguishes a description (that creates space in time) from a narrative (which creates one space in another space) (Metz & Taylor, 2007, p. 18). The sphere –with its omnidirectional and contemporaneous visual nature– is opposed to the linear and directional nature of time executed by human experience and the cognitive logic of the human organiser of that experience in a sequence of events. In narrative, time is understood in its duality: the time of the signified or story-time and the time of the signifier or discourse-time. While story-time travels independently, the X axis relates to discourse-time. In cinema, it arises from the activity of sequencing called montage, a procedure that filmmakers have been using to tell their stories (Gaudreault & Jost, 2007, p. 58).

Discourse time operates a central role in determining the rhythm, narrative tension, and the *evenementielle* density of the discourse, elements that influence the aesthetic perception of the story. Discourse-time in cVR is related to cinematic time and its duality. Keeping Eisenstein terminology, we can use the vertical/ horizontal duality again. Vertical Time relates to the time in which actions occur simultaneously within the scene-space. In contrast, horizontal time regards the sequentiality of shots, scenes, and sequences, and, in Interactive Fiction, the sequentiality of the Narrative Units chosen by the interactor.

"The narrative instance is organised as a sequence of signifiers that has a certain duration (for the literary narrative, the time it takes to read it; for the cinematographic narrative, the time it takes to see it, etc.)" (Metz & Taylor, 2007, p. 19). In computer-based narrative experiences, discourse time acquires an ulterior layer: the HCI-time, which is the time in which human-computer interaction happens. HCI time presents a duality: (1) the interactors' time to coordinate perceptive stimuli with the story development and (2) the system's time to process interactors' input and give feedback. In optimal conditions, this exchange should not present obstacles by system delays. If interactors must make conscious decisions, they must have enough time to process information and think about the decision. In the case of unconscious decisions, the system should be able to read interactors' physiological data and change the course of the story in a short time, so as not to affect the flow of the experience.

For both cVR and IFcVR, Figure 1 presents the time duality mentioned above: Cinematic Time Duality and HCI Time Duality.

Cinematic Time and HCI time work in a co-dependent relationship due to the interactor's ability to build her own discourse by choosing what to see within the sphere and which hotspots to activate, in the case of IFcVR.

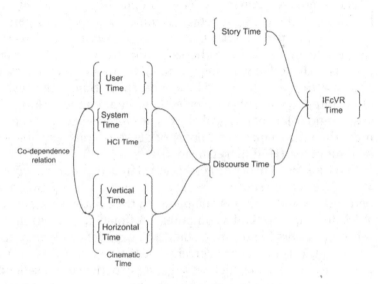

Figure. 1. Time in IFcVR

2.3. *From the KinoGlaz to The All-Feeling Eye*

Vertov's masterpiece *Man with a Movie Camera* from 1929, marks the beginning of a new relationship between man and the moving image, where the role of the camera is recognized no longer as an external and mechanical element, but as an organic element that does not need further action mediations to transmit the phenomenology of the act of seeing and constructing meaning through the sequentialization of images. The identification and recognition of the camera as an autonomous entity, the *Kino-glaz* or *Kino-eye,* 'is directed towards the creation of an authentically international absolute language of cinema on the basis of its complete separation from the language of theatre and literature' (Vertov, 2004, p. 318).

In VR, the concept of Kino-eye acquires a new level of meaning. The user's experience is lived through a dual device (hardware-software) that tries to simulate the natural mechanics of the human eye. However, concerning the replication of the experience, the process of visualizing the sequence of images resembles filmic phenomenology, akin to a "cinematographic process directed by oneself [...] creating a detached mind-eye capable of perceiving mental constructs that manifest as sensory perceptions only through technological prostheses" (Diodato, 2005, p. 8). In fact, there is no big difference, in perceptual terms, between seeing reality or a virtual reality, 'for H. Sapiens, space-time is the desktop of the interface, and physical objects are icons on the desktop. The shapes and colors of physical objects resemble objective reality no more than the shapes and colours of desktop icons resemble files in a computer' (Hoffman et al, 2015).

The Interface Theory of Perception claims that our perceptions are not veridical reports of reality, the relationship between our perceptions and reality is analogous to the relationship between a desktop interface and a computer (Hoffman et al, 2015). In this sense, it is possible to understand the experience of the virtual world in the same way we perceive the real world. From a Narrative point of view, in which we organise experience as a sequence of events, it is possible to conceive the experience as an "extension of the experience of the film viewer" (Diodato, 2005, p. 110). In both cases, in VR, the Kino-eye as a technological prosthesis is not limited by the visual aspect. Keeping the image as the central core, the Kino-eye expands itself and includes in its perceptive nature the other senses. Depending on the technical complexity of the interaction design, the Kino-eye becomes a sort of Eye of Horus, that not only sees but feels everything. This symbolic eye represents the unification of all senses in our construction of the world. Some storytellers[5] use the Eye of Horus as the icon that represents the interactor on the storyboard of VR experiences. The 'all-feeling-eye' presents itself in contraposition to the 'all-seeing-eye' (Koenderink, 2014) while at the same time enhancing the conception of

---

5   https://external-mxp1-1.xx.fbcdn.net/safe_image.
     php?url=https%3A%2F%2Fs3.amazonaws.com%2Fstatic.oculus.com%2Fwe
     bsite%2F2016%2F06%2FFigureo.png&_nc_hash=AQBUURZGMww2hhM6

the *Kino-glaz* in its search for the *KinoPravda, that is, the truth that cannot be reached by the naked eye.*

Even though for Vertov the concept of KinoPravda wanted to bring up social realities, the conceptual weight that Vertov gave to technology as a mediator between the eye and reality unleashed another series of questions that delve into the concepts of reality, credibility, and perception in the film image.

The impression of reality has been one of the main issues of VR as it is for cinema (Bazin, 2004; Metz and Taylor, 2007). The core activity of the technological development of VR has been to recreate with the highest level of fidelity possible the nature of human sensory perception. A vast number of studies in VR focus on testing the level of presence, immersion, and agency within VE. The outcome of these studies has shown that the more natural the quality of the visual experience, in the organicity of the human eye together with the visual refinement of the virtual environment, its objects, and agents; the more the sensory stimuli (haptic, auditory, olfactory), the faster the interaction with the virtual environment, the greater the level of presence, immersion, and agency of the interactors' experience.

Metz finds in motion the distinction between object and copy 'because movement is never material but is always visual, to reproduce its appearance is to duplicate its reality [...] In the cinema the impression of reality is also the reality of the impression, the real presence of motion.' (Metz and Taylor, 2007, p. 9). Metz goes further by noticing that movement is insubstantial, and that we relate our feeling of reality with its quality of being tangible. This is what the *all-feeling eye* looks for: the materiality of virtual reality. A dream pursued by cinema but towards which it recognizes its impossibility. 'One of the factors that determine the difference between looking at a motion picture and looking at reality is the absence of the sense of balance and other kinesthetic experiences' (Arnheim, 1957, p. 102). Even in 3D movies, spectators, when watching a film, do not confuse the space of the film accessed by a display with their own space (the movie theatre)[6], in the same

---

6   Albert Michotte van den Berck called it 'segregation of spaces The space of
     the diegesis and that of the movie theatre (surrounding the spectator) are
     incommensurable (Cited in Metz, 2007, p. 10)

way they do not confuse a film with a real theatre spectacle. In event-based arts or narrative arts -to use Bazin terminology- the perception of reality requires interactors' affective, perceptive, and intellective activity, furthermore, the Kinoglaz through its plasticity finds the truth. It is worth asking to what extent will interactors be able to distinguish reality from spectacle in VR or cVR? The answer of Bazin (2004) referring to cinema highlights again its link with cVR:

> It is montage, that abstract creator of meaning, which preserves the state of unreality demanded by the spectacle (p.45).

The concept of the *all-feeling eye,* as the Kinoglaz did, poses interesting questions that go beyond its technological nature and enter the field of narration in its objective to seek the sensation of the real. We can consider the *all-feeling eye* as the mediator between the virtual (story)world and reality, the receiver of the articulation of all the systems that interactors perceive, the cinematic form of VR.

2.4. *The Issue of Point of View in cVR*

For the ordinary person in everyday life, sight is simply a means of finding their bearings in the natural world (Arnheim, 1957). The same happens in novels: 'When a novel begins with "I am alone here, now, sheltered", the reader immediately asks: who is this "I"? When is "now" in the story? and what defines "here" and being "sheltered"?' (Gaudreault & Jost, 2007, p.47). In any narrative art, no matter its sign system (verbal or audiovisual), there is a process in which the story becomes discourse. During this process, the creator chooses someone to delegate the mediation of the discourse, especially in fictional narrations. This mediation on the transmission of the story has long been recognized by narratology as Point of View.

The conceptualization of the Point of View in narrative arts has been a crucial conflict in narratology. The mere term 'Point of View', as Genette pointed out, is not enough to designate so many and so different aspects of the discourse: which is the story, who tells the story, who perceives the story, with whom the viewer feels the story, how much story information have characters and readers if they are close or distant from the main actions. These aspects, among others, make a difference between speaking and perceiving. This theoretical issue depends on which type of narrative art is being analyzed: literature, film or theatre, and currently also new media. Depending on each narrative art, it is possible to identify perspective, focalization, ocularization and auricularization. Studies in comparative narratology aim to develop a system of categories under the umbrella term Mediation: 'Such a system would make it possible to identify features common to all forms of mediation as well as the features characteristic of and peculiar to each specific medium and mode of narration' (Meister & Shonert, 2009, p. 8).

As we have seen, vision as a human act, by recognizing space and what happens within it, is the core of VR. Vision allows us to understand where we are and at the same time, on a cognitive level, it allows us to understand who we are in a certain context. Since this study is based on a medium whose interface to the VR storyworld is cinematic, studies on the cinematic point of view are the closest insights that lead to the understanding of this topic. Following this idea, cVR presents itself again as the middle point between cinema and VR, thus these considerations support the definition of a medium-conscious narratology for VR. In this sense, we can find that all VE builder software in their documentation and guidelines[7] suggest in the very first lines to locate the camera-user at the 0°0°0° position, which means locating the all-feeling-eye at the center of VE. The visual position of the interactors in a distance relation with objects and agents within the VE determines the quantity of visual-auditory information that interactors perceive from the scene-space, and this fact does not deal with the camera position as a viewpoint but is a result of authorial decisions in terms of narrative mediation. Hence, interactors can be invited to enter and explore space, but that does not mean that they are actually agents of the storyworld.

---

7   Daydream, Unity, Unreal, Oculus

2.4.1. *Discoursivization in cVR and IFcVR*

Narrative is the outcome of a completed process: it is a product (Meister & Schonert, 2009, p. 12). In cinema, this process has been called by Gaudreault (1988, p. 199) 'filmic discoursivization'. In the dichotomy story/discourse, discourse is the representation of something that is not materially present (Meister & Shonert, 2009), but virtually present. The filmic discoursivization is developed as a layered activity, as a big orchestration of different expression modes (Gaudreault & Jost, 2007). In cinematographic terms, Gaudreault & Jost (2007) proposed a categorization of the narrator according to the division Vertical/Horizontal montage that has been mentioned above.

To what is shown in the Vertical axis, resulting from the combined work of *mise-en-scene* and framing, is limited to what has been called *monstration*. The second layer of cinematic narrativity corresponds to the horizontal axis, at a level superior to that of monstration, as a function of temporal modulation, it becomes the *narrator*. At a higher level, these two instances would be modulated and regulated by the filmic *meganarrator* responsible for the *meganarrative*: the film itself (Gaudreault & Jost, 2007, p. 58).

At this point, it is pertinent to add an extra level, due to the interactive nature of cVR and IFcVR, to the role of the Meganarrator: that is the HyperMostrator. The HyperMostrator acts on both vertical and horizontal montage, and it includes within the cinematic interface the interactive hotspots, as well as the decision-making moments within the narrative. However, in the category of Filmic Narrator, composed as a function of Meganarrator, it is not included in the HyperMegaNarrator, because this takes place when the creator delivers part of his authorial power to the interactors. Figure 2 shows the distinctions between the different functions, and the independence between Meganarrator and HyperMegaNarrator.

The HyperMegaNarrator comprises the hyper montage of both vertical and horizontal axes. In cVR, the interactors choose the fragments of the sphere that they want to see, and this means to create a sub-sequence within the same shot; this level of interactivity corresponds to the vertical montage. While in IFcVR the interactors will choose the path to follow by taking conscious or unconscious decisions, creating the ultimate sequence and therefore their own experience, this higher level of interactivity corresponds to the horizontal montage. Hence, in cVR and IFcVR, as in cinema, the Meganarrator is responsible for the grand-image making, while the *HyperMegaNarrator* is the constructor of the final narrative experience.

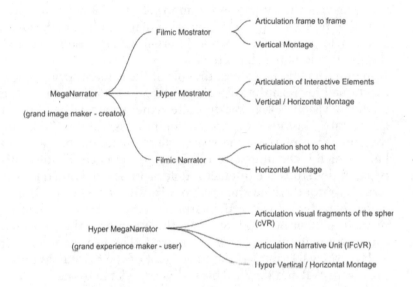

Figure 2. Hyper Filmic Narration in cVR and IFcVR

2.4.2. *The Narrator Type or Interactor Role in cVR*

'Whether it is a question of cinema or any other form of narrative, it is impossible, without taking useless risks, to do away with the notion of the narrator' (Gaudreault & Jost, 2007, p. 62). To understand the concept of Point of View in cinema, Francois Jost and André Gaudreault, in their book *Le Récit Cinématographique,* find a theoretical basis on the concept of Focalization proposed for the study of literature by Gerard Genette. Focalization designates the cognitive relationship between narrator and character, it answers the question 'who sees?', 'who is the character whose point of view orients the narrative perspective,' (Genette, 1980, p. 186) and the 'regulation of narrative information' (Genette, 1980, p. 162). In cinematic analysis, the term point of view is often understood as the viewpoint, that is, an optical paradigm, while Francois Jost (2004) names 'ocularization' the phenomenon that determines both the position of the camera and the vision of a homodiegetic or heterodiegetic character. 'Ocularization has to do with the relation between what the camera shows and what the characters are presumed to be seeing' (p. 74). External ocularization puts the characters before the camera, while Internal ocularization recreates the visual field of the character.

In omnidirectional videos, the role of the camera acquires new functionalities regarding Focalization and Ocularization, as the interactor vision *viewpoint* is the same as the camera. Depending on the narrative instance, the production process will vary. To locate the camera within the scene-space, the cinematographer needs to know which is the interactor role in the experience. To solve this issue, in this study the Interactor Role is proposed. I opted for the term Narrator distinguishing it from Focalizator. The Focalizator is the character who leads the narration, who will restrict the narrative to his/her perspective, while the Narrator is the voice that carries through the narrative. As shown in Figure 2 the Interactor as HyperMegaNarrator is the final agent of the discoursivization process in cVR and IFcVR. This role is not related to the Focalizator but to the narrator.

The NT item indicates who is the viewer inside the scene. The framework proposed by Cleanth Brooks and Robert Penn Warren (1943), also used by Gerard Genette for drawing the concept of Focalization (1976), describes the different types of narrators in literature. Brooks and Warren's framework offers a simple division of narrator roles that can vary on the levels of information restriction of the focalizer. However, such restrictions deal with the literary screenplay rather than having an effective role on technical filmic issues. Based on Brooks and Warren (1943) narrator types, a proposal to interactors' point of view in cVR experience is presented. The interactor type defines where the camera will be placed in the scene, in accordance with the director's intentions.

1.   Protagonist: Interactor live their own story as the main character. They can embody someone else's story, or they can be a player-character.

2.   Secondary Character: Interactor and main character interact. They can embody a character, or they can be a player-character.

3.   Omniscient Interactor: Interactor is analytical regarding the story, having access to characters' feelings and thoughts, or having information that is unknown to the characters.

4.   External Interactor: Interactor observes the events without access to characters' feelings and thoughts.

The narrator-interactor role in relationship with characters, as is noticed in the Routledge Encyclopaedia of Narrative Theory (Herman, 2008), seems to present the same difference between narrators and characters, as a matter of hierarchy, function, and representational authority, not of different mental processes. Narrator Types are differentiated according to whether they are *intradiegetic* (they are characters of the storyworld) or *extradiegetic* (they do not belong to the storyworld) in Genette terms, and according to the degree of information that they can have from the storyworld. Based on the Genettian division between *homodiegetic* and *heterodiegetic* narrator, the distinction of first-person narrator or third person narrator and the different levels of focalization, different combinations can be extracted. These combinations regard script and *mise-en-scene* rather than the camera position, or the use of a voice over. However, in VR, interactors are always homodiegetic, as they are constantly building the story around their own experience, no matter who is the focalizer of the narrative.

2.5. *Narrative Distance in cVR*

If in this moment we look around at 360°, we will find hundreds of elements that offer information about the world, about reality; these elements can be part of the environment as objects or can be perceptive ocular phenomena as vanishing points and diminishing lines, colour, lights, and shadows. The arrangement of all these elements makes up a situation to which we exist at this precise moment. This wealth of information and the lack of intermediation between us, as interactors of this 'real interface' and the situation that we build by arranging all the elements, is related to the concept of Narrative Distance (Genette, 1980). As we have seen before, borrowing concepts from word-mediated narratives is not always the best way to proceed; if these concepts are forced into a new medium, narratological concepts, as narrative art forms themselves, are in a continuous evolution and adaptation.

In HMD-driven VR, immersion, both perceptive and narrative, is often taken for granted. Reaching a perceptive immersion passes through the system's ability to link multiple senses to the VE, while a narrative immersion passes not only through the content of the story but through a form that is so natural it is almost invisible. Classical narratology suggests that the lower the mediation between story and and interactor is, the lower the feeling of reading an artefact and the higher the level of narrative immersion. Narrative immersion in cVR finds interesting insights in classical narratology: the absence of a mediator, the low speed, and a large volume of 'free' information (Tornitore, 2013). In fact, it is already possible to find these insights in blogs and tutorials about VR and cVR. For example, before it's sunset, the Oculus Story Studio[8] offered some suggestions based on their experience in creating some of the first high-quality VR short movies, related to the concept of narrative distance.

In cVR, depending on the level of authorial control that the creator desires to have upon the narrative, the 'filmic monstrator' must know how to guide the experience of the interactors and their montage of the story. Until now, the Holy Grail of cVR storytelling has been the dichotomy between interactors' gaze freedom and authorial control. In other words: How to be sure that interactors are looking in the right direction at the right time, retaining respect for the interactors' visual freedom?

2.5.1. *The Mediator Presence*

Every discourse presupposes a mediation, but a strong notability of the Mediator increases the distance between storyworld and

---

interactor. The mediator can be a facilitator of the discourse, or an obstacle in experiencing the story. It is not possible to think that the only act of wearing a HMD eliminates the role of the Mediator, both for fictional and non-fictional VR experiences.

The term Mediator indicates all the narrative strategies that the Meganarrator uses to guide the cinematic discourse. Again, Genette understands mediation as a two-fold element: mediation on the discourse, which involves the use of language and literary techniques to convey the story, and the narrator's act of telling the story. Like in cinema, in the cVR discourse cinematic elements are included in relation with the *mise-en-scene,* such as the creation of the atmosphere with lighting and sound, characters and props disposed to guide interactors' gaze; the position and the movements of the camera; the insertion of graphics that enrich the scene-space; as well as visual and auditory interactive elements. On the narrator's act of telling, we can find the use of a voice over, or audiovisual insertions (texts, animated figures, etc.) that verbally narrate past, present, or future events, thoughts or feelings, or instructions.

In cVR, as a spatial medium, the mediation in the two dimensions (filmic discourse and verbal narration) is also used for instructive purposes, besides the diegetic narration. Some of these functions are:

1. To contextualise interactors in the storyworld.
2. To guide interactors in space.
3. To give instructions on how to live or navigate the interactive experience.

An interesting example can be found in the study of Mirjam Vosmeer and her team, about the use of the voice over in cVR experiences. In the paper *Who Are You? Voice-Over Perspective in Surround Video* (Vosmeer et al., 2017) they present the results of using first person, second person and third person voice over:

> Our experiment showed that of the respondents that were given a choice between second- and first-person perspective, and second- and third-person perspective, a large majority (75%) preferred the

second person perspective. After the test, [...] many respondents stated that the third person narrative felt more like listening to an audio book, and that this perspective gave them the sense of just having to sit back and listen. Apparently the third person perspective did not stimulate them to engage or to look around, and they did not feel actively involved in the movie. With the first-person perspective, on the other hand, many respondents indicated that they had a hard time identifying with the voice that was telling the story. With the second person perspective, most of the respondents experienced a strong sense of presence. They indicated that in this version, the visual perspective that was provided by the surrounding video content seemed to relate closely to the perspective that was given by the voice-over narration. This version also triggered them to look around and actively engage with the surrounding video content (p. 229).

Another insight that tries to answer the main question how to visually guide interactors' gaze into the right event (author[itarian] point of view) is given by the former Story Study of Oculus[9]:

We tried guiding the audience's view through audio cues. We had a bird fly by the viewer to capture their attention and guide their gaze towards a point in the scene. We also tried to design the set in a way that guides the viewer's gaze to the right areas. However, each time we implemented one of these dictatorial tools too heavy handedly, the storytelling started to feel forced, staged, and artificial.

To embrace VR as its own unique medium, we must let go of our almighty control of what the audience sees. Instead of instantly pushing the story onto the viewer, we take a step back for a while and let the viewer take part in discovering the story themselves. We call this 'The Letting-Go.

By not forcing the viewer to look somewhere and making the surroundings interesting in all directions, we incite the viewer's curiosity in the world. And through this curiosity, have them take a more active role in experiencing the story. We give the audience time to look wherever they want and get used to where they are. Then, after 40 seconds or so, a time we felt was enough for most people to feel settled and relaxed, we start utilizing things like the bird to get the audience's attention back. But by now, because we gave them time to

---

settle in, they are willing to listen to us.

The more information without a mediator, the greater the narrative immersion (Tornitore, 2013). This claim by Tornitore referring to literary narratology also applies to cVR, with a twist: the presence of the mediator will be more notorious, especially in spatial and interactive environments where the interactors need clues and guides that allow him to build the experience. However, the less invasive and authoritarian this mediation is, the greater the sense of agency will be, and therefore, the immersion.

2.5.2. *Evenementielle Density and Discourse Speed in cVR*

This last piece of advice from the Oculus team offers two special insights related to the two last components of Narrative Distance:

Evenementielle Density (ED): To make interesting surroundings in all directions.

Discourse Speed (DS): To give the audience time to look and get settled in.

These two components have been placed together since they are closely related. The greater the amount of visual and auditory information in all 360°, the longer the interactors will need to be able to perceive and understand the information within the storyworld; therefore, the speed of the filmic discourse will be slower.

In cVR, a VE with little information around can be perceived as empty. Emptiness without a narrative purpose can generate boredom, a feeling of being lost, and even anxiety. The *Evenementielle* Density refers to the number of audiovisual stimuli within the VE, including both diegetic and extradiegetic elements, and it is also related to the Points of Interest (POI). POIs are on top of the *evenementielle* hierarchy of ED. From a cognitive point of view, interactors, as *HyperMegaNarrators*, connect and give meaning to the elements they find, whether they are related to the story or to the discourse. In this sense, all these elements play an *evenementielle* role, since the cVR is a *corpo-evento* and interactors are narrating their own experience. We need to choreograph what happens in the sphere to develop the ED and push the story forward.

A great density of audiovisual information means a slowdown in the Narrative Time as in the HCI Time. The decrease in discourse speed induces the interactors to a greater participation, either because the increase in the flow of information requires an active participation in recognizing and semantically connecting the audiovisual signs within the experience, or because the decrease in discourse speed is understood by the interactors as the request for greater attention in the presence of an important moment of the story, without forgetting the reactions of intolerance caused by long descriptions.

The regulation of both ED and DS are subject to the creator's narrative intentions, and there is no mechanism or rule to follow. As it is highlighted in the article *The Storyteller's Guide to the Virtual Reality Audience,* Kate Newton (2016) developed some experiments on the design of the scene-space and noticed that little visual information can generate three cases:

- When interactors have limited visual information, they will work twice as hard to make meaning out of every detail they see.

-If something doesn't correspond to their expectations, it takes them out of the experience.

-It sends them into detective mode, investigating the scene from a distance.

3.
INTERACTIVE FICTION IN
CINEMATIC VIRTUAL REALITY

3.1. *Bringing Interactivity into Cinematic Virtual Reality*

While current research is largely focused on unveiling the film language and production methods of the linear cVR, this still offers a limited level of interactivity if compared to what VR can reach. It is fascinating to be 'present' inside the scene; excellent results in this respect can be achieved because cinema's spectatorial voyeurism is enhanced in cVR, together with the contextualization of the immersive filmic work by means of performances in real spaces. However, an extra level of interactivity to the filmic immersive experience can overcome the incongruence generated by being immersed but having little agency within the scene-space. Through the implementation of an interactive fictional narrative structure, interactors can directly manipulate both the course of the story and the discoursivization of the filmic experience, besides looking at the omnidirectional image.

Interactive Fiction in cinematic Virtual Reality (IFcVR) can be defined as an Interactive Digital Narrative (IDN), placed at the intersection of Interactive Fiction (IF), the computer-mediated interactive fictional narratives, and Cinematic VR (cVR), i.e., the creation of virtual experiences that have a cinematic interface of any kind: 360º video (stereo and monoscopic), 2D 360º animations, 3D 360º animations and video, volumetric video in 360º VEs. cVR is distinguished from VR by not allowing the interactors to modify the VE or to interact with its agents in real time. In cVR, interactors can only observe the VE and activate interactive objects overlaid upon the interface. Even in 6DOF[1] cVR experiences,

---

1   http://www.onsetfacilities.com/virtual-production/360-6dof-volumetric-

the cinematic interface does not allow user manipulations. It is a fixed and finite object. It is, after all, an enhanced film (or video) experience. Although the reception of the IFcVR passes through the cVR aesthetics, a non-linear narrative structure offers the possibility of counteracting the limited interactivity of the cinematic interface. In IFcVR. interactors can manipulate the transmission of the discourse by making decisions that modify the course of the story, stimulating their interest in repeating the experience to look for missed details or discover different endings.

In this chapter, I will approach the narrative definition of IFcVR, through the analysis of the convergence between interactive cinema, interactive fiction and cVR. Starting from the hypothesis that IFcVR should be the type of filming experience of VR, the creation of IFcVR goes through the integration of the latest developments in Human Computer Interaction (HCI). The innovation in connecting the story with different ways of interacting with it would be the key to success of an IFcVR experience. Possible interactive structures and today's HCI possibilities are presented in the next sections, to display the spectrum of possibilities of interaction between human and narrative in cVE. Regardless of the types of interaction, I reaffirm IFcVR as a narrative form, and consequently as an IDN, through the adoption of the latest advances in the field of IDN.

3.2. *The Interactive Film*

The idea of creating an interactive film experience by hybridizing it with other analog media and art forms is as old as cinema itself. It is not a fashion that came along in the digital age.

When researching interactive cinema in books, journals, and conferences, or just by googling it, one word jumps out above all OR one word stands out above all the others: Kinoautomat. Kinoautomat is an interactive cinema created by Raduz Cincera in Czechoslovakia in 1967 and presented at the Expo 67 in Montreal. Kinoautomat was designed to screen a 35mm film with numerous narrative pathways in which the audience voted for the alternative paths for the film. This voting system 'brought a novel democratic aspect to the cinematic experience' (Hales, 2014, p. 143). As Hales points out, Cincera's Kinoautomat was not intended to be a one-screening interactive film but a movie theatre for interactive movies, a 'system designed to function with any non-linear film that had been created correctly for it' (Hales, 2014, p. 153). Years later, at the Osaka *Flower Expo* from April to September of 1990, Cincera presented another filmic interactive experience: Cinelabyrinth, a theatre with eleven rooms called 'show spaces' and a total of 22 (video) projection screens. Within the Cinelabyrinth, spectators have the unique freedom to navigate between show spaces, curating their viewing experience by selecting sequences of their choice (Hales, 2014, p. 160-163). In a groundbreaking event reported by the LA Times in 1992, an innovative creation was introduced as 'the world's first truly interactive motion picture.' This revolutionary film, titled 'I'm your man' (Bejan, 1992), enabled audience members to collectively shape and direct the action using Nintendo-like pistol grips, akin to the concept proposed by Kinoautomat. The interactive film, or Interfilm as they called it, promised to be 'the most revolutionary technological development in film since Al Jolson ushered in the talkie era with *The Jazz Singer* in 1927'. Just six years later, The New York Times published the article *Interactive Filmmakers Hope to Make a Comeback*[2], noticing the failure of *I'm your man*, as Lisa Napoli wrote:

> Ideas that are ahead of their time don't necessarily die. If they're lucky, they get reincarnated as new technologies are invented. Take for example Interfilm, an attempt to create 'interactive' films that failed, for a variety of reasons, earlier in the '90s. Its creators hope the concept will make a comeback thanks to the increasing popularity of digital video disk (DVD) technology.

Two decades after, we know that interactive films in movie theatres, DVDs or browser-based, never got the attention that they dreamed of receiving. Nonetheless, the importance of these attempts does not rely only on the fact to change the course of the filmic narrative but in how it established a new relationship

---

2   https://archive.nytimes.com/www.nytimes.com/library/tech/98/08/cy-ber/articles/17dvd.html

between public and medium, at a time when audiences timidly began to exercise their power over devices and media more frequently and with greater control. In interactive narrative texts, both content and support are constantly shouting to the public: go ahead, manipulate me!

We can say that *Kinoautomat*, as Interactive Cinema, is the direct grandfather of the IFcVR, since they share two fundamental characteristics: the filmic content and the push-button logic (Huhtamo, 2014, p. 181). In IFcVR, the filmic content has a new aesthetic form, but it keeps its cinematic interface, and yes, we are simply pushing buttons and clicking options on all interfaces from all devices on the reality spectrum. The name *Kinoautomat* is in fact inspired by the push-button logic of the 'coin-operated drinks vending machine with multiple choices (of drink configurations) by pressing a combination of buttons' (Hales, 2014, p. 145). Nonetheless, the name also reveals a hidden potential of the cinema, something that sounds almost an oxymoron when the adjective 'automatic' is added to the word 'cinema'. Even though it connotes indirect or limited human control, it refers to a machine or system able to act on itself autonomously.

One main difference marks IFcVR from *Kinoautomat*: the individual experience. In Kinoautomat, as in cinema, spectators were 'together alone' (Huhtamo, 2014, p. 175) in a physical space where spectators voted the alternatives and afterward watched a sequence that was voted by most of the current audience but perhaps not by themselves. This kind of democracy is no longer necessary in new media. In the one-to-one relationship between a user-device, the user's decision-making capability, or even just their clicking activity, is an individual process. This fact has strong repercussions on the concept of show as a social and collective event, where social and collective translates into 'many people in a single space'. In this sense, we are living a metamorphosis of virtual crowds, where the connecting point to virtual networks is supplanting corporeal participation in public spaces (Huhtamo, 2014, p. 187).

But the individual logic did not stop the evolution of the hybrid see/hear and choose; on the contrary, it traced its course by finding good ground in computers. The fact that 'the mouse was designed 'for an individual user sitting in front of a computer terminal' (Huhtamo, 2014, p. 183) freed the interactive audiovisual from the chain that had it tied to democracy, and at the same time it accomplished the democratic utopia in which each one can have what they choose. In this way, the idea of Kinoautomat as a theatre for interactive films was abandoned. New proposals combining cinema and interactivity consist in temporary artistic installations, with no intention of evolving as a unified artistic form. With the massification of the personal computer and afterwards, with internet access, along with the constant evolution of the digital audiovisual supports, a new format emerged: the interactive video.

Interactive video was born as the counterpart of linear playback videos, in which interaction consists in the manual video search, play, stop and pause. In *Interactive Video: Algorithms and Technologies*, Riad Hammoud (2006) presents it as the promise of video formats by offering interactors 'nonconventional interactive features, powerful knowledge-acquisition and teaching tools, efficient storage, as well as non-linear ways of navigation and searching' (p. 3). In 2005 YouTube appeared, a game-changer in video consumption. Since then, VOD (Video on Demand) web platforms for computers and smart TVs entered the mass market, modifying forever how people consume audiovisual content. Although VOD systems and strategies were already proposed in the 90's, the shift accomplished through the internet had a bigger impact. While VOD is a consumption mode (it gives interactors what they want, whenever they want, the times they want) interactive video is an audiovisual format; it is enriched video content.

Hammoud indicates three definitions of interactive video depending on the complexity of its interactive structure and elements:

1. Interactive video is a digitally enriched form of the original raw video sequence allowing viewers attractive and powerful interactivity forms and navigational possibilities.
2. Interactive video presentation is a form of interactive video document that is centered on enriched video but is not exclusively video.
3. Interactive video database is a collection of interactive video documents and interactive video presentations (Hammoud, 2006, p. 6).

In recent years, the possibilities of interactive video have aroused the interest of video makers and web developers, proposing browser-based experiences whose backbone is video, or audio-visual content. Interactive video also has become a tool for story-telling, from which two genres have had humble success among web surfers: (1) the Interactive Music Video, in which interactivity pushes the boundaries of a ground-breaking audiovisual genre. Some examples are Bob Dylan's *Like a Rolling Stone* or Jack White's *Black Liquorice*; and (2) the Webdoc, proposed as an audiovisual genre by Arnau Gifreu Castells in his PhD thesis *The Interactive documentary as a new audiovisual genre*[3]. The webdoc moves along the thin line between documentary and journalism, and mixes multimedia content in a browser-based product. It is possible to find great webdocs from independent filmmakers as well as others produced by well-known media conglomerates.

Something interesting about these formats is the change entailed in their aesthetic reception as audiovisual content. In many webdocs, for example, the quantity of multimedia materials, such as text or still images, moves the documentary reception away from the film experience. In these cases, the hyperreading dynamic prevails over the feeling of 'watching a film', removing relevance to audiovisual content and giving it to navigation. However, other webdocs and interactive videos propose interactive experiences in which the video content is the core of the experience. This is the case, for instance, of the webdoc *I love your work*; the *360° video for browser and HMD A Way to Go* (2014)[4]; *Turbulence: A Hypernarrative Interactive Movie* (Knoller & Arie, 2009); the mainstream productions from 2017 Black Mirror Bandersnatch (Netflix) and Mosaic (HBO), and the recent Immortality (2022) directed by Sam Barlow.

New frontiers of Interactive Cinema are moving towards the non-conscious interactivity, in which interactors' biofeedback and brain activity change the course of the story. In this way, the final output of non-linear film is perceived by the interactors as linear, granting the filmic experience but removing the decision-making process. Pia Tikka (2008) has called this type of new cinema Enactive Cinema. This already differentiates from interactive

---

3   Original title in Spanish: *El documental interactivo como nuevo género audio-visual: Estudio de la aparición del nuevo género, aproximación a su definición y propuesta de taxonomía y de modelo de análisis a efectos de evaluación, diseño y producción.*

4   http://a-way-to-go.com/

cinema by its very name. Enactive cinema is rooted in cognitive-constructivist film theory. According to cognitive-constructivism, 'viewers are cognitively active and aware when watching films [...] narrative cinema complex engagement is not due to its simple linearity but to the films' rewarding play with the spectators strive for coherence'(Ben-Shaul, 2008, p. 10). In her web page[5], Tikka explains that while viewers are immersed in the film's narrative, a system called 'Eisensteinian montage machine' tracks their unconscious emotional and bodily responses and modifies the film based on these changes. Following this idea, in recent times research and creation is moving in the direction of enactive cinema rather than interactive cinema (Ramchurn et al, 2018).

It should be noticed that, despite the obstacles, failures, and little recognition, the idea of Interactive Film has existed since the conception of cinema. The Interactive Film is content, an autonomous interactive narrative text, independent of its reproduction support, whether it is an interactive cinema with a democratic voting system, a video installation connected to brain sensors, a DVD, or a webpage, and it can present a fiction story, a documentary, a mockumentary, or an experimental art film. The divergences between interactive film media (interactive cinema, interactive video, enactive cinema, etc.) seem to be rooted in the kind of interactivity that is required from the interactors: whether it should be a collective experience in a physical space or an individual experience through a desktop computer or a HMD; whether interactors' input should be conscious, stimulating participation and active role during the filmic experience, or if the storyline should vary based on physiological data, without involving interactors' decisions. The common points, on the other hand, are (1) to separate the film, as narrative entity, from the single outputs and from one-time readings, and (2) to involve interactors' thoughts and/or emotions in the filmic discourse.

---

5   http://www.enactivecinema.net/

3.3. *Fiction Meets Interactivity*

IFcVR looks for an interactive fiction film experience. The Interactive Fiction (IF) is the underlying narrative structure of IFcVR, in which its interactive feature is the multiplicity of pathways, while fiction is the core of the narrative. Fiction is the essence of a storyworld, whether it is narrated in linear cVR or IFcVR. It is a tough task to recognize fiction from nonfiction because fiction represents events that we absorb through nonfictional modes of understanding. Furthermore, narrative is an artifice, and this fact presupposes that all narratives contain some fiction, because through narrative 'Possible Worlds' (Ryan, 1991) can exist. To explain the difference between fiction and non-fictional narratives, Ryan separates the actual world we live in from possible realistic or fantastic worlds created by imagination. In this sense, non-fictional texts refer to the actual world, while fictional texts create non-actual possible worlds (Ryan, 2013b).

As Ryan (2011) notes, fiction is based on the pretence to represent reality, not on being a representation of reality. Nonetheless, fiction's reality takes a new form in photography, cinema, or video, in opposition to literary fiction. These media capture realities visibly and audibly, defying in a further degree interactors' cognition in separating fiction from nonfiction, because fiction films present simulated events relying on the pretence that the actors are the characters. According to Ryan (2011), fiction literature differentiates from fiction cinema, in how we access the storyworld. In fictional verbal language, we hear a report of the events through a narrator, while in film we are looking at the events that someone, the *GrandMegaNarrator* or *GrandImageMaker,* is showing to us. Ryan also notes that this fashion has an alternative: the idea that film is unmediated, and that we feel as a spectatorial voyeur, not as an embodied witness within the scene, but as a 'disembodied consciousness that moves around the fictional world as freely as the camera' (Ryan, 2011).

Ergodic Literature (Aarseth, 1997), Interactive Fiction[6], (Blank & Lebling, 1980; Reed, 2012), Hyperfiction (Douglas, 2003; Bell,

---

6   Mary Ann Buckles 1987 UC San Diego Ph.D. dissertation *Interactive Fiction: The Computer Storygame 'Adventure'* was the first book-length aca-

2010), or Text Adventures, are some of the names that have been used to describe the fiction narrative with alternative storylines, in contradistinction to Interactive Narratives or Hypernarratives, that designate nonfiction interactive narratives. Since the advent of digital supports, these terms reflect the intersection between hypertext (Nelson, 1987; Landow, 1994) and narrative: hypertext and fiction. Yet, IF was born before the digital era. Most research on Interactive Digital Narratives (IDN) points to Jorge Luis Borges' *The Garden of Forking Paths* (1941) as the seed of interactive narratives. Even though the tale itself was not an interactive text, it presents the idea of a book that is, at the same time, a labyrinth:

> Ts'ui Pên would say once: I retire to write a book.
> And another: I retire to build a labyrinth.
> Everyone imagined two works;
> nobody thought that book and labyrinth were a single object

And the idea of multiple futures, forking paths in time, possibilities that give rise to other possibilities, and possibilities that converge in one time:

> ...the garden of the forking paths was the chaotic novel;
> the phrase several futures suggested to me the image of the bifurcation in time,
> not in space.
> [...] It creates, in this way, different paths, different times, which, too, proliferate and bifurcate

Afterwards, books themselves became labyrinths, as the narrative artefacts became interactive: the reader had to physically manipulate the book to assemble chapters, segments, and pieces of the story. Some examples are *Composition No. 1* (Saporta, 1963), *Rayuela* (Cortázar, 1966), *House of Leaves* (Danielewski, 2000) or *4321* (Auster, 2017). With the digital support, the Hypertext Fiction appears, a genre of Electronic Literature or e-literature. This era is opened by Judy Malloy's *Uncle Roy* (UNIX version: 1986, BASIC version: 1988) and *Eastgate* writers as Michael Joyce with *afternoon, a story* (1987) and Stuart Moulthrop with *Victory Gar-*

---

demic work on the form. (Rettberg, 2017, p. 34)

den (1992). But as was the case with interactive cinema, hypertext fictions never had either 'an operable business model, nor a significant cultural apparatus' (Rettberg, 2017, p. 174). This fact did not mean the end of interactive fiction narratives. Even though no genre or product really landed on the mass public, something probably better happened: IF established itself as a narrative method and continued to migrate to new digital platforms with new human computer interfaces.

There is a prejudice that eclipses the potential of the IF, that of the gamebook or Choose Your Own Adventure. This idea should be abandoned, as IF 'is not a simple 'Choose Your Own Adventure' scenario [...] since hypertexts can include hundreds or even thousands of narrative episodes or segments, connected with an even vaster number of links [...] a single work can have thousands of permutations' (Douglas, 2003, p. 24). On the contrary, IF is the theoretical and technical basis for the creation of intricate and complex narratives, which means great authorial work for the creation of meaningful interactive digital experiences. With the arrival of faster telecommunication standards, and the development of new and better platforms for VR, MR and AR, narratives will continue in this reformulation path, and IF is one of the main links between narrative and hypertextuality. This is how IF also broke through a format that seemed to be far from novels and books: video games. This perceived distance, however, could not be more wrong, since all video games unfold in a storyworld, even though they do not obey classic narrative mechanisms. This 'narratology vs. ludology' debate (Koenitz et al, 2015, p. 3), opened a branch of study within the field of IDN: Narrative in Video Games, also called Ludonarrative (Aarseth, 2012; Koenitz, 2018). Aarseth (2012) in *A Narrative Theory of Games* points out the two main issues at the core of the debate: 'Games, as a metonymic label, is the wrong term for ludonarrative software, and that narrative theory, while necessary, is not sufficient to understand these new forms'.

In fact, one of the first questions that emerged was if IFcVR would be enjoyed by interactors as a videogame or as an interactive film, as its interactive nature has a ludology component. This question led to the production of a prototype to measure if the user experience of IFcVR is closer to a videogame or to a filmic experience.

It is relevant to underline what I consider the main difference between narrative VR video games and IFcVR, that is, how the experience moves forwards: in videogames narrative experience is pushed by interactors' accomplished missions or goals; while in IFcVR, narrative leads interactors' experience and their interactions are based on the displayed events. In games, the communication between creator and player is different than the one that gets established in films. A game writer is always communicating with the player, by offering narrative context, passing on game information regarding goals and missions, or tutoring the player on the game mechanics. Instead, communication between filmmaker and spectator moves in other terms: narration does not pass information but generates experience; narration is complete only when it is experienced by the spectator, as Carlos Ruiz Carmona argues in *The Role and Purpose of Film Narration* (2017):

> It is the experience of the narrative that provokes the emotion during the act of communication [...] film narrative evokes abstract dimensions of human experience which don't necessarily translate into data or need to be understood or explained [...] Experience cannot be or does not need to be understood or processed rationally or emotionally to communicate. Thus, film narration only needs to provoke experience to communicate. This is why I argue that film narratives only complete themselves after the audience experiences them. Before the viewer's experience, the narrative remains an intention to become something (Carmona, 2017).

Following this idea, the IFcVR examples share the cinematic interface and the interactive fiction structure, and, excluding the last example, they have not been catalogued by their creators as video games or narrative video games, but under the tag 'interactive VR film / movie', reaffirming a distinction that lies in the experience of film narration. In a video game, interactors have the responsibility to trigger the flow of the events, to discover, to win, or simply to try not to die, in the same way the interactors are expecting not to get bored. In IFcVR, interactors have a privileged position in being present in the space where the events take place and in manipulating them according to their interpretation, but with the awareness that they are attending a film that is an autonomous narrative. The fact that interactors are living an external independent narrative should not give them a passive role, as there is always the risk of them getting bored and taking off the HMD. On the contrary, an IFcVR experience must maintain curiosity and suspense, and make interactors feel that the events are evolving, that something will happen when that door is opened, that in the end their participation in the story will bring cognitive and emotional satisfactions. This sensation is called 'dramatic tension' and is one of the great issues that IDNs must face.

3.4. *The Issue of Dramatic Tension*

The process of construction of a unified theory of IDN is still ongoing and with it, a theoretical basis for all the artistic forms and platforms included under the IDN concept. As Koenitz summarised in *Towards a Specific Theory of Interactive Digital Narratives* (2015), since the beginnings of the intersection between narrative and computer-based media, several researchers have developed frameworks and methodologies that allow the understanding and production of this type of narrative texts. First approaches for IDN are based on the first dramatic theory, Aristotle's Poetics (Laurel, 1986; Mateas, 2001), while a Narrative Theory for VR (Aylett & Louchart, 2003) finds a primary basis on Plato's distinction between mimesis and diegesis. Subsequently, the narrative basis for computer-based media were heavily influenced by the narratology studies of the second half of the twentieth century conducted by Gerard Genette, Seymour Chatman, Gerald Prince, and Mieke Bal as proposed by Espen Aarseth, Nick Montfort, Henry Jenkins, and Marie-Laure Ryan. During IDN history, the issue of narrative vs interactivity keeps re-emerging, from mainly two points of view: (1) level of authorial control vs level of user agency and (2) narrative coherence and engagement vs level of interactivity.

As authors are shifting from an over authoritarian attitude to embrace Barthes' death of the author, the second issue seems to be the most controverted of the two: 'for hyper-narratives to be comprehensible, coherence within narrative threads and between them must be maintained' (Ben-Shaul, 2008, p. 31). Hence, the returning question is: how to create an engaging and coherent interactive story? How to achieve that feeling that keeps up our attention and emotion towards the story? In this respect, the keyword is engagement. Novels, films, theatre plays, video games, TV series, and oral storytelling have achieved this challenge as they stimulate the receiver's need to know what is happening next. Propp (2003), followed by Campbell (2008) and Vogler (2008) have recognized some patterns in folk storytelling that raise empathy with the protagonist and their endeavour. These patterns were combined in the popular Hero's Journey, a series of stages that the hero must overcome to master his challenge. Hollywood blockbusters scripts, on the other hand, have been using a three-acts structure to guarantee a climax; this structure is known as Syd Field's paradigm (2005). Both Hero's Journey and Field's Paradigm share a structure often labelled as dramatic arc or story arc.

In the article *'The Story Arc', a Ghost of Narrative Game Design*, Koenitz demystifies the dramatic arc as a narrative standard, 'the notion of the 'Aristotelian story arc' is at best loosely connected to the original texts. This status provides an explanation for contradictory positions on the suitability of the Aristotelian model for analysis and for the design of narrative-focused video games' (Koenitz, 2017). This rejection of using the 'dramatic arc' in the design of IDNs was presented by Pamela Jennings, who instead proposes the study of multi-climax narrative structures, as in African storytelling, for interactive digital narratives. The 'story arc' responds to Brooks and Warren proposal of breaking down fictional narratives into plot-stages: exposition, complication, climax, and denouement, tracing the experiences of storyworld participants who are faced with some sort of conflict, whether external or internal (Herman et al, 2008).

The implementation of a narrative structure, such as the Field's paradigm or the Hero's Journey, responds to the authorial need of 'narrating' or 'showing' the storyworld. During the discoursivization process undertaken, interactors will expect conflict to happen. For Brooks and Warren, conflict is what links plot with character (1943 p. 172), but, as Iser (1997) remarks, the immersion is not accomplished by the mere presentation of conflicts but includes the multiple solutions that the text can imply, thus 'the more explicit the text, the less involved the interactors will be, leading them to the feeling of anti-climax' (p. 46). This concatenation of conflicts creates a dramatic progression in time. During this time in which interactors live the storyworld, there is hope or desire to reach a peak moment in which s/he finds the message, lives a strong emotion, or discovers the truth. The arrival into a narrative (experiential) discovery - a climax - represents a reward for the interactors after taking the decision to access the proposed storyworld. The debate, beyond the underlying temporary structure, falls back on having a narrative climax or not. This opens different concerns: Why not talk about multiple climaxes? or even, is it really necessary to reach a climax?

If narrative, as Bruner has suggested, is about the vicissitudes of intention, it is also, as historian Hayden White argues, about seeing events display the coherence, integrity, fullness, and closure... that [in life] can only be imaginary. The ways in which interactive narratives map and yet do not map onto this concept speak eloquently to potential for future development in hypertext fiction and digital narratives alike. And to the reasons why we listen, read, or watch fictions in any medium unfold, climax, and resolve for no purpose aside from the unalloyed pleasures they give us (Douglas, 2003, p. 151).

The issue is about creating and releasing tension. Vogler, for example, suggests the insertion of several climaxes, one for each act, and even one for each stage of the Hero's Journey. The objective of the climax is to change the hero's direction, assigning a new goal. He also suggests a differentiation between 'crisis' and 'climax', the first one related as a 'point in a story or drama at which hostile forces are in the tensest state of opposition', and the latter as 'the crowning event of the whole story' (Vogler, 2008, p. 156), and expands the conception of climax by describing the 'quiet climax'. In opposition to 'an explosive, dramatic, loud, or dangerous moment of the story, a quiet climax can give a sense that all the conflicts have been harmoniously resolved, and all the tensions converted into feelings of pleasure and peace' (Vogler, 2008, p. 202).

The challenge is to create interesting interactive stories that take interactors into a narrative experience leading to enjoyment, transformation, and satisfaction without discarding the conception of the climax but embracing it and multiplying according to the number of possible paths, scenes, or narrative nodes that the predefined structure engages. Today, most IDNs prototypes and experiences are based on a fixed structure of predetermined hyperlinks, a structure that can be limited in terms of user agency. In Interactive Films, the predetermined hyperlinked mind map is the most common structure, if not the only one since each audiovisual node's production costs are higher than other media. The same happens in IFcVR.

Since IFcVR is based on an interactive fiction structure with pre-recorded narrative units, the creator effectively has more control over the narrative text. The variety of navigation outputs relies on two features: (1) the richness of auditory and visual inputs within each scene space and (2) the multiplicity of links between nodes. In IFcVR, the fictional pact implies the fruition of a cinematic experience rather than a game. These characteristics change the position of the creator towards an experience that finally seeks a linear and fluid output and frees the creator from proposing an experience in which interactors assume a player role. The success of the final linear output, like in a film, depends on the coherence between all details and events so as, at the end of the experience, interactors can draw conclusions from a unified whole. Interactivity cannot be created in the same way in games as in hypernarrative films, because the first ones bring simultaneity to the fore while the latter ones rely on the evolution of a storyline. Divergences from coherent storylines result in less satisfying stories. Likewise, "restrictions for players result in less satisfying games" (Ben-Shaul, 2008, p. 55). In fact, assembling a coherent story that can take different paths is hard creative work. There are, however, interactive structures that facilitate this task and better adapt to the narrative's need for coherence.

3.4.1. *Non-Linear Narrative Structures*

The interactive fiction film is built upon a predetermined structure composed by single narrative nodes with multiple in and out links connected to each other. This interconnected structure acquires the shape of a network, and according to this shape, the navigation can have different behaviours. Despite its underlying interactive structure, IFcVR, as an Interactive film, searches for a consistent linear narrative, in which the jumps between audiovisual nodes are imperceptible and the navigation becomes a cognitive activity rather than a playful attitude (Ryan, 1999). The final output is a linear film. In this sense, this final output is not different from any film, the only difference is that interactive films sequences and scenes are organised by the interactors. In film history, non-linear films have become a genre on itself. In non-linear films, the storyline has been broken down and gets re-organized with a different diegetic temporality, thus it is the spectator's task to rearrange the sequences in a cause-effect order. The article *How the Brain Reacts to Scrambled Stories* (Green, 2016) published by the newspaper *The Atlantic*, relates to some experiments that show how people enjoy paying attention to disruptive narratives in which they must assemble the pieces.

When creating either a traditional non-linear film or an interactive film, the screenwriting must follow the chosen interactive structure. The screenwriting occurs in a second moment guided by the mental map of the sequences that make up the story from beginning to end. The interactive structure can be found in the literature as in blogs or software, with different names: mind map, mind tree, hyperlinked structure, networked structure, etc. Marie-Laure Ryan (2015, p. 165-175) has summarised the interactive architectures as follows:

1. The Vector (with optional side branches): This structure remains linear and works as a 'string of pearls', a succession of narrative units with a cause-effect relationship. Interactivity is added by means of extra multimedia material but does not influence the course of the story. A great example showing that a simple interaction should not mean an insignificant experience is Vincent Morisset's *A Way to Go* (2014)[7].

2. The Complete Graph. In this structure all nodes are linked to all the other ones. This is the most interconnected structure and contemplates all possible navigation paths, and therefore, higher level of interactor's autonomy. However, as Ryan notices, this structure cannot guarantee a perfect narrative coherence.

3. The Network. According to Ryan, this is the most used structure for interactive narratives as it allows more authorial control over the course of the story. Nodes can be accessed through different routes allowing interactors different navigation alternatives. Although the network structure is intended for the creator to restrict the navigation pathways, the structure does not guarantee

---

7   http://a-way-to-go.com/

narrative coherence as interactors risk returning into previous nodes, creating loops and circuits that can break the temporal unfolding of the narrative.

4. The Tree. This architecture is based on branching plots, in which there is no risk to create loops or circuits, since once a pathway is taken it will develop independently of the others. The big problem of this kind of architecture is its exponential growth. A higher level of interactivity requires a vast number of nodes that results in a great amount of creative and production work, on one side, by designing all the narrative possibilities, and, on the other side, on producing such a high number of audiovisual nodes.

5. The Database. Ryan refers to the database as the typical structure of informational websites, in which a homepage offers a menu with different options. In a database structure it is possible to randomly choose a narrative node, turn back and explore another one. This structure activates interactors' cognition while connecting at a semantic level the selected nodes. The database organisation has become a cultural interface.

> After the novel, and subsequently cinema, privileged narrative as the key form of cultural expression of the modern age, the computer age introduces its correlate: database. Many new media objects do not tell stories, they do not have this purpose; they don't have beginning or end; in fact, they don't have any development, thematically, formally, or otherwise which would organize their elements into a sequence. Instead, they are collections of individual items, where every item has the same significance as any other' (Manovich, 1999).

However, database randomness is not incompatible with narrative, as interactors organise sequentially and semantically each node.

6. The Maze. This structure is common on quest adventures as it is goal driven. Interactors can choose different navigation paths that take them into different endings, so there can be 'one or more ways to reach the goal'. This structure has two positive features: it allows a great level of authorial control and narrative coherence as the creator foresees all the possible pathways, and it also stimulates repetition as interactors may want to repeat the experience to live a different ending.

7. The Flowchart. According to Ryan, this structure is the best way 'to reconcile a reasonably dramatic narrative with some degree of interactivity, as the system prescribes an itinerary through the storyworld, but interactors are granted some autonomy in connecting the various stages of his journey'. It eliminates the risk of running in circles or hitting a dead end. As Ryan suggests, if this structure is run by a system capable of keeping a memory of interactors' past choices the events of a specific node can be influenced by this memory allowing or denying some possibility.

8. The Hidden Story. This architecture is a two-level structure: an atemporal interactive network of choices and a fixed chronologic linear narrative. Interactors move in the first interactive network. In this network some nodes are connected to the first linear structure, thus interactors have access to hidden information that they must assemble. This structure is commonly found in mystery stories.

9. The Braided Plot. This structure is often called 'parallel structure' as over time, interactors can jump between different parallel plots. In literature and cinema, it is possible to find several examples of parallel plots, commonly used for change between characters' points of view, spaces, or temporalities.

10. Action - Space. 'In this model, interactivity takes place on the macro-level and narrative plotting on the micro-level as interactors move freely within the geography of the virtual world finding self-contained adventures, events, pieces of information, or episodes. Usually, this model offers a backstory that is completed as interactors act within the experience and are often used by MMORPGs (massively multiplayer online role-playing games).

For IFcVR, the architectures that contain links to past nodes can be problematic as interactors might not be bothered about watching repeated scenes, this is the case of The Complete Graph, the Network, and Action-Space models. The Maze, the Hidden Story, and the Flowchart can present the same problem if returning points are contemplated. In this case, an alternative version of the node should be shot or created, thus interactors will not see the same video. The audiovisual medium, comprising animation, live action, or CG, entails high costs in terms of time, financial resources, and production complexity, therefore the greater the number of scenes, the greater the costs; therefore, the Tree structure is not recommended. However, this can also be considered a 'weak point' for IFcVR when shot in live-action 360º video: few scenes mean little interactivity and few alternatives for the interactor.

The interactive structure underlies, waiting for the path that the interactor traces through it. To work its way, the interactor must pass from one node to another and activate key elements to understand the story. Within each node, the system presents decision-making moments or time lapses in which the interactor's feedback is expected to push the story forward, creating a rebound dynamic between system and user: interactivity. This is mediated by the Human-Computer Interface (HCI).

3.5. *Forging the Path: HCI and IFcVR*

Interactivity is a conversation between two agents. One of them says something while the other is expected to respond based on the interlocutor's input. As IFcVR spectators are humans, and IFcVR travels through a computing system, there are interfaces that allow the conversation between both agents: human and computer. VR HCI developments can allow unsuspected ways to interact with a film (imagine that you must literally run to escape from danger, or that the film becomes frightening depending on your heart beats) maybe we can speak directly to the characters to make them take one or another direction, we even could move objects with our thoughts to help the protagonist. Movement, biometrics, voice recognition and brain interfaces are some of the interactor's inputs that can be given to the VEs through current HCI. This section presents current developments in HCI that can be used to compose the IFcVR experience, catalogued into conscious and non-conscious user inputs.

VR HCI can be divided into two settings: inputs and outputs. Inputs in VR are in the first place related to the user's position in space; this means that Tracking positions and orientations of user's head, user's limbs, and interaction devices (such as gloves, mice, or joysticks) provide input to the VR system. Besides spatial user inputs, users can also send Action or Event inputs to the system (Raycast, 2018), by activating an Interactive Item or Object. By utilising the participant's facial expressions, tone of voice, gestures, and posture as inputs, a higher degree of natural interaction could be achieved. Additionally, participants would be able to engage with more intricate objects, such as virtual characters and deformable objects.

Given the system inputs, the resulting VE (visuals, audio, tactile information) is output to the participant through visual and audio hardware, an HMD, or a CAVE. The HMD can be connected to a computer or can be a stand-alone device. The HMD works by tracking the user's head movements allowing 3DOF or 6DOF depending on the device. VR tracking systems need to accurately determine the participant's pose and to display the appropriate images in under 90 milliseconds, and preferably under 50 milliseconds. Otherwise, the VR system induces a 'swimming' feeling, and might make the participant disoriented and hamper the quality of interactivity.

Action inputs have two main functions within the IFcVR:

1. Jump between alternative narrative units (NUs).

2. Access or Activate extra-information: multimedia material that contains diegetic information that enrich interactors' knowledge about the storyworld and its characters, or extradiegetic information with instructions on how to navigate the experience or paratext (Genette, 2001). The multimedia material can be of different nature: text, images, audio, flat videos, 3D objects or even minigames.

Action or Event inputs can be catalogued as conscious or unconscious, according to the type of HCI that activates the interactive object. This distinction obeys to the type of input given to the system: in the first case, interactors' input involves the reflection and conscious coordination of their cognitive abilities (e.g.: moving head or body, talking, applauding, thinking, using a joystick); in the second case, data on the physiological functions of the interactor are collected by the system without requiring a conscious action of the interactor to modify the course of the story, only their emotions expressed by physiological changes will control the experience. Such a creator's choice is at the root of the design that runs the IFcVR experience and is related to the artistic and narrative purposes of the creator.

IFcVR systems can be multi-sensory and multimodal, since the design of the system can foresee the integration of one or more

HCIs to receive interactors inputs and to send them back the system's outputs (e.g.: a sound, a vibration, or a change of temperature to confirm an action or to contextualise interactors in the storyworld). However, it is important to think of the interfaces not as mere technological instruments, but as an integral part of the storyworld; they must have a role and a meaning within the narrative experience. The selection of the interface(s) changes the relationship between interactor and system, and between interactor and storyworld. In the next sections, current HCIs will be presented. They are divided into HCIs that require the conscious coordination of the interactor and those based on the physiological data of the user. Some of the presented HCIs not only allow the reception of user's input but also can send output to the user. Some interfaces such as the brain-computer interface (BCI) or the respiratory feedback, although based on physiological data, can also allow a conscious interaction.

3.5.1. *Cognitive Interaction*

In this type of interaction, interactors decide whether to activate an interactive object. The decision-making process hence requires a conscious activity on the part of the interactor, either reflecting or reacting to a specific event presented in the story. The depth of the interactors' thinking activity at the decision-making moments will depend on the creator's artistic intentions, as interactors' decisions may require an exhaustive reasoning, or can be a fast reaction to the environment, as Stephen Cowley and Frederic Vallée-Tourangeau argue in *Cognition Beyond the Brain: Computation, Interactivity and Human Artifice* (2013). They challenge the conception of thinking, separating it from an isolated brain activity and describing it as a response to environmental inputs. In this order of ideas, interactors' horizon of expectations, together with their socio-cultural background, will react to the events presented in the scene, pushing them to take one path or another. As in life, some decisions will be harder than others, requesting more time to analyse the possibilities provided, while others will be based on simple intuitive reactions to the sensory or narrative stimuli of the VE.

Decisions, especially difficult ones, take time. In IFcVR, as in IDNs in general, the decision-making time becomes part of the time of the discourse. It is not a time detached from the narrative experience, but a time that connects discourse and experience. When creating an IDN, narrative time can be a tricky issue to solve due to the quantity of interactive elements, agents and decision-making moments that run through the narrative experience. Hence, the writing and development of the narrative system need to design the time of the story and of the filmic discourse (construction of the scenes), as well as to plan the time of the user interaction, which will become part of the time of the interactive discourse. Several research studies have explored the issue of time in IDN (Porteous et al, 2011; Schoenau-Fog, 2015), proposing time planning frameworks to organise narrative actions and events in an IDN system, especially for advanced types of IDN systems based on artificial intelligence (AI) software. Hence, during the development of the interactive fiction, and afterwards during the setup of the system, the creator must respect decision-making time in order to ensure that, from a UX standpoint, interactors know what they are doing and feel in control, so as no one would select something by mistake, even by compromising immediacy if the creator chooses to ask user's confirmation through some type of visual or auditory feedback to user interaction.

Current HCIs for VR allow different types of conscious interaction by the user. IFcVR can make use of any of these interfaces to make interactors act and by acting, have agency within the experience. The way in which the HCI is connected to the story or the use of multiple HCIs lies on the creative capacity of creators and their artistic intentions. As technology is in constant development, the following HCIs for VR are in different stages of development and adoption.

Head Tracking. This is the most common type of HCI for interactive applications in VR as every HMD in the market has a built-in head tracker, including headsets for smartphones as new generation smartphones contains an inertial measurement unit (IMU), a combined device that merges accelerometers and gyroscopes, sometimes also magnetometers. Interactors can activate hotspots by gazing at an interactive object with a cursor on the screen that they can move with their heads (Lavalle et al, 2014).

Controllers. These are joysticks with an integrated 3 or 6 degrees-of-freedom (DOF) tracking sensor that reports the device's position and/or orientation, with numerous buttons for the participant to provide input, they are cheap, easily adaptable for different tasks, and familiar to many users. However, they might not provide the required naturalness, feel and functionality for a given task (e.g.: object manipulation in simulations or training). To face this lack of 'naturalness', VR companies are working on special design and tracking systems to enhance the VR controller. The objective is to give interactors a fuller hand motion range through a special design that adapts to the hand and avoids dropping the controller. New generation controllers are equipped with capacitive sensors (KAS) that detect when individual fingers are touching the controller, so interactors can do things like picking up objects by naturally closing the fist, instead of hitting a trigger or grip button.

(Full) Body Immersion. Full body immersion is the holy grail of VR. The purpose is to make interactors feel and be bodily present in the VE, also being able to move and interact with their body within the storyworld. This is a bi-directional communication between interactors and VE. The body immersion has been a never-ending process since the beginnings of VR, in which it is possible to find two branches: (1) those that are focused on hands presence and ability, a hard task if we consider the versatility of human hands and (2) those that are working on the Full body immersion, creating a virtual body that performs as accurate as possible as the real body, including hand work.

To achieve full body immersion, it is necessary to combine different technologies, to give user's input to the system by translating body movements in VR, as well as to give feedback to the interactors of their actions within the VE. Within this set of technologies, it is possible to account motion sensors powered by Infrared Light Emitting Diode (IR LEDs) or radar chips, position tracking sensors (IMU), gloves and suits with tactile sensors and haptic, force and temperature feedback, and even EMG (Electromyography) sensors to enable real-time selection of operational commands together with recognition of interactors' motions and gestures. These technologies are being used and merged by VR companies in a series of diverse wearables and accessories.

Eye Tracking and Facial Expressions. Another way of interacting with the VE is making use of eye movement. The mechanism, even at a lower stage of development with respect to the HCI seen above, works through an eye-tracking camera located inside the HMD that recognizes the movement of the eye (Geiselhart et al, 2016). These same cameras can be used to detect and categorise the facial expressions of the interactor's eye contour, that is, the face part enclosed within the HMD (Chen et al, 2018; Hickson et al, 2017).

Natural Language Processing (NLP). Through voice commands, it is possible to interact with the VE, either for selecting interactive objects (e.g.: Dorozhkin, 2002), to interact with storyworld agents and objects (Bellassai et al, 2017), to manipulate objects within the VE (Zhao et al, 2005) or even to create intelligent VEs (Kamath et al, 2013). Current research in this area is merging NLP together with other types of HCI to create a multimodal interaction with virtual worlds (Olmedo et al, 2015). This convergence is being already applied in conversational gameplay and interactive narratives.

In *A Speech Interface for Virtual Environments*, Scott McGlashan, and Thomas Axling (1996) propose a spoken language interface (McGlashan & Axling, 1996). To enable this type of interaction, they put forward three technical aspects that also belong to the creator's sphere and can be extrapolated to other types of human-computer interfaces: speech recognition, language understanding, and interaction metaphor.

3.5.2. *Biofeedback Interaction*

This type of interaction relies on interactors' biofeedback, the measurement of physiological functions as brainwaves, heart function, breathing, muscle activity, or skin temperature. Physiological signals are sent into the system as a response to a specific activity or situation in which interactors are immersed. In IFcVR, the system will receive interactors' biofeedback as an emotive response for what they are experiencing in each NU. This type of interaction relies on several research studies that identify a 'biological basis of cinema as embedded in the emotional simulation dynamics of the mind' (Tikka, 2008, p. 235). Pia Tikka summarises these research studies looking for an 'embodied cognitive model-ing' approach (Tikka, 2008) that functions as the foundation for enactive cinema:

> The recognition of otherness in cinema based on mirror neuronal imitation, which links to dynamical views on action and perception in an embodied goal-driven survival system. The integration of the senses, neurophenomenological views of perception, the dynam-ics of 'as if' body loops, the 'narrator in the brain', image-schemas, and the neural basis of conceptualization enable a description of the continuous unfolding of enactive cinema in terms of embodied simulation (p. 235).

If we consider the human being as an emotion-driven organ-ism, and this characteristic as the core of the filmic experience, an interactive system or emotion-driven cinematic montage system, in which interactors do not make conscious decisions but let their pure emotions choose the way to go along the film, Pia Tikka's En-active Cinema proposal would be the theoretical basis for an IF-cVR system that works through unconscious interactions.

Biosignals measure the behaviour of the autonomic nervous system (ANS) in situations that move along a spectrum that goes from relaxation to stress. VR is the perfect medium to expose the interactors to simulated situations, thus making it possible to car-ry out studies on stress treatment (e.g.: Ridout et al, 2017; Bullinger et al., 2005), and leading to the development of therapies in dif-ferent areas, including social psychology (Blascovich et al., 2002). The following types of interfaces can be used for two purposes:

1. To induce sensations that enhance the experience and contex-tualise the interactors within the VE (i.e.: thermal, olfactive).

2. To modify the story course during run-time.

Often, different types of biofeedback are combined to obtain accurate data on the user's emotive response to the VE (Cho et al, 2017). Self-efficacy feedback is another tool often used in physi-ological HCIs, so as interactors can track their own performance within the VE (Weerdmeester et al, 2017).

Brain-Computer Interface (BCI). In the human computer inter-action field, the ability to control machines only by mental activ-ity, or to be able to transmit thoughts and sensations to another human brain (Jiang et al, 2018), used to be a sci-fi dream. Brain-Computer Interfaces (BCI) development is now making great steps in brain-to-computer and brain-to-brain communication. Neural Interfaces allow interactors to send commands to computer-based systems through brain waves (electroencephalographic (EEG) signals) and VR is a fertile field for the design of interactive applications in which the BCI system is used to control, navigate, or perform within the VE just by thoughts (Amores et al, 2016; Renard et al, 2010; Ron-Angevin & Díaz-Estrella, 2009; Guger et al, 2009). Researchers in the BCI field 'imagine a future in which users have total intuitive control of remote virtual environments within a think-and-play user interface (Lecuyer et al, 2008). BCI developments expand from rehabilitation applications to artistic purposes (Nijholt & Nam, 2015). Even though controlling one's own EEG signals is very difficult and requires training, it needs a conscious activity to successfully control or modify the VE.

Thermal or temperature biofeedback. Temperature has proven to be a reliable factor in measuring the sensation of embodiment in the VE (Tieri et al, 2017). Skin temperature (SKT) changing over time can be used in both ways during an interactive experience: (1) On one side, body temperature data can be the input that modifies the course of the story or that activates interactive elements, (2) but it can also be the system's output or response to a user interaction, or can help to contextualise interactors inside the virtual environment; for example: interactors are able to 'feel' the weather of the VE, through specific devices as the 'thermal taste machine' or a thermally enriched HMDs (Chen et al, 2017) interactors can be able to experience pleasant or unpleasant sensations related to the thermal stimulation.

Sweat - Electrodermal biofeedback. Skin conductance or Electrodermal Activity (EDA) measures the amount of sweat on the skin, and it is often used to measure the level of users' stress. The stress level of the interactors can be used as an input to create interactive VR applications, for example by generating a run-time adaptive dialog (Blankendaal & Bosse, 2018). This type of interface has been widely used in VR therapy for stress management especially post-traumatic stress (Rothbaum et al, 2001; van't Wout et al, 2017); for the management of different types of phobias or anxiety disorders (Ayala et al, 2018; Gorini et al, 2010), or to measure emotions during decision-making moments (Beck & Egger, 2017).

Heart variability biofeedback. Heart rate variability (HRV) can be measured through different systems as photoplethysmograms (PPG) or electrocardiographs (ECG). HRV data represent another way to both measure interactors' reaction to the virtual scenario and to send the input to the system to activate some command during the virtual experience. Current studies analyse multiple stress levels in virtual reality environments using heart rate variability (Cho et al, 2017) while developing different applications supported using a HRV fitness shirt (Gradl et al, 2018) or fit trackers. Heart rate can also be delivered to the interactors as an output during the virtual experience, so as they can be aware of their own heart rate in different types of heart-rate representations. A recent study shows that 'audio-haptic feedback was the most preferred while visual feedback was reported as being distracting' (Chen et al, 2017).

Respiratory Biofeedback. Heart rate variability is closely related to breathing, and breathing pace is also related to anxiety or relaxing states. It is possible to intercept respiratory biofeedback through a pneumography or respiratory strain gauge with a flexible sensor band that is placed around the chest, abdomen, or both, providing feedback about the relative expansion/contraction of the chest and abdomen, and measuring respiration rate (number of breaths per minute). A 2018 experiment, BreathVR (Sra, Xu & Maes, 2018), uses respiratory feedback as physiological input to enhance single and multiplayer VR games. In the experiment, they apply different types of intuitive active breath control actions as additional input channels in a VR game, offering insights for the design of Interactive VR applications controlled by breathing inputs. Below, some insights are summarised, whose validity can be applied to the use of any biofeedback HCI in the design of interactive VR narrative and gaming experiences:

Providing Narrative for Gestures. Authors argue that creators must strive for the interactor's narrative immersion, hence the actions interactors perform within the experience are related to their role within the narrative (e.g., relatively explain the reasons for using breathing actions and for wearing a sensor).

Relevance of Effects to Actions. Author encourages creators to give some type of feedback to the interactors once they have performed an action. Audio feedback is as important as the visual effect to connect the physical world action with the virtual world effect (e.g., some breathing actions trigger fire-breathing or a wind force in the game).

Managing Suitable Physiological Load. When using biofeedback interfaces, especially those controlled by the interactor (such as brain waves and respiratory feedback), creators must moderate the use of the actions performed by the interactors to avoid fatigue from overuse.

3.6. *Interactive Fiction in Cinematic Virtual Reality*

One of the first questions that emerged during the conception of this study was if Interactive Fiction in Cinematic Virtual Reality can be considered an Interactive Digital Narrative (IDN), or even if, in its essence, it can be considered a narrative text. Whether an IDN work can be considered a text or not, is not a superficial question. As Barthes points out, there are countless forms of narrative in the world, genres, media, vehicles, and the expansion of this variety is closely related to technological development. It is fair to claim that the new fields in narratology and new media that emerge within the sociocultural mini revolutions caused by technological novelties are guided by this simple question: Can we consider this artefact a narrative text? What makes this artefact a narrative text? Which tools do we have to analyse the artefact in its narrative quality? This section aims to contribute to this discussion.

IDN as a study field has not developed yet a series of conventions for the study of its own narrative artefacts, in part due to the novelty of the field, in part due to the wide spectrum of narrative forms, genres, media and vehicles that it covers, and in part also because narratology itself is a young[8], extremely alive field.

---

8   If we take into consideration that the study of narrative structures had an important flourishing in the 20th century, and the term 'Narratology' just appeared in 1969, coined by Tzvetan Todorov.

After all, when we talk about narratives, we are talking about an essential human activity. The absence of a canonical set of narrative structures specific to IDN (Koenitz et al, 2015) raises a variety of issues when trying to identify a narrative text within the field. The core of the discussion (are IDN experiences narrative tests or not?) resides mainly in two aspects of the technological hypertextual nature of any IDN experience: the abolition of the fixed output (the possibility that each time an IDN experience is enjoyed by an interactor in different ways), and the fact that 'the text is the only element directly accessible to the reader, and the text of any digital work is accessible to the the interface' (Knoller, 2012). Both characteristics have an impact on the levels[9] of creation, enjoyment and meaning of the narrative quality of any IDN text. From now on, considerations on the narrative structure of IDNs will be done through its application to IFcVR, to identify its narrative features.

In *Language of New Media*, Manovich translates Roland Barthes concept of text into the logic of computer-based products. He indicates that no matter how interactive, hypertextual, distributed or dynamic a product, the 'text' is in any case a finite object (Manovich, 2009, p. 209). An IFcVR experience is a fiction film whose sequences or scenes have been detached from a single timeline organising them one after the other. Instead, these unique sequences or scenes constitute a Narrative Unit (NU): pieces of narrative disseminated in a cyberspace, that are organized in a linear form by the interactor. The links between Narrative Units and extra material (multimedia as graphics, photographs, 2D videos, written texts, 3D objetcs, etc.) creates a form in cyberspace: a mind map. The mind map is a structure whose conformation gives it a specific way of behaving, modelling the way to navigate through it. Interactors assemble the NUs and inscribe them in a finite temporal experience, other possible outputs remaining potential. In IFcVR, possible outputs are not infinite as there is a X number of NUs and a Y number of pathways. In this sense, IFcVR finitude makes it a text. This consideration applies also for any type of IDN, since so far there is not a system powerful enough to generate all the possibilities.

9   The term *Level* is intended in Roland Barthes' conception: 'Levels are operations: a system of symbols, rules, etc., which must be used to represent expressions' (Barthes, 1975, p. 242)

A narrative text, however, contains other characteristics besides finitude. As Genette (1990) points out, by narrative we can understand: the narrative statement, the discourse that relates a sequence of events and actions; the subject of the discourse, the sequence of events and actions themselves, be they fictitious or real; and the act of narrating itself. Christian Metz (2007) elaborates a definition of narrative:

> It is a closed sequence, a temporal sequence. Every narrative is, therefore, a discourse [...] What distinguishes a discourse from the rest of the world, and by the same token contrasts it with the 'real' world, is the fact that a discourse must necessarily be made by someone (for discourse is not language), whereas one of the characteristics of the world is that it is uttered by no one (Metz & Taylor, 2007, p. 20).

In *Story and Discourse: Narrative Structure in Fiction and Film*, Seymour Chatman (1978) proposes a structuralist model for the study of the structure of narrative texts. The model is based on the distinction between Story (a sequence of events plus its setting) and Discourse (the expression of the story, how it is narrated). Such a structuralist approach for the study of an interactive narrative is needed, because as it happens in narratology, the only object of study that we have is the text itself, the signifier of the story, which Genette (1990) simply refers to as narrative.

How to study, then, a signifier that mutates from person to person, from iteration to iteration? In IFcVR, for instance, different media are contained within one another, in a matryoshka-like style: a literary script inside film, film inside VR, VR inside a multisensory and multimodal interactive VR work. This matryoshka-like combination of different media poses the challenge in distinguishing which media 'transmits' the story, and which one 'manifests' it. In this sense, it is of great help the distinction that Chatman does between Content and Expression, and its crossing with Substance and Form (1978, p. 24):

- Substance of Expression refers to the type of media that vehicles the discourse
- Form of Expression stands for the organization of the narrative elements, that is, the narrative discourse.
- Substance of Content refers to the representations of objects and

actions in real or imaginary worlds, under the creator's view of the world.

- Form of Content describes the elements of the story: the relationship between events (characters that perform actions and make things happen) and existents (characters profiles and settings of the storyworld)

Unlike narratives with a fixed output, like films or books, IDNs are based on the technological system that allows both creation and usage of the experience. Koenitz's theoretical framework on IDN uses the distinction established by Nick Montfort, between the computer program as the material artefact and the narrative as its output (Koenitz et al, 2015, p. 96). Studies focused on creating a theory for IDNs cover a wide range of approaches. It is possible to account approaches that:

- apply narratology theories related to the Form of Content[10] to IDNs.

- identify intrinsic characteristics of IDN works.

- categorize the existing IDN artifacts mapping and organizing what has been done.

- propose new models that step away from legacy media models and take into consideration both system (the digital artifact) and process (the user interaction with the system) (Koenitz, 2010).

- discuss the extent to which narratology theories can inspire interactive narrative technologies (Cavazza & Pizzi, 2006).

Legacy media produce an enclosed fixed output, while IDN texts exist by running a code and each version of this output can be fixed only by recording it.

From a structural standpoint, we must examine the run-time narrative text, which is the narrative that interactors receive. This endeavour begins with an understanding of interactive narrative as narrative. This entails breaking it down into story and discourse. The story is the narrative's content, and the discourse is how that content is communicated. 'Interactive storytelling relies on a predefined story, a specific plot concerning facts and occurrences.

---

10 These theories are based on the ideas of narratologists like Propp, Greimas, Campbell or Jennings, who propose conceptual tools to understand archetypal characters and their relationships, dramatic progression, hero's stages, all elements that belong to the content.

Only the telling of the story is done interactively.' (Spierling et al, 2012). In Fig 4, I am proposing a structural approach to understand the composition of the IFcVR text. Based on Chatman's proposal, I divided the IFcVR into Story and Discourse, and, at a second level, both content and expression are divided into form and substance. Next, a differentiation is presented between what is part of the storyworld and what is part of the system, understood as Ted Nelson's literary machine.

The Storyworld is an abstract space where characters and time coexist. Characters with goals and dreams, which are related to each other, creating conflicts or pleasant situations. The creator takes specific moments from the storyworld and transforms them into reality by recreating them through cinematic VR. At this point, we find a degree of complexity superior to that of linear cVR: we find ourselves at two levels of transmission narrative structure that belongs to the Substance of Expression, that is, to Manifestation instead of Transmission. The authorial control of the creator arrives at this point.

1. Narrative structure of transmission of the cVR unit: The filmic moment (scene, sequence) that will constitute a single narrative unit.

2. Interactive narrative structure of transmission: The connections that the creator makes between cVR units, giving a form and a specific behaviour to the network or mind map.

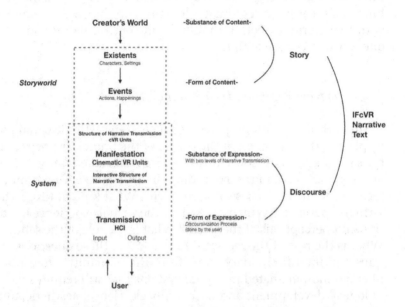

Figure 3. Elements of the IFcVR narrative text.

Finally, the Form of Expression is a task that an interactor must perform. It communicates with the Storyworld via the System while also being controlled via a human-computer interface. A discoursivization process is initiated when interactors send inputs to access new cVR units or extra content and receive a response. The interactor's action sequentially aligns the narrative units of the mind map during the process. Storyworld and system merge on the Transmission level, which is also the Form of Expression.

To close this theoretical journey, I believe that the path that VR films will now take will abandon linearity in order to delve into the creation of interactive structures for the transmission of the immersive filmic narrative. Not only because interactivity heightens immersion, but also because of the contrast created when we are completely abstracted and surrounded by an alien reality while having no control over it. We can be spectators in a movie theatre or at home, but when we are asked to make a fictional pact to give

full control of our cognition to a system, and thus to someone behind the creation, a legitimate demand is to be able to interact
with that world, or better, to fully be in control. IFcVR could be
one way to accomplish this.

3.7. *Applying Reception Theory to IFcVR*

Similarly to how VR proposes a change in an aesthetic paradigm
by placing the interactor at the centre of the frameless image and
transporting human consciousness to an alternate reality, it also
alters the act of coding and decoding the artistic text. The communication act in VR, raises some concerns: What kind of text is the
virtual experience? Which codes does the virtual experience use to
transmit perceptions of the world? What is the role of the sender?
What is the role of the receiver? An answer to these questions requires an interdisciplinary effort from the humanities towards a
phenomenon mediated by digital systems that still requires technological development and user feedback. Hence, aesthetic, and
literary reception theories offer a starting point for the analysis of
the dynamics of artistic creation and aesthetic reception that are
found in the VR medium.

Art is a creative-productive, receptive, and communicative activity, in which an artistic/narrative text acquires life and meaning
during the process of reception or 'reading'. Hans Jauss (1982) suggests that the text itself does not have inherent meaning or value,
but it is constructed by readers and their 'horizon of expectations'.
The horizon of expectations is determined by their socio-cultural
background and the context in which that text is received. Umber-
to Eco (1992), on the other hand, conceives the text as a *macchina
presupposizionale* that is open to multiple interpretations coming
from multiple readers and multiple contexts. The fragmentation
process of the artistic text happens to be the mechanism to find
meaning as an intersemiotic and heterosemiotic event (Ruthrof,
1997). Stuart Hall (1997) argues that 'things don't mean: we con-
struct meaning, using representational systems – concepts and
signs' (p. 11). Hall (1986) also observes our historical period full of
a multiplicity of codes, readings and discourses that produce new
forms of self-consciousness and reflexivity.

The act of reading, defined by Iser (1980) as a function of text construction, is posited as an efficient and necessary condition, having the same importance as the creation of the text itself. Iser distinguishes two poles in the literary work: 'the artistic pole is the author's text, and the aesthetic pole is the realisation accomplished by the reader' (p. 21). In general, the various trends of the Reception Theory of the second half of the 20th century balance the weight of the textual operation, conferring to the receiver an active role in understanding, updating, and interpreting the text. Nowadays, we acknowledge that the text, even from the moment of its creation, foresees this kind of participation on the other side of the communication act (Eco, 1992). In the communicative act posed by new media, reading is a digital travel around multimedia fragments floating in the cyberspace. Reader function becomes 'Hyperreading' (Hayles, 2012) the reading act of hypertexts. Hyperreading entails a form of communication in which readers build relational logics. In the introduction to Derrick de Kerckhove's conference presentation *La Rete ci renderà stupidi*[11] (2016), Massimo Arcangeli uses the word pun *'nodi da scegliere, nodi da sciogliere'*[12] to define hyperreading. In Hyperreading, meaning is not contained only in each single text node, but in the semantic connections that may exist between nodes, multimedia materials, urls, etc, and at the same time, on an upper level, between the relationships that exist between the final output of the navigation process and interactors' background and motivations.

VR, as omnidirectional image-event, can also be considered a hypertext: audio and visual information is spread around the sphere and the way in which interactors elaborate their own narrative path is through the same mechanism that hyperreading applies. Moreover, in VR, the metaphor of McLuhan (1964) that conceives the medium as an environment, acquires a visual representation. VR is itself a visual-spatial environment, in which interactors find themselves spatially immersed in the message, and the way to decode the message-medium is through the multiplicity of sensory stimuli that they experience. If the VR text is consistent

---

11   In Italian: 'Will the web make us stupid?' presented at the Futura Festival (July 30, 2014)
12   In Italian: 'Knots to choose knots to loosen'

with human experience, reception passes through the coordination of the senses involved in the experience together with what occurs within the scenic space. Though Cinematic VR is not interactive as computer-generated VEs, it still can be considered an IDN, as the very act of looking around and choosing what to see within the visual sphere is a type of interaction. However, the increasing integration of cinematic VR artefacts with contextual performances such as *Carne y Arena*[13] (González-Iñárritu, 2017), or the enrichment of the cVR space-scene with layers of multimedia elements, enhances the VR experience. IFcVR uses an underlying Interactive Fiction (IF) structure to deliver an *enactive* immersive cinema.

In Figure 4, a visual representation of the VR communication act is proposed. The representation is based on the polarisation between creator and interactor. On the Aesthetic Pole, the Actual Reader -with their horizon of expectation- is situated. The meaning construction process is located between Text and Actual Reader, and it is mediated by the feeling of Telepresence (comprising perceptive immersion, narrative immersion, and agency) during the acts of hyper-reading and living the Experience, i.e., the VR text.

On the Artistic Pole, we find the Creator who, through the mastery of the platform, translates the Imagined Storyworld into sensory codes. Through a user-centred design, creators need to put themself, simultaneously as author and reader, at the centre of the perceptive storyworld. This act corresponds to the conceptualization of the Implied Reader. The imagined storyworld is the starting point of the creation process, it is the mental space with narrative content, and by narrative content we intend humans to be able to generate multiple events that unfold in time and change the state of things (Fludernik, 2010, p. 6). The theory of the *Possible Worlds*[14] expands this idea by defining reality 'as the sum of the imaginable rather than as the sum of what exists physically, a universe composed of a plurality of distinct

---

13   'CARNE y ARENA' defined by its creator as a VR installation, was awarded at the 70th Cannes Film Festival as the first virtual reality project to be featured in the festival's history. https://carneyarenadc.com/

14   Possible Worlds | the living handbook of narratology. (2018). lhn.uni-hamburg.de. Retrieved 31 July 2018, from http://www.lhn.uni-hamburg.de/article/possible-worlds

worlds' (Ryan, 2013). 'If a storyworld is anybody's world, it is the world of the characters' (Ryan, 2014, p. 32).

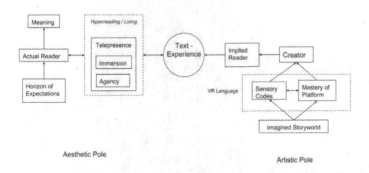

Figure 4. Communication Act in Virtual Reality

3.7.1. *Who is the IFcVR receptor?*

In IFcVR, the cVR are the recorded scenes or sequences that constitute the narrative units of a hyperfiction or interactive fiction structure. To enjoy an IFcVR experience, the interactor of the system needs to experiment two levels of reading, as described by IDN theory (Roth & Koenitz, 2016): local and global. The local reading regards the current narrative unit or story beat, that in this case corresponds to each cVR NU, while global reading corresponds to the final output or journey created by the interactor's choices.

The pragmatics of hyperreading in IFcVR occurs in a multilayer activity, in which the first level of interpretation of each narrative unit comprises:

1. The recognition and exploration of space.
2. The coordination of the multiple sensory stimuli disposed into the scenic space that is related to the intuitive use of the HCIs.
3. The recognition and identification of the story that is being told in a 360º VE.

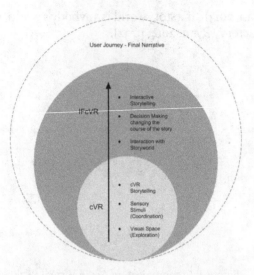

Figure 5. Levels of 'Hyperreading' in IcVR

Afterwards, there is a second level that travels along the inter-active elements in each cVR unit and through the links between narrative units:

1. Interaction with the storyworld through hotspots.
2. Decision-making processes that are based on their own inter-pretation of the information that is received by the fictional scene.
3. User's construction of the story throughout the Interactive Storytelling.

The third reading layer regards the final interpretation of the ultimate journey, the single output formed by interactors' choices. This linear output is intimately related to the interactor's socio-cultural context and to her own horizon of expectations.

It would be difficult to identify a type of reader/user of an expe-rience like the one proposed in this study. Not only because of the lack of other similar experiences, but also because, in general, VR audiences have not been defined and speculations about potential publics and markets emerge. Despite this, through the articulation of the history of new media (Wardrip-Fruin & Montfort, 2003), the point of view of who receives and interprets information, and manipulates media artefacts, has been a constant. This person is often called *User*: the one who uses something. In Human-Computer Interaction (HCI) theory, the third wave of HCI where technology moves from the workplace to our homes and viceversa (Bødker, 2006), extends the User Centred Design (UCD) (Vredenburg et at, 2002), to a broader conception that is the Human Centred Design (HCD), a framework based on the recognition of human needs and desires during the ideation, development and prototyping of a service or product. The essence of UCD - and HCD - lies in the awareness and anticipation of the user's interaction with the system: it is not possible to design a system outside the user's point of view. New media has made an important contribution to the conceptualization of today's humans; we are all users of a technology that is striving to become invisible (Krishna, 2015). The UCD has spread in all areas of application turning the term 'user' into 'human', reaffirming our position at the centre of any technology.

Users in their role of pure interactor do not care much about the technology itself, about its components or code, the user only interacts with the perceptual surface. 'User has no direct contact with technicalities. The technicalities underneath are simply the means whereby certain exact and simple services are rapidly performed' (Nelson, 1987, p. 444). Something similar happens with traditional audiovisual content. Even though the fruition of audiovisual content has become a naturalised activity; when audiovisual content is consumed, little attention is given to the construction of the content so that what is absorbed is what is immediately happening on the screen. In the same way it happens when an HMD is used: our audiovisual education tends to read the content as it reads cinema or television, and the coordination of vision and hearing with other senses such as spatial perception or the use of joysticks belongs to the media education that VR has yet to develop in their publics. About hypertext reading, Kerckhove (2016) considers that 'today's readers can read like a cinematographic montage, to acquire images with a hypertextual approach and to put them together using phenomenal intellectual abilities. "Hypertextual intelligence" is the ability to know things quickly, when needed: it is a thought that shares the global knowledge of the Internet through a screen' (p. 33).

A definition of the IFcVR reader takes into consideration both components of the artefact: its cinematographic component and its interactive component. The IFcVR readers, in its cinematic connotation, are spectators, viewers and listeners. All these definitions imply a passive attitude, as they seem to be only receiving information. In IFcVR, however, at the same time they are using, manipulating, operating, and modifying the VE, within the new media connotation. The VR component deepens this interpretation of the user while they explore, interact, interpret, and experience. These considerations relate to the conceptual shift from User-centred design to Human-centred design.

3.7.2. *Who is the IFcVR Sender?*

A medium that contains another medium requires a complex analogue and/or electronic support that presupposes a further challenge for creators. On one hand, creators must know the technology they are using and the techniques to compose an artistic text on that specific platform. On the other hand, media involving different perceptive stimuli usually require an artistic dialogue between different arts and diverse media. A scriptwriter may not be the director of a film, as an actor may not be the writer of his monologue. This has been one of the most relevant debates raised in film theory: In cinema, who is the author? (Meskin, 2008; Caughie, 1981). The one who imagines and writes the storyworld and plot or those who translate them into audiovisual signs? This dichotomy takes place also in literature but in a more abstract way. In literature's narrative universes, the author of the book is often recognized as the creator of the storyworld. This dichotomy was well expressed by Jorge Luis Borges in *Borges y Yo* (1960):

> To the other one, to Borges, is to whom things happen. [...] I live, let myself go on living, so that Borges may contrive his literature, and this literature justifies me [...] Thus my life is a flight and I lose everything, and everything belongs to oblivion, or to the other [...] I do not know which of us has written this page.

When talking about the VR creation process, the creation of alternative realities is implicit. Each storyworld/VE is closed in its oneness as a complete and autonomous universe but open at the same time; interactors can navigate, explore, and create their own experiences. The same debate about authoring emerges in cinema, hence the cybernetic and interactive aspect adds a new layer or dimension from which to think about the act of artistic creation and communication. The technical aspects involved in the construction of virtual digital worlds usually unite the artist and the engineer in a single role. In computer-based media, a new kind of artist has emerged, who 'masters the technical details to control the actual platform on which the space-making happens' (Heim, 2012). The construction of these virtual worlds, whether as hyperstructures or artificial audiovisual worlds enclosed, is in the first place in what Kerckhove calls multimedia writing that 'tends to the iconicity rather than to the sequentially' (2016, p. 29).

In this study, I am relying on the conception of the author proposed by Pia Tikka in *Enactive Cinema: Simulatorium Eisensteinense* (2008). Tikka explores 'the very grounds from which the phenomenon of cinema emerges [...] the intrinsic dynamics of a cinema author's mind in the process of creating a moving image' (p. 23). She distances herself from the debate of authorship in cinema (individual author, (co-) authorship, or multiple authors), focusing her study:

> [...] on the hypothetical imagery aspects of the author's mental working process. This set-up implicitly excludes the other potential agencies of authorship, and the collaborative teamwork of cinematographers, sound designers, scriptwriters, set designers, actors, and other film professionals is understood to converge into a single holistic embodiment of expertise, as exemplified by Sergei Eisenstein's own use of the word 'author' or 'creator' (p. 28).

It is difficult to find a specific term to refer to the person that creates complex digital environments, and in the literature, we can find a vast variety of terms depending on the discipline or area of study that is analysing the creation of VEs. From a spatial point of view, we talk about space maker, space shaper, void developer, architect, designer; from a (hyper) narrative point of view we refer to: author, hyperwriter; from a technological point of view, we can speak of a developer, programmer. However, there is one holistic term that transcends the craft work and embraces an ulterior meaning: Creator. The connotation of creator has an intrinsic religious implication; thus, the creator must conceive all the single aspects of both virtual environment and storyworld. This study has been built from the point of view of those who feel and translate their feelings into IFcVR, independently of the interdisciplinary nature of the production of this type of artefacts. Therefore, the term adopted in this book will be 'creator'.

In IFcVR, the creation process occurs in the opposite way to the reading process. The process, from the point of view of the creator, follows a two-moment sequence.

The first moment relates to the creation of the Interactive Fiction:

1. Definition of a storyworld (characters, atmosphere, context, etc.).

2. Definition of an Interactive Fiction (hyperfiction) structure from which it is possible to trace divergent storylines.

3. Definition of the HCI system and design of the interaction moments in relation with the storyworld.

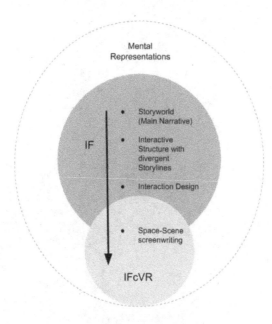

Figure 6. Writing process of IFcVR

The second moment relates to the creation of each cVR Narrative Unit, in which the creator does the screenwriting of what happens within each scene-space. This writing takes into consideration not only what happens on the scene but in the whole space at the same time. The process of creation is traversed by a continuous dialogue of creators with their mental representations, understood as perceptive stimuli and not only visual mental images of the storyworld.

4.
DEVELOPMENT

4.1. *The System Design*

In the chapter Understanding the Process of Authoring, Sofia Kitromili and myself (2023) propose a process for the creation of IDNs composed of four stages: ideation, pre-production, production, and post-production. The proposed model looks for an unified understanding of the process of authoring for all kinds of IDNs. For IFcVR, I have decided to follow the traditional film workflow, where in the Development stage ideation and preproduction merge, considering aspects already related to the system's design. In IDNs it is not possible to separate the system from the storyworld. Therefore, when creating an IFcVR, the first step is to design the system that will contain the possible stories to be delivered during the 'discoursivization' process. The protostory model is a conceptual framework proposed by Hartmut Koenitz (2023), that gathers all aspects to consider during the ideation phase of any IDN project. By using the protostory model, the IDN not only focuses on the narrative design but provides an overview of the aspects that will be managed by the IDN system. As the etymology of the word suggests, the protostory is a root, the original element from which the other elements develop, the starting point that allows us to pursue a medium-conscious narratology taking into consideration the technological nature of IFcVR, even if it is not an emergent narrative, but a pre-scripted one.

In cinema, the screenplay starts with an idea that is embodied by a character (who the story is about) and an action (what is the story about) (Field, 2003, p. 32). In literature, cinema, and theatre, an assumed premise is leading to a conclusion (Lajos, 1972, p. 4). In the same way, all IDNs start with an idea, a message that will remain on the interactor's mind; the difference is that, in IDN, the idea does not have the form of a typical drama or film subject, it goes further. If the premise in cinema is the initial situation that drives the plot, the protostory is the fictional space that gathers all the possibilities, technical and narrative, of an interactive digital narrative. Koenitz proposes as a starting point the Protostory model: a procedural blueprint that defines the space of potential narrative experiences contained in one IDN system.

Once these concepts are defined, one can then move on to thinking about Narrative Design, the creative moment in which the interactive screenplay is written. In AI-based IDN systems, programming can take place almost simultaneously with the creation of the final product. In IFcVR, as a pre-scripted filmic experience, the protostory is placed before the phases of film production: protostory, development, pre-production, production, post-production.

Using the Protostory model, Figure 7 illustrates the primary components of a IFcVR project.

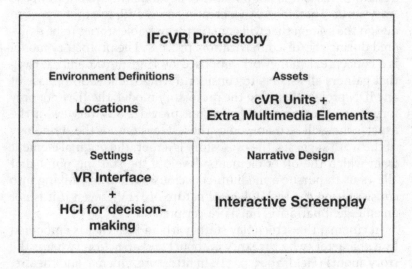

Figure 7. IFcVR Protostory Model

Environment Definitions. In IFcVR, the environment corresponds to the locations in which the scenes of the story are going to be shot or animated. Again, a cinematic term is used to designate a component of the IFcVR system design. I propose that this direction of art for the environment should already be considered during the Protostory phase. Therefore, key considerations like photography, design of spaces, etc., should be described in this phase.

Assets. The assets of an IFcVR experience are, in first place, the cVR units, the independent scenes that deliver parts of the story. In second place, it is possible to deliver extra information through multimedia elements (text, animated characters, still images, videos) layered upon a 360° moving image.

Settings. As the main interface of the IFcVR project is VR, the settings correspond to the integration of the VR system with the interface designated for interactors' decision-making moments.

Narrative Design. The narrative design is the interactive structure of the interactive VR film. This structure is created by the screenwriting of each narrative unit and followed by the connections between them. The resulting graph of the interactive structure will determine the number of the possible output stories or paths that interactors can take within the storyworld. In the next section, a framework proposal for the screenwriting of interactive VR fiction films is presented.

4.2. *The Narrative Design: Screenwriting Framework for IFcVR*

The narrative design of an IFcVR project can be related to screenplay for cinema; both are conceptual tools for the shooting of the scenes. At the same time, the IFcVR narrative design is indeed the IF of IFcVR: Interactive Fiction. However, the screenplay of an IFcVR experience needs to preserve narratological consistency on one side and to grant real interactive experiences on the other side. In this section, a screenwriting framework is proposed that aims to become a conceptual tool for the authorship of a pre-scripted interactive narrative with multiple navigation alternatives. The main contribution of the framework is to support the design of an interactive narrative that is independent of interactor's decisions within the storyworld: the plot is always conducted into a dramatic climax, so as the filmic experience can be received by the viewer as a fluent and coherent story. The question that served as a guideline for the development of this proposal is the flagship question of interactive digital narratives: *How to tell an engaging interactive story without compromising its dramatic progression?*

To achieve a fluent interactive VR movie, we need to consider three main elements:

1. A well-structured pre-scripted interactive story with special attention to its dramatic arc based on the classical cinematographic structure (Field, 2003)

2. The *interactivization* of the narrative structure (e.g.: The Hero's Journey (Campbell, 2008; Vogler, 2008; McKee, 2010), other narrative structures as proposed by Koenitz, 2018).

3.The immersive nature of cVR.

Interactive Digital Narratives should also pursue the Principle of Unity, 'the absolute and essential relations of all the parts of the whole' (Price, 1908, p. 56). As it happens in films, the ultimate linear sequence formed by the narrative units that interactors have chosen needs a dramatic tension to conduct the story and keep the viewer's interest alive during the experience. To achieve this goal, an interactive screenwriting framework is proposed that it takes as its foundation, the classical cinematographic narrative structure summarised by Syd Field in his book *Screenplay: The Foundations of Screenwriting* (2005); hence the final experience can have a dramatic progression like watching a film. In this sense, Field's paradigm becomes a canvas, upon which the narrative structure can be 'interactivized'.

4.2.1. *A Time Paradigm as a Canvas*

> What is the common aim of all dramatists? Twofold: first, as promptly as possible to win the attention of the audience; secondly, to hold that interest steady or, better, to increase it till the final curtain falls (Baker, 1919)

Also, for interactive structures, as it has been used for theater, radio, cinema and tv, a starting point for creation is to set periods of time that will help creators on their way to guarantee a series of events and complications that character(s) will live during the time of the experience, driving the story and the interactors along the ups and downs of emotions, independently of interactor's choices. In this way, the creator can set the rhythm of the narrative and keep a great level of control, not by telling the interactors what to see or to choose, but by controlling the temporality of the events. Interactors will live the illusion of freedom of choice, while the experience is already built: each temporal segment has an objective, complications, turning points, its own climax, and a final climax that fills and rewards the interactor's struggle.

Of course, this idea is nothing new; already in 335 BC, Aristotle recognized a narrative structure of three acts, by identifying the anatomy of a *whole* action, which is composed of 'a beginning, a middle, and an end'. Afterward, he split the play into two parts: 'complication and unraveling'. Returning to the thought of Aristotle, Gustav Freytag represented the action in the form of a pyramid and identified five moments for its completion: exposition/prologue, conflict, rising action and climax, falling action, and resolution/denouement. Freitag locates the climax where rising action and falling action split. This is not perfect mathematical timing, as each action can have different timings, moving the climax across the acts. Since the time of Aristotle, there have been theatrical and literary works that develop their stories in one (Lewis, 1918), two, three, four, or twenty acts. Analogously, a lot has been theorized about the number of acts that a story should have. However, beyond the number of acts, the important concept is the division of the plot and plot actions into 'periods of progression' (Price, 1908, p. 78). Each period of progression or act should have an object and a proposition, and 'carry it out' (Price, 1908, p. 79). Following this idea, we can think of each act as an independent and complete dramatic event, with its own structure, plot points, and even a climax. By doing this creative exercise, the interactive story will not only ensure a final climax, but multiple climaxes that interactors can live through during the filmic immersive experience, besides the interactive structure of the story and the number of narrative units that integrate it.

In the same flow of ideas, I propose to base the writing of the interactive screenplay on time and its subdivision into acts, which in the case of ZENA was done by using Syd Field's Paradigm which is

the traditional Hollywood film structure. The notion of time and its subdivision on periods of progression will work as a canvas, in which the interactive narrative structure will be designed. In this structure, the story develops in three acts: setup, confrontation, and resolution. Generally, the time of the whole film is divided as follows:
- Setup (1/4)
- Conflict (1/2)
- Resolution (1/4)

Each act contains specific turning points and stages that continuously add tension and contribute to interactors' engagement: 'at the end of each act you have reached a predetermined stage of your journey' (Price, 1908, p. 79). The turning points, or narrative vectors in IDN terms, will be distributed on the single narrative units that will make up the interactive structure's graph. The creation of the Time Paradigm canvas is summarised in the following steps:

1.   In a blank space (paper, computer screen, board, etc.), draw a straight line that will represent the total length of the story and make time divisions that will separate the story into acts or periods of progression of the whole experience. Each act has its own duration according to its importance or complexity.

2. Once the canvas is divided into acts, assign to each act an objective, this can be represented by a word or a sentence that answers the question 'Which will be accomplished in this act?'

3. Then, assign when the plot points or narrative vectors will take place on each act. To this end, creators can help themselves by using Hollywood established plot points, or other narrative structures or simply creating them on their own. At this moment, the creator can foresee several climaxes, anti-climaxes, or even a maxi-climax and locate them on the timeline.

The next step is the creation of the interactive fiction structure, by organizing the narrative units with a brand-new logic, different from theatre or cinema.

4.2.2. The Screenplay as Mind Map: Interactivization of the Narrative Structure

This conceptual framework provides a way to 'interactivize' a narrative structure to create a pre-scripted interactive digital narrative. At the time, most cinematic VR experiences are linear with little interactive opportunities or agency, besides looking around selected elements that do not change the course of the story. Changing the course of the story means creating multiple stories, multiple parallel universes, and multiple 'What ifs'. And this is just creative work, one of the critical parts of the conception and subsequent writing of an interactive story. While there are online tools for writing interactive fiction, such as *Twine* or *Inform7*, which allow us to create hyperlinked words or phrases that branch off the story -which can be also done with any text editor- the concept behind creative work is the same, i.e., to shape a story with different possibilities.

In this sense, the story is itself a mental map that covers points where the development of the story can diverge.

IFcVR is based on single pre-recorded audiovisual narrative units or nodes, especially 360° videos. Therefore, to create a non-linear story with multiple navigation alternatives, the proposed framework creates a graph-based preconceived structure formed by various unique video clips that correspond to a scene or sequence. Each video clip represents a narrative unit (NU).

Regardless if it is a scene or a sequence[1], it has already been edited in post-production. Each narrative unit (NU) can be the source or destination of another one or of multiple units; this is a crucial aspect to keep in mind when developing the narrative events that occur on each NU. Whether it is a scene or a sequence of scenes, each NU must be an independent and coherent narrative element; this will make it possible to easily connect each NU with other NUs.

At this moment, the creator may or may not have decided if their NUs are individual scenes or sequences; this division will

---

1   The terms Scene and Sequence are conceived in the cinematographic sense (Field, 2005).

take place in the next phase of the screenwriting. Here, the creator is at a middle point between the division into acts and the division into scenes-sequences: "the division into narrative units".

The step-by-step process for creating and locating each NU is described below, and it will be exemplified through the interactivization of a well-known Hollywood structure: The Hero's Journey. The same creative method, however, can be applied to the interactivization of non-western-like narrative structures[2].

'Narrative events have not only a logical connection but a logic of hierarchy. Some are more important than others' (Chatman, 1980, p. 53). This sentence of Chatman illustrates very well the task of mentally placing on an empty canvas the events that will push our interactive story forward in time. These narrative events take place inside the NUs. In the previous step, the whole experience time was segmented into acts and in the timeline of each act the turning points were pointed out. In this step, questions such as 'What are those important narrative events? What occurs in them? At what turning point do they correspond to?' trigger the creative process.

In the case of the Hero's Journey, there is a characteristic that facilitates the creation of the NUs: the time division of the hero's journey is the same as Field's Paradigm. The hero's journey is represented as a circle with three acts: the departure from the ordinary world (setup), the entering the extraordinary world (confrontation) and the return to the ordinary world with the achievement of the main purpose, that brings peace, mastering the two worlds (resolution). Each act – 'Separation from the ordinary world', 'Extraordinary world' and 'Return' – is divided into stages of conflict, illumination, fear and overcoming barriers, victory and wisdom. Using the linear structure divided into three acts as a canvas, each stage can be located as an independent NU inside its correspondent act. The division of each stage and its location on the timeline allows the creation of a non-linear structure where the order and connections can be made by following the specificities of the plot.

---

2   It is important to note the difference between *narrative structure* and *interactive structure*. The narrative structure concerns the content of the story, while the interactive structure refers to the disposition of the narrative units and the form and behaviour of the graph.

In this study, a non-restrictive way to locate each NU within the correspondent act is suggested, presenting different alternatives to diversify and combine stages. Below, I am describing how the process of interactivization was undertaken during the narrative design of ZENA.

Act I: The Departure – Setup. In Act I, the first possibility of interaction is related to the acceptance or refusal of the call that represents the inciting incident. These two possibilities (accept or refuse) are presented in one single scene: the help of a supernatural agent. The simplicity of the interaction in this first act obeys not only to the narrative beginning of the story but also to the progressive multiplicity of the choices that the interactor will make along the development of the story. In this case, no matter what the interactor's choice is, the hero must be conducted to begin the adventure. The call to adventure corresponds to the inciting incident, while the first plot point coincides with the first threshold, the entering the extraordinary world.

Act II: The extraordinary world – Confrontation. The second act begins after the hero's arrival in the extraordinary (new) world and entry into the "belly of the whale", it is in these stages that the hero descends into darkness and discovers new truths, to emerge at the end as a reborn hero. In ZENA, these two stages, such as "preparation" and "call", are consequent scenes. These stage-scenes were edited as one narrative unit in post-production. After the stage "The Belly of the Whale", several trials are proposed; all these scenes belong to the stage "The Road of Trials". The Road of Trials is a series of obstacles and tests, but also the moment when the hero finds allies and friends. Three situations corresponding to the Road of Trials are presented in ZENA: an "inner confusion" of the hero, the encounter with some ally(s) as well as the encounter with some enemy(s) and threats.

Specifically, the scenes "encounter with an oracle" and "obstacle/threat" are placed at the "Middle Point" of the experience, since, according to Campbell, it is the moment in which the hero finds key information that will be useful to him on the way to the climax. The Midpoint closes the first part of the story and opens the second.

At this moment, an example of a double stage is introduced: the approach to the 'Ordeal', which has two alternative scenes for the same stage: the "Right Approach' and the 'Wrong Approach', each stage adds dramatic tension before getting into the Ordeal, which in this case, it is also the climax. This duplicity can be adapted to any stage of the journey.

Act III: Return – Resolution. The last act begins with the climax of the story, the moment when the hero is near to reaching the key element that will bring peace and happiness. But as it happens in video games, reaching the reward can be related to the behaviour of the interactor, its attention to details and commitment with the hero's goal. In ZENA's interactive structure four possible endings are presented: two negative endings where the hero does not achieve his mission and two positive endings where the hero gets the reward and can choose between two options for a happy life, mastering the two worlds: ordinary and extraordinary world. An interactive story with only one possible end would spoil the curiosity of the interactor to try other alternatives in subsequent usages of the interactive story.

The process of creating the mind map or interactive structure of the interactive screenplay can be summarised in the following steps:

1. Generate and identify the NUs that correspond to the turning points or narrative vectors. Write a sentence describing what happens in each NU and place them in the canvas in the corresponding plot point or narrative vector.

2. Create the NUs that build the rest of the story. Write a sentence describing what happens in each NU. Place them in the canvas in their correspondent acts or stages.

3. Identify in which NUs, interactors will face a decision to move forward in the story.

4. Identify which NUs can have multiple outcomes. i.e.: The call in Act I can be accepted or rejected; the approach in Act II can be right or wrong; the road back in Act III can be positive or negative.

5. Identify which NUs can be a hub so that the interactor can go back and forth. E.g.: The New World, at the beginning of Act II, offers three different possibilities. At this point, as ZENA's creator, I gave my interactors the possibility to come back to the New World NU, so as they can choose a different path. This is the only time in which interactors could go back in time. A different video version of the NU was shot so that interactors will not see the exact same

video of this scene space when they pass here a second time. Figure 8 illustrates the interactive structure with the interactivized version of the hero's journey.

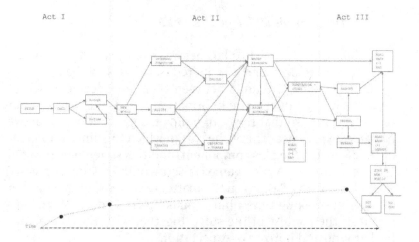

Figure 8. ZENA's Interactive Narrative Design

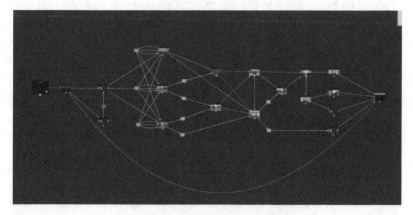

Figure 9. ZENA's Interactive Structure

By following this method, the result will be a mind map canvas that works as a visual tool for the creator, offering an overlook of the whole interactive structure. The mind map can be used as a starting point to consider navigation options when writing the actual scenes, or it can be used to interactivize an already written story. The following step is to link the Narrative Units.

4.2.3. *The Audiovisual Language of cVR*

At this point, the creator has before their eyes a map of events that are hierarchized and distributed in time. Now the task is to connect the narrative units between them and decide which of those events can offer more information to the interactors about the storyworld, so that they can build an entertaining interactive narrative experience. This is the part in which the film component of IFcVR meets the play component, and this statement from Sid Meier confirms it: 'A good game is a series of interesting decisions' (Hiwiller, 2016, p. 84). It is not a matter of increasing the number of decision-making times, but of making those decisions meaningful in the context of the story, together with the interactor's background and horizon of expectations.

Although IFcVR is a pre-scripted narrative, the success of the experience lies in the cleverness of these decisions. In IFcVR, the interactive options are mainly two: the power of the interactor to select the next scene or to access additional information that enriches the experience. Therefore, interactions can occur between NUs (external link) or inside the narrative node (internal link). Interactions can be activated through elements that belong to the storyworld or elements that are external to it.

As the frameless image frees viewers' eyes and gives them autonomy to explore the space, during the screenwriting, but also during the shooting, many film and video makers ask themselves: *How can I direct the viewer's attention to what I want them to see?* During the realization of this study, I have been able to follow the curve of interest on the part of the academy in specifically analysing the cVR language for storytelling, and this has been the most recurrent topic regarding cVR's narrative immersion.

This need for control is caused by the fears that come with the frame disappearance, which is frequently related to a possible disappearance of the direction role. However, from my perspective, the director's intentions in a VE can have a greater reach on the viewer's experiential level. Film and videomakers should abandon the controlling logic of expecting the viewer exactly what they need when working in VR. as that this attitude underestimates interactors' willingness to immerse themselves in the story, and visually follow the narrative events and interesting elements that creators are presenting to them.

The creator's intention lives in the narrative action and then translates into the images according to the point from where the camera is located. Hence, to organise the technical possibilities of directors during the *mise-en-scene*, we can identify different types of shots that can be achieved by the position of the camera and its distance from the key elements and events, and the type of semiotic intention that they can transmit. The shots consider four different conditions that can be combined, to determine the position of the camera. In relation to the given condition, these are the possible types of shots that can be achieved:

Interactor Type: This condition is based on the Interactor Type (IT), that is the role of an interactor that belongs to the storyworld. If the interactors are the protagonists of the story or a supporting character, thus belonging to the storyworld, this type of shot would be a first person shot, also called Point of View (POV) shot.

The interactor can be a human, and in this case the first person shot needs to recreate the human characteristics of that specific character, or can also be a non-human character, in the same way the camera position will need to adapt to the physical characteristics of this non-human character. Locating the camera as a 'live' character has technical consequences: it requires a special rig to be placed on a person or object in a way to recreate the embodiment of the first person's point of view.

Height of the Camera when Perpendicular to the Ground: If the camera is located perpendicular to the ground, it offers the natural vision of a human being standing. Depending on the height of the camera in relation to the ground and the characters and elements that surround it, the shot can have different semantic meanings. We find three cases:

1.   Normal height to the surrounding world, in the natural eye line. The intention can change according to the distance between camera and elements.

2.   Low angle shot that means little distance from the ground, below the eye line.

3.   High angle shot, when the camera is located at a great distance from the ground, above the eye line.

Distance between Camera and Key Elements/Events: Since the camera is at the centre of 360 degrees, the objects around it are visible depending on how distant they are from the camera.

From 3 to 10 metres - Extreme Wide Shot or Long Shot

From 1.5 to 3 metres - Wide Shot ot Full Shot

From 1 to 1.5 metres - Medium Wide Shot

From 0.5 to 1 metres - Medium Shot

Within 0.5 metres - Close Up (Interactors might need to exert their eyes to focus)

Position of the Camera in relation to the Ground: The viewing axis of the camera may not be perpendicular to the ground, as it can also be located parallel to the ground. This positioning gives us three types of natural vision but not very common to humans:

Observe the world at ground level - Nadir

Observe the world from above - Zenith

Observe the world on a horizontal axis (i.e., lying down, with the turned head).

The location of the camera in horizontal position in relation to the ground can give a feeling of flying, lying on the ground or falling. This choice is very delicate, as losing the horizon and the sense of standing on the ground can lead some people to suffer from motion sickness.

4.2.4. *External and Internal Links*

External links connect a NU with others. They represent a change of scene or sequence, a dramatic situation that is different from the previous one, a new event. The external links are the ones that make interactors move forward in time, proceeding towards the end of the experience. To jump from a NU to another NU, interactors will need to decide at the end of the event, as we are working with pre-recorded units. It is also possible to insert the decision-making moment at the beginning of the NU, but in this case, interactors should be informed that the NU continues, so as they can choose to live it or skip it.

An external link that returns to a previous narrative node can present two possibilities:

1. What in movies is called a flashback. The narrative need for a flashback responds to the search for key information to fulfil the story. This information could have been already given but requires a second look or can be added by doubling the narrative node creating two versions of the same scene: the first narrative node and the flashback narrative node that contains the new information.

2. A return that enables the possibility to make a different choice. The return to a previous narrative node that enables the possibility to take another path, requires several versions of the same narrative node in correspondence with the number of links that this specific narrative node offers. In this way, it is possible to add free information and new details to each version of the narrative node (e.g., a non-fundamental character that says hello or some casual situation).

Internal links connect diegetic or extradiegetic elements inside a single NU. Technically, a diegetic or extradiegetic hotspot is linked to a multimedia element (video, image, sound, text) that can be overlapped to the current 360° video or can transfer to another 360° video that returns to the same NU. The purpose of the internal link is to offer useful information to the interactor. This information can be:

1. Diegetic. Multimedia elements that belong to the storyworld and enrich the understanding of the story.

2. Extradiegetic. Multimedia elements that do not belong to the storyworld but give useful information to the interactor, i.e.: instructions, credits, further information material.

4.2.5. *Hotspots*

The IFcVR hotspots are areas of the video with a linking function. When clicking, tapping, or hovering a hotspot, the player will jump to the video segment linked to by the hotspot or will display multimedia material. When interactors face decision-making moments, they will have to choose between hotspots, or select one to access some information. Hotspots are generally visual, images overlay above a segment of the video that contains a link, hence creating a hypervideo. Depending on whether a hotspot belongs to the storyworld (characters, objects, places, sounds), it will be considered diegetic or extradiegetic. Hotspots can also be used to start over a 360 video or to transition to a specific time in a different video.

Dynamic Hotspots. An issue posed by hypervideo, especially for narratives based on interactive video, is the lack of software with dynamic hotspots, that is, hotspots that move frame by frame. Thus, in a shot with camera movement, a hotspot located on a door, for example, can always remain on the door and not in the upper layer that fixes the hotspot in a single area of the video. During the realisation of ZENA, Gabriele Fusi (2017), a bachelor student of software engineering of the University of Genova, developed Prometeo 360 an editor for interactive 360° video that not only allows the creation of interactive immersive experiences, but also allows the creation of dynamic hotspots. With Prometeo 360, creators and editors can 'redefine the interactive areas using key frames; hence the areas will follow the objects in the videos while they move' (Fusi, 2017).

Auditory Hotspots. In cVR, hotspots can also be auditory using Spatial Audio. They work in the same way as visual hotspots with the difference that there is a sound source associated with the active area that is visually transparent. In this way, the interactors will make their choice by recognizing the audio source and then hovering or selecting that invisible area. Auditory hotspots can be combined with a visual element within the environment. Auditory hotspots can also have interactive functions as modify volume levels, stop or play the track, fade the sound or reproduce effects.

4.3. *The IFcVR Screenplay*

Once the narrative design has been developed that is the interactive architecture of the IFcVR project, the next step is to write what is going to be seen: the cinematic screenplay of the immersive interactive film. At this point, each Narrative Unit has been created, associated with a narrative event (a scene or a sequence of scenes), and connected with other NUs, hence creating the whole interactive structure. Now, with the overview of each step, the creator can write how the events unfold in cinematic form, visually describing the actions that characters perform. The writing of the screenplay for an immersive film needs to consider in the first place the aspects related with the 360º environment.

This conceptual exercise creates narratological issues, related to the cinematic VR narrator:

Who tells the story? Who is the interactor within the storyworld? Is the interactor part of the story at all?

Some other challenges in relation with the Interactive Fiction structure are:

What kind of interactions are going to be used? In which way will they affect the story? How to write a fluent and coherent story where a single narrative node is both source and destination of one or several other nodes?

This section will describe how these issues were tackled during the development of ZENA, proposing a format for the script master head.

4.3.1. *IFcVR Screenwriting*

Each NU has been identified with a logline that describes its narrative event. Now, it is time to write the screenplay, which includes the detailed visual description of what happens in the scene: the characters, their actions, their movements in space and their dialogs (Field, 2005). An IFcVR Narrative Unit needs to consider two aspects: the cVR and the IF aspect.

The cVR aspect is related to the 360º space. At this point the first step is to define who is the interactor within the NU: it can be diegetic and be the main character of a supporting character; or it can be extradiegetic, being omniscient or external, having little or no information about characters' internal monologues. It is possible that the role of the interactor during the whole experience will be always the same, or change depending on the dramatic needs of the experience. For example: in one scene interactors experience it in first person the story while in the next scene they can see themselves as an external third person character. Once interactors' role has been selected for the NU, it is possible to locate the camera within the stage.

As in cVR the scene is the stage, the creator will have to imagine from which physical point of view the interactor is going to experiment the scene. If the NT relates them with a character of the story, the creator will have to think, for example, how tall is that character or the distance from which the character interacts with the other characters. If the NT does not belong to the storyworld, the creator will choose from which area of the stage the interactor will have the best visual field of view (FOV) to undergo the events, and narratively, how to offer the information from which the interactor will build up the understanding of the events. The selection of the NT not only will have a narrative impact but also a technical impact during the shooting. The logline of the NU, together with the creator's dramatic intention will determine the location of the camera and how close this will be to the objects and characters.

Since the scene is the stage, during the screenwriting it is also important that creators describe the stage in 360°. The description of the stage will allow us to integrate visual and auditory elements (characters, extras, props, or interactive elements) that enhance the experience in the whole visual space, and consequently the movements of the characters within the scene/stage, e.g. from which area the characters enter the scene and from where they will exit, in which area of the stage the main action will take place, where the hotspots will appear, and to which objects/characters they are related in relationship to space.

From the Interactive Fiction (IF) point of view, the screenplay needs to clearly describe how the interaction is going to be activated by the interactor. In this sense, the screenwriting logic turns away from cinema and develops itself in a different way. A good IFcVR, as all interactive narrative experiences, requires an intense creative work to bring together the dramatic weight of the scene into a meaningful decision for the interactor and the development of the story. Driving towards the decision-making moment must be achieved organically and according to what happened in the narrative unit.

Another aspect to take into consideration is that one NU can be both destination and source of multiple nodes, and this ambiguity must be handled not only from a strictly narrative point of view but also from a visual one. The story logic must be maintained despite the multiple possibilities, as well as the cinematic continuity and the visual flow between NUs. This narrative and visual harmony should be maintained so as the interactive film will have unity and flow.

4.3.2. *The IFcVR Script Model*

In traditional linear cinematic screenplays, a heading is assigned to each master scene to show: the scene number, if it is shot in *interiors* (INT) or *exteriors* (EXT), the main location in which the scene develops and if it occurs day or night. Underneath, the body of the scene is included, together with the detailed visual description of the stage, the emotional state of the characters, their movements, and their words. At the end of each scene, the type of cut that connects the master scene with the next one is written on the right margin, if any. In the same way, IFcVR screenplays keep the same logic in which the script translates the narrative events into visible and audible actions.

However, the IFcVR screenplay has two different characteristics from the cinema screenplay (cVR and IF). It is important that the script clearly shows these differences to guide the actors and the crew during the shooting. Some useful information to be displayed on the IFcVR is listed below:

From the cVR point of view:
1. The Interactor Role will indicate the position of the camera within the stage.
2. The 360° environment, especially if there are objects or elements within the cVE that will be useful for the scene.
3. The number of shots/scenes contained in one single NU.
4. Spatial audio specifications, so as it is possible to determine in which area of the sphere the audio sources will be located.

From the IF point of view:

1. The screenplay needs to indicate the path that the story is following: current NU, previous and next NUs.
2. The type of interaction: number of hotspots, visual or auditory hotspots, internal or external links, diegetic or extradiegetic hotspots and the location of the hotspot.

I propose a Master Scene Heading format, composed by the number of each NU, its logline, the location, its number of scenes and shots, which characters are participating, the precedent NUs (Inputs), the sequent NUs (Outputs), a space for the description of the audio setting, and the types of interaction (number and types of hotspots).

The screenplay is completed by the body of the scene, which describes the actions of the characters, their dialogs, their physical and emotional states, as well as the physical space. It reports what can be seen or heard and the movements of the characters inside the stage. At this point, the screenwriter must take into consideration the whole space in 360° when locating characters and props, to create a rich scene for the viewer to explore. At the end of each scene, the body of the interactive screenplay also reports the interactive choices and how they are presented to the interactor, e.g., if they include text or only visual symbols. To write the body of the scene, I suggest using the guidelines of traditional movie screenplays, to write the body of the heading of the scenes, the action description, dialogues, and cuts.

5.
PRODUCTION

5.1. *Pre-Production*

During the IFcVR pre-production phase all the necessary elements are settled for shooting; these include crew, locations, props, actors, technical equipment, as well as financial arrangements, and a detailed schedule for production and postproduction. However, in addition to the tasks of preparation of the necessary elements, as well as the financial tasks, during the pre-production a breakdown of the script is made. This breakdown produces two important tools for production: the storyboard and the shooting script. In this section, some insights will be given to elaborate both storyboard and shooting script, as we prepare to go to production.

5.1.1. *cVR Storyboard*

In cinema, the storyboard is the visual storytelling of the film. For each shot, the storyboard draws what is going to be shot and seen in the final film. It is a visual tool especially useful for the director and photography director during the shooting process. It not only shows the type of shot, but also communicates its intention. Storyboards are the blueprint of films, animation films, video games, commercials, and TV shows (Paez & Jew, 2013). The question that arises is: how to storyboard for an omnidirectional, frameless image, even with multiple events happening at the same time?

At this moment, most of VR and cVR producers and directors are self-taught; surfing the web, it is possible to find the knowledge that the new communities of VR creators are sharing and constantly updating[1]. In the same way, both academia and industry are sharing insights and tools for sketching and storyboarding for VR (Henrikson et al, 2016). As far as storyboarding is concerned, we can summarise some principles:

1. Areas of Interest. The sphere can be divided into 4 main areas according to the FOV: front area (0°-360°), is what the user clearly see without moving the head; the right (90°) and left (270°) areas can be clearly seen by moving just the head to one side or the other, and the curiosity zone (180°), users needs to turn the whole body to see what is happening behind them The sphere can be also divided according to the distance camera-object. The minimum comfortable viewing distance in an HMD is 0.5-meters while beyond 10-metres the sense of depth perception diminishes rapidly until it is almost unnoticeable beyond 20-metres. This gives us a good focal space between 0.5-meters to 10.0-meters where we can place important content (McCurley, 2016). When it comes to direct the interactor's gaze, theatre has tackled many of these challenges using light, motion, and sound. All these cues should be located on the spherical storyboard, as well as hotspots or other types of interactive areas with thermal, haptic, or auditory cues.

2. Framing Points of Interest. When points of interest (PoIs; important objects and characters as denominated by Brillhart) have been located within the sphere, it is possible to draw how these PoIs are going to be seen by the interactor's FOV. By storyboarding how PoIs are going to be framed by the interactor vision, the art department and cinematographer will be able to set the elements according to the creative intention of the scene. These drawings can be compared with the storyboard of traditional cinema, which considers the different types of shots that can be produced depending on the location of the camera, the distance between it and the objects, and the height of the camera in relation to the ground and the objects.

5.1.2. *The Shooting Script*

The shooting script is the schedule of the shooting, the timing to shoot each scene, the order in which they are going to be shot, and production breaks. It takes into consideration aspects

---

1   https://medium.com/cinematicvr

related to cinematic continuity, so the scenes' order during shooting does not necessarily follow the order in which they will be edited together, but a new order established by production needs: distance from one location to the other, time of the day (morning, afternoon, or night) or special needs related to effects, costumes, actors.

The shooting script also gives information about the technical requirements of each scene: number of shots, camera movements, audio information. For IFcVR, it is suggested to include the number of the NU, the number of takes, if lighting key corresponds to daylight or night, the location, if it is exterior or interior, the characters called for that NU, the Interactor Role in order to know where the camera is going to be located, and if there are special requirements for that NU from the art department or from the team.

When screenplay, storyboard and shooting script are ready, it is advisable to do a read-through of the screenplay with cast and crew before shooting and to share the storyboard and shooting script to all members of the crew.

In the next section, I will describe how the shooting of ZENA was conducted, giving general information about each stage of the production: the setting of the scene, the action moment, the role of the director, and the reformulation of the frameless image.

5.2. *Production*

Cinematic VR finds itself opening a new space between cinema and theatre. The history of these two narrative arts have always been interlaced, not only by the connection that cinema has with theatre as its predecessor, but also by the intermediality that has emerged from the influence that cinema has had in theatre. A first approach can see the relationship between cVR and theatre as a legacy brought by cinema. Cinematic VR, as the recorded image/sound of the real, connects with space in a way that cinema cannot do. During its history, cinema developed a new conception of stage, choreography, and performance, being forced to cut the space into frames. Cinema composes space by delivering fragments that interactors must arrange in their heads.

Some of the main distinctions between cinema and theatre are pointed out by Pudovkin, as cited by Fisher (2007). For Pudovkin, 'the theatre director works with "reality", while the film artist's 'active raw material is no other than those pieces of celluloid'. Hence, film craft is more plastic and material than theatrical art" (p.69). Pudovkin also recognizes that, due to editing, screen acting requires a different skill from that of the stage. These two first distinctions take us directly to what cVR does differently from cinema, even though both are based on space. Cinematic VR delivers the recorded moving-image of what happens inside this scene-space. It forgets its cinema legacy to go back directly to the theatre itself. As in theatre it is the duty of the director to interpret the content of the dialogue, for the eyes of the audience through colour, shape, and motion, through the appearance and gestures of the actors, through the spatial organisation of the setting and the way the bodies move within this space (Arnheim, 1957).

We can divide this setting into two components: (1) one related to the location and (2) the other related to the performance within the location.

5.2.1. *Shooting Workflow*

The Scene-Space Design is the composition of the scene-space as location, and this composition is developed as a two-fold structure: The Scenic Space and the Spatial Space. The Scenic space is related to the *Evenementielle* Density; it includes all the elements that creates the diegetic space and the organisation of these elements in relation with the camera, so its positioning respects vision's comfort. The scenic space considers the order of the POIs and the *evenementielle* hierarchy of all the visual and auditory stimuli.

The Spatial Space, instead, is related to the laws of physics and the positioning of the all-feeling-eye (the camera) within the scenic-space, creating a comfortable environment for the interactor, avoiding vertigo or nausea. It considers the horizon, the interactor role (NT) within the experience, to locate camera, lights, and microphones, not only in relation with the narration but in relation to the feeling of presence.

However, just like Cinema, cVR is also plastic and material. As a recorded image, cVR can also maintain the fourth wall, even though it is shot in a theatrical way, that can even generate some level of alienation for a generation of filmmakers without knowledge of theatre stage management.

The IFcVR shooting workflow takes into consideration characteristics from both IF and cVR; however, the spatial condition of cVR will be the aspect that settles the shooting. The cVR condition sets the mental framework for director and crew: we are shooting all the space contemporary. Everything is being recorded and therefore, every single angle will be seen by the interactor. There are no hidden spaces. This frame elimination brings some issues to the shooting process: the scene must be developed in its entirety in the same shot, reminding cinema's *sequence shot* which requires that actors and crew choreograph the performance together with the technicalities of the scene; this includes cinematography, lightening, audio recording and art direction, and, when referring to an immersive digital narrative, also the spatial audio, as well as the graphic and interactive assets that will be added in postproduction. The spatiality of the scene and the performance of the narrative event in one single shot move the cVR shooting towards the lands already dominated by theatre.

Although the cVR component predominates during the shooting, on behalf of the Interactive Fiction component, two aspects are fundamental:

(1) The Cinematic Continuity: The record of the cinematic continuity is crucial to maintain the visual and performative coherence between NUs that could have been recorded in different moments or days, and not in sequential order. This continuity especially includes the performative intention and emotional charge of the actor at the end of one node, therefore, no matter the interactor's choice, the character's emotional state must always be consistent.

(2) The Decision-making Timing: When at the end of a scene or NU the interactor will have to make a decision, this decision will be made within a video in a limited time, thus it is important to allow a prudent time for the decision-making in the recording, and, if this moment involves the presence of one or more characters, all those

characters will need to stay in position until the cut.

The shooting itself can be divided into two moments: the preparation of the scene and the actual shooting, when "action!" is given. The preparation of the scene comprises three moments:
- Setting of the Scene.
- Measurement of Distances.
- Rehearsal on Set.

Setting the Scene

The configuration of the stage comprises of the location of the camera according to the description of the scene and the location of the key elements and characters in relation with the area where the narrative event will take place. When deciding where to put the camera, it may be useful to remember the words of Sidney Lumet (1996) 'If my movie has two stars in it, I always know it really has three. The third star is the camera' (p.75). This claim takes on a new life in VR, where we know that the vision of the camera is in fact the vision of our interactor, who is therefore the 'third' star of the movie. The location of the camera raises technical issues regarding lighting and sound. For instance, light sources need to be visual elements that are part of the diegesis while working with recorded 360° images. As far as audio is concerned, the on-site audio sources also need to be part of the diegesis, while the spatial audio capture must be close to the camera, so as the interactor's vision and hearing are faithful to natural embodiment.

For the shooting of ZENA, two cameras were used, each with a field of view of 180º, which gave rise to two stitch zones merged in one *stitch zone* all around the sphere, the area in which the images of both cameras merge. Depending on the characteristics of each camera, it is possible to have from none to multiple stitching zones, therefore, during the setting of the scene, it is important to take into consideration the stitch zones so as no key element will be located on it.

The front camera is directed towards the place where the central event of the scene will take place. The back camera is directed towards the area where the character Lorenzo will enter the scene/stage. Lorenzo's final position will be next to the Master, who is already in place. In this case, while the master remains fixed in a single area of the sphere, Lorenzo enters the scene from the area of curiosity shouting *'Maestro, Maestro'*. Lorenzo's voice forces the interactor to turn around to understand what happens, and then the interactor will follow Lorenzo until he joins the master in the area where the narrative event will take place. In this scene, the camera is slightly shorter than the master's and Lorenzo's eye lines with the intention to make the interactor feel in front of two important characters. This is the third scene of Narrative Unit 1. In this NU, Lorenzo is introduced in Scene 1; in Scene 2 he receives the call through a dream, and in Scene 3 he runs to his Master to ask for some suggestions. Scene 3 was shot in St John's church, located in the complex of *La Commenda di Pré*, a location dating from the year 1180. Within this Scene, Lorenzo needs to make the first choice: whether to accept or to reject the challenge. When he accepts, the Master gives him some indications along with the magic cane, through which the knights of Saturn (the interactor) accompany him and guide him, and with which he can make his trip to the future.

Some scenes of ZENA were recorded in the streets of Genoa during the daytime. Depending on the scene, passersby were allowed to walk through the filming, as it happens in the daily life of a city. Some other times, especially during the scenes with dialogue, we closed the entrances to the zone in which we were shooting. Due to the small size of the camera, most passers-by did not notice that we were shooting. Therefore, when the actors were performing, passers-by would cross the scene without reacting. This would preserve the life-like sense of a scene set in the busy old alleys of Zena. In other cases, when a scene was being performed, most of the time passers-by would react to the character's actions. The setting of the scene depends on the relevance of the location; it can help to ask, 'Why is it important to shoot in that specific place?' By answering this question, the director, cinematographer, and art director should be able to determine the areas in which the narrative events will take place within the space, where the camera will be located and how actors will move within the space.

Measuring Distances

Meaning in cVR is a distance-perspective matter. The spatiality of VR and the close relationship between scene and stage that exists when recording in 360º puts a semantic value on the distances between the camera and the objects or characters present in the scene. Unlike cinema, in VR the camera does not get close to the elements and the particulars but is 'naturally' located in a strategic position from where interactors observe and participate in the scene. The position of the camera will determine the interactor's embodiment; this awareness also differs from the cinematographic practice where the montage of the different types of shots builds meaning and narrative flow. Given the bodily presence of the interactor in the scene, and the sequence shot that is the long take of the entire scene, the positioning of the camera along with how objects are distributed in space will dictate the semantic value of each character/object in space.

Once the camera was located, we used a metre to suitably position characters and objects in relation with the camera; distances should be consistent with the director's intentions and the storyboard of the scene. In the scenes where there is a camera movement, and especially where there is some movement of the actors in space, we found it necessary to mark the starting and ending points of the movement. The distance between the starting and destination points were slightly marked on the ground with tape. These marks had two functions: (1) To give the actors a guide to move in the space, and (2) To keep a record to assure cinematic continuity among scenes.

Rehearsal on Set

Akira Kurosawa maintained that the thoroughness of the rehearsals makes the actual shooting every time very short, and that the rehearsal not only included actors, but every part of every scene – the camera movements, the lighting, everything (1983). As Kurosawa points out, the rehearsal makes the recording more fluid when everyone involved knows the role they should play during the scene. In cVR, the rehearsal has many functions: to choreograph actors and/or camera movements; to characterise the emotional intention of the scene with the actors; to make technical adjustments, and in general, to control how the scene and stage work together. In cVR there is also another motivation for rehearsal: anyone who does not belong to the diegesis cannot remain visible on set.

During the shooting of ZENA, we did not have a real-time monitor to check how the performance was developing during the shooting, or a place to hide inside the scene to watch what was happening during the recording, hence all the team had to leave the stage except actors. In some cases, we did have a place to hide from the camera (for example, in the old church I hid in the confessional) so we could look if the scene was fine or not, but most of the time this was not the case. The actors rehearsed beforehand, not only for performance purposes but also to show to the director and the crew how the scene was going to develop, especially in those scenes that were designed for the actors to move across the stage so as the viewer is forced to move around following the characters.

Sound Recording

The missing element during the creation of ZENA was the spatial sound. At that time, we did not have the material possibility to involve a space sound specialist in the production and postproduction of the prototype. Without 360° audios, we could not experiment with the inclusion of auditory hotspots, with the creation of narrative environments based on the placement of sound sources in space or being able to guide the interactors with their audition more than with their vision. Spatial audio would be very important to create realistic atmospheres and to enhance both perceptive and narrative immersion. Spatial audio can play a fundamental role in the creation of IFcVR, and in general of VR experiences.

Even if we could not work with spatial audio, we were very careful to consider from where the interactor would have listened to the dialogues and the other sounds inherent to the cVE, or diegetic sounds. The sound treatment of ZENA includes both diegetic and non-diegetic sounds. Within the diegetic sounds we find: the ambient sound of each location, natural sounds of the characters (steps, gestures, and movement-generated sounds), dialogues, music played by one of the characters on stage. The non-diegetic sounds comprise background music for Lorenzo's presentation scene and all four possible endings, music for the decision-making moments, few sound effects in some cases at the beginning of a new narrative unit.

Another sound that had a particular role in the experience is the voice over. This was used twice: the first one is the non-diegetic voice-over of an omniscient narrator that introduces the story, telling where the interactor is, in what time and who is Lorenzo. The second moment of voice over is diegetic; this is the voice of Chronos, the magical helper, who reveals to Lorenzo the reason for the mission and how he must act to achieve his assignment. As a filmmaker, I have noticed that voice-over is frequently overused in cinema, as it is very effective in facilitating the narration; I took it as a personal challenge, and tried to avoid the use of voice-over during the development of any type of audiovisual work. But during the realisation of this study, we had the opportunity of enjoying many VR and cVR experiences that are built upon a voice-over. In this sense, VR is very effective in creating a soundscape around us, but also a story that is being told. In fact, regarding the voice over, VR poses the question for the interactor *Who am I listening to?*

ZENA then had two moments of recording: the recording on location, and the recording of the voice over. The voiceover was recorded after the three days of shooting, a studio with a bidirectional microphone, and later it was 'spatialized' with an effect in post-production. During the recording on location, we placed three microphones: a pair of binaural microphones, one in each ear of Lorenzo, and a bidirectional sound recorder located just below the camera, on its same axis. . The choice of the microphones and their location during the recording have an important role for the narrative immersion. The binaural microphones used were key to create role identification, one of the components that enhanced narrative immersion. Having microphones in the ears of Lorenzo allowed us to create a closer relationship between the interactor and Lorenzo, especially during the scenes in which the interactor was identified with Lorenzo (NT1) or in which the interactor was positioned at the magic cane that accompanied and guided Lorenzo (NT3). The binaural microphones also allowed the interactor to listen more clearly to Lorenzo's breathing, the sound produced by his body gestures, his voice, the thoughts that he sometimes expressed aloud to himself, and gave a better clarity of the dialogues between Lorenzo and the other characters. The binaural also allowed a more accurate stereo post-production, emphasising the sounds coming from Lorenzo's left or right side.

The sound recorder, located on the same axis of the camera, had three functions: (1) to simulate the natural hearing of the interactor, as it is attached to the camera/eye of the interactor, picking up ambient sound and dialogs from the location of the camera, (2) to create a safe additional track to binaural microphones and (3) to record a wild track for ambience audio. The sound recorder that we used had an integrated bidirectional microphone. It was placed in the same way our ears are in relation to our eyes, therefore depending on the front lens of the camera we located them at the right and left side of the microphone. Afterwards, all sounds were worked out in post-production: the environmental ones were spatialized, while sounds with a specific source in space were worked in stereo.

Action!

At this point, we are ready to shoot. Once microphones, audio, cameras, as well as actors and crew, are in position, the *Action!* is given. 'Action! says it all. Internal Action. External Action. Perform. Do, Acting is active, is doing. Acting is a verb' (Lumet, 1996, p. 116). If we had had a place to hide on the location, everyone would already be in their places, otherwise, and for most of the cases, before the *Action!* We left the stage for the actors. I had to trust my actors in those scenes in which the crew did not have a chance to directly check the development of the performance. The actors helped the director to know if the scene was shot as rehearsed. When one of the actors pointed out something that could have been better, I always repeated the scene. We kept the record of every single take we shot, specifying why we made another take. However, as we rehearsed before the shooting, we decided to always shoot two takes, most of the time the first take was a print, while the second one was more like a safety take. Further repetitions were sometimes requested by the actors, or because there was some intromission.

The actors played an essential role during this shooting: they performed, remembered all dialogs and movements on scene, and they told us when they felt OK or not with the take. Beside this, they had some other instructions related to the IFcVR type of film we were shooting. One of the instructions was related to the decision-making moments, i.e., when the interactors must decide which way to follow. In general, the actors were requested to always wait at least 30 seconds after the *Action!* and to remain in position until the camera operator would stop the recording. The decision-making moments represented a critical aspect. Actors were asked to keep the emotion of the final moment, especially the avatar character, Lorenzo, the one who performs the actor's choices. Lorenzo had to express the moment of choice with his face and body movements, e.g., by pointing gesturally where the hotspots were located or showing indecision between two characters, while the other characters were holding the last emotion or situation.

One of the main mistakes that was made in this movie had to do with this precise moment. The fact that the video is of limited duration, many times interactors felt that they did not have enough time to reflect on their decision. Certainly, deciding which way to proceed is an individual matter and varies from person to person, which makes it difficult to determine how much time is enough; however, this aspect should receive particular attention in future projects, allowing more time for decision making. Lorenzo, protagonist, and avatar character, also had to remember where the hotspots would be in space, and act having these invisible objects in mind.

Something important to mention is that Lorenzo was also often the camera operator, not by starting or stopping the recording, but operating the camera movements. Interactor Role 2 corresponds to an interactor that is part of the diegesis without being the protagonist of the story. In ZENA this role was interpreted by the magic stick that guides Lorenzo in his journey. In some scenes Lorenzo had to walk with the cane/camera in his hand with stable and slow movements to avoid interactors to suffer from motion sickness, and at the same time, he had to remain in his character, being also aware of the presence of the interactor who was, literally, in his hand. In some scenes, he had to hold the camera and to interact with other characters and people passing by. In ZENA's case, even though in some cases we protected our locations from external interferences (e.g., street loud sounds or people passing through), one of the intentions was to give a sense of the real city during the experience, so we kept some scenes with passers-by talking on the phone or looking at Lorenzo with perplexity.

5.2.2 The Experience Director

> The intentions that motivate an act are contained within the action itself. You will never escape this. Even though the 'why' of any work can be disguised or hidden, it is always present in its essential DNA (Bogart, 2008, p. 30).

Although the type of artefact that is being proposed and analysed is an interactive experience that differs from both the film and the video game, when trying to work out its own identity we are moving in a land that has already been well explored by theatre and film. This claim arises from the fact that, although the interactor has a higher level of agency within the cVE than in 360° linear videos and linear VR experiences, in IFcVR the narrative weight falls on the scene, and from this the interactor makes the decision that will model his unique narrative outcome. Likewise, during the development of the study, we have seen how the creation process distances itself from the cinematic workflow at first, but at this moment of the creation, the cinematic and cVR methods are very similar again. For this reason, I return to the role of the director to refer specifically to the moment in which creators leave their studios and find themselves on the set to direct the production.

When I say director, I am not only referring to the film director but also to the theatre director, as characteristics from both roles merge in this case: the term 'Experience Director' comes to my mind to describe this role. The Experience Director is, in the first place, a director who works in a real environment with real actors; in this sense, the Experience Director moves away from a creator who works only with computer-generated agents and spaces. Secondly, the Experience Director works with a different conception of his audience: the theatre director directs the work towards an audience that is physically present in the same space as the play; the film director directs for an audience that will receive the film through a screen in a movie theatre; the experience director directs for a person who is embodied in a VE and is actively involved in the narrative event. For everyone of these three types of directors, the conception of the audience is completely different.

Sidney Lumet points out the limited control of the film director over certain areas, 'one of these areas is the operation of the camera' (1996, p. 116). In cVR, this aspect is less problematic as the camera does not always need an operator during the recording and it does not have to cut the scene in multiple shots. However, the Experience Director, especially when working with VR[2], needs to physically see from the place from which the interactor will see the scene. Only by doing this, creators will understand how the audience will live the IFcVR experience. By 'living' I understand all the aspects that interactors will be in touch with during the experience, not only what happens in the scene but also the way in which they are going to interact with the storyworld. Akira Kurosawa points out that all the occupations on a film production 'melt together under the heading of direction': actor's coaching, cinematography, sound recording, art direction, music, editing, dubbing and sound mixing (1983, p. 192). The experience director has to do with all of this, but also with the sensitive dimension of the audience as well as the care of the relationship between the interactor and system.

Regarding the direction of the scene during the shooting, all the aspects related to what is going to be seen and heard (the setting of the scene, the movements of the actors, the distances between characters and objects, and the performance of the narrative event playing along with the location and height of the camera), concern only the experience director and their intention, and this is something inherent to the artistic creation. Although the direction of the IFcVR content, i.e., the film takes us to the cinema grounds, there is a primordial physical connection between VR and theatre that transcends cinematography. This connection is pointed out by

2   I consider that the phrase Experience Director can be used to name directors who work with hybrid environments, such as VR, MX, AR.

Anne Bogart (2008) as: 'The theater is always about what it means to be alive now, present at this particular moment in the theater' (p. 106). Analogously, VR is about what it means to be present at a particular moment in a particular virtual space, as well as the relationship between that virtual experience and both creator and interactor's personal and historical context.

The director role in cVR is a mixture between the directors in cinema and theatre. Tarkovsky regretted that 'a vast number of clichés and commonplaces, nurtured by centuries of theatre, found a resting-place in the cinema' (1987, p. 24). He referred specifically to the concept of *mise-en-scene* and argued how this concept was a simplistic way to express the idea of a scene by giving it the depth that the meaning requires, a 'violence to the living texture of the artistic image' (p.24). His claim was to conceive the *mise-en-scene* not only as the design made up of the disposition of the actors in relation to each other and to the setting, but also the scene construction by filling it with the life, beauty and with the emotional and psychological states of the characters.

The *mise en scene*, in Tarkovsky terms, does not make a distinction between theatre, cinema or cVR; it regards transmitting emotions and beauty. This entails a synergy between directors and actors. With regards to cVR, acting and directing are rather related to theatrical acting methods that need a different approach to corporality and expression of feelings. The fact of being able to perceive the body of the actors in relationship with one's own body changes the approach of director and actors regarding the camera and the performance, establishing a distance, for director, crew, and actors, between cVR and cinema. In cVR, everything happens around the *all-feeling eye*, the camera; according to the Interactor Role, the performance will involve the interactor as part of the diegetic space or not. Thus, there is effectively a disposition of the bodies and actions on the stage which follows a theatrical corporality that keeps a cinematic role for the camera.

5.2.3 *The Actors' Presence*

Christian Metz (2007) pointed out a main difference between the theatre actor and the film actor: 'the bodily presence' (p. 10).

This also turns out to be the difference between the film actor and the cVR actor. In VR and cVR in general, we can measure and feel the corporeality of the actors in relation to our own.

The materiality of the human body, especially in cVR movies made with 3D stereoscopic video or volumetric video, and even animated characters in 3D, enhance the willingness of belief, the feeling of realism and presence. These sensations are related with the self-consciousness of being bodily in the world (Legrand, 2007). In some cases, when interactors do not have a physical body within the VE, the own body recognition passes through the corporeality of the characters and the dimensions of the objects and elements that form the VE. Legrand (2007) argues that 'the fundamental form of self-consciousness cannot rely on self-specific information. It rather relies on self-relative information, information about the world that is relative to the self/body' (p.514).

It is possible to account two dimensions on the role of the actor in cVR:

1. The performative act during the production.
2. The relationship between character(s) and interactor during the experience.

The first dimension is related to the disappearance of the frame; the performance for the cVR moves away again from the cinematographic logic and turns towards the logic of the theatre. This theatre method is reflected in the management of the stage and the ability to deliver long and coordinated performances. In some cases, the different types of cinematography shots (i.e.: close-ups, American shots, etc., unlike high angle or low angle shots that depend on the height of the camera) are reached by the distance of the actor from the camera, thus it is the actor's jobs to move across the space to give the semantic meaning related to the cinematic different types of shots, within the scene-space. During the production, the cuts in a scene are very rare, so actors must perform in what is called 'Sequence Shots' in which actors are asked to perform for long times and in perfect choreography. In cVR, actors must also be aware that there is someone else in the scene, the interactor. Especially in cases where interactors play a role in the story, actors must involve them in the scene, and sometimes address them directly.

The second dimension is related to the cinematic interface of cVR. Unlike computer-generated VEs and computational agents, in cVR interactors cannot interact in real-time with the characters. In this sense, the cinematic nature of cVR predominates and works in the same way cinema does. 'Metz argues that the cinema installs the spectator in a situation in which his gaze is inoculated from reciprocal awareness. Spectatorial voyeurism is further promoted by the keyhole effect of the screen which suggests we are looking through an aperture/apparatus upon the actors' (Allen, 2007, p. 130). This sense of spectatorial voyeurism, even though this can seem a conflictive term, could be the hidden weapon that can develop the potential of cVR.

When producing an Interactive Fiction in Cinematic Virtual Reality (IFcVR), the actor role acquires a new nuance. The actor's performance influences the decisions that interactors will make in the task to assemble the filmic discourse. Within the IFcVR, we can identify two main types of actors:

The Avatar Actor: interactor's decisions will have direct consequences on the future of this character (or characters in the case of a narrative with multiple focalization). This type of character drives the narrative. The avatar actor takes the feeling of empathy and identification of the interactor to a higher level. The fact of being a character subject to the decisions of the interactor requires the actor to sometimes perform like a videogame character, giving gestural signals to the interactors about their state of mind. The actor also accepts their destiny, and this docility must be reflected in their performance.

The Non-Playable Actors: these are characters who belong to the storyworld on a secondary level, or, most importantly, characters who are fundamental for the development of the story even though their role and behaviour do not change based on interactors' decisions. The non-playable actors in any case will have to interact with the avatar actor(s), and likewise will have to respect interactors' decision-making time. They, in some cases, may be the trigger for a certain decision or present alternatives that will have consequences on the development of the story of the avatar actor (s) (e.g.: they can give advice, need help, etc.).

5.3. *Postproduction*

Since we are working with video files, moving from one space to another is what we technically call "transition" in film/video making. The cinematic transition is the juncture that connects one shot after the other. It is already established during the screenwriting: as there are different types of shots, there are also different types of transitions, and each of them has a semantic value within the audiovisual discourse. Transitions play an important role in organising time: the time of the story, the time of the discourse and even the psychological time of the film, by establishing dynamic relationships between shots, scenes, and sequences (Mitry, 2000). Although the post-production work comprises of aspects related to audio, colour, graphic and subtitles, in this chapter it seems essential to draw from the filmic editing of the IFcVR experience as the temporary organisation of shots, scenes and sequences, and how transitions or travelling can be done between them.

Film directors must often battle with the impulse to edit or not to edit, as Lucy Fischer (2007) states citing Siegfried Kracauer in her chapter *Film Editing* about these opposing tendencies when creating an audiovisual work. The debate resides in how much is taken from reality and its interpretation through the shot, and how much is created by the juxtaposition of shots. This internal debate is another issue that traditional film/video makers face when they start working with cinematic VR (Zhang et al, 2018; Kjær et al, 2017; Moghadam & Ragan, 2017), but neither the cVR discourse nor the IFcVR discourse are created by what Eisenstein (1949) called the *collision* of different shots. On the contrary, these collisions or conflicts are created within the single shot (through the performance, the location of key elements and characters, the design of the stage, etc.) and when the shot arrives at the computer, it already has an irreducible life.

Shot and montage are the basic elements of cinema; montage has always played an important role in defining what is cinema itself. The Soviets called it 'the nerve of the cinematographic art' (Eisenstein & Leyda, 1949, p. 48). I must warn, however, that the montage of the object of study of this study has very little to do with the montage of traditional video or traditional cinema, both technically and syntactically. This deflection from the cinematographic concept of montage is rooted in the conception of shot, the cell or molecule of the cinematic discourse. While cinema 'combines shots that are *depictive*, single in meaning, neutral in content, into intellectual contexts and series' (Eisenstein & Leyda, 1949, p. 30), in IFcVR, and in cVR in general, each shot is an *image-space* with narrative actions happening within it. The shot becomes a window to a specific time-space that can be cut, linked, or juxtaposed according to the events unfolding within. The montage, at this point, deals with little worlds that contain semantic framings already designed by the creator during the development and/or the shooting phases. Thereby, in cVR, the cinematographic montage, as film theory has defined it, is done by the interactor as the ultimate *MegaGrandNarrator*. Going up a level, in IFcVR, the interactor links these small worlds, one after the other, becoming what I have called the *HyperMegaGrandNarrator*.

To approach the process of montage of an IFcVR experience, we must divide the process in two moments in which there will be two types of different montages: (1) the montage of each narrative unit, and successively, (2) the montage of the interactive experience. Each of these types of montage has a unique mechanism, and both move away from the cinematographic montage in its intellectual sense. This chapter faces technical aspects approached by the mechanism through which an IFcVR experience can be built as a fictional filmic experience, where the narration of events prevails, and where interactivity joins the flow of events as a narrative element, and not as a disruptive one.

5.3.1. *Editing the Narrative Unit: Linear cVR Montage*

As a pre-scripted interactive narrative, IFcVR has an underlying structure that is immutable. The interactor delineates its passage through this structure, which is formed by single Narrative Units each of which is, in a strictly technical sense, an already stitched[3] 360º video file, be it monoscopic, stereoscopic, or 3D[4]. The possibilities of interaction are basically two: (1) accessing extra information within the same NU and (2) being able to choose the next NU.

---

3   If the scenes were shot with multiple cameras.
4   Animated video should also be considered, in future studies.

At this moment of the creation of the IFcVR experience, creators find themself in the editing room with the raw material, both audio and video, that has been recorded during the filming, and it is time to put it together to create each single NU.

As a filmic experience, an IFcVR story is divided into scenes and sequences. A scene unfolds an action or event at the same time-space, while a sequence contains a series of scenes. A NU can contain a single scene, with one shot or multiple shots, or can contain a sequence. If the NU contains a scene with multiple shots or a sequence of scenes, there will be cuts within the same video. In an audiovisual narrative sense, I do not find the cut between a scene and the next one problematic, because it simply implies a transition between one time-space and another, led by the events that happen in each of them. On the other hand, cuts within a single scene can be tricky. To cut is to change camera position in a single scene/space, and that means to change the interactor's position in space. This can be done to offer the interactor different perspectives over the same event or space. However, even though it is a valid mechanism to strengthen the narrative by giving more information about the place or event, it will slow down the discourse time as in cVR, interactors need time to understand where they are standing, who they are in the experience, and what they are looking at. And in the same way, the creator will have to give time to the events or actions to fully evolve from that camera position.

These notions about the cut also give us valuable information about the cVR shot. When referring to the cinematographic shot as material for composition, Eisenstein (1949) describes it as "more resistant than granite, with a resistance that is specific to it, and with a tendency toward complete factual immutability that is rooted in its nature" (p. 5). If already in cinema the shot has this indivisible and strong quality, in cVR it acquires an even greater robustness because it must allow the sense of location for the interactor and the flow of events, and it must contain all the elements, conflicts and collisions that the creator needs to locate and coordinate in the time-space to set up the scene. Taking a look at cVR projects and videos, through a HMD and even through YouTube or Vimeo, most of them treat the scene with a single long-shot, thus the whole narrative event unfolds in that single shot. This means that the creator just chose a camera position and let the action happen in space. This one-shot is reminiscent of cinema's long-takes or sequence shots. Referring to Orson Welles' sequence shot in *The Magnificent Ambersons*, Bazin (2004) notices 'his refusal to break up the action, to analyse the dramatic field in time is a positive action the results of which are far superior to anything that could be achieved by the classical cut' (p. 34). This same spirit should guide the creator during the screenwriting and later during the shooting.

The montage at this point is a careful sharpening of each shot. While cinema's montage 'creatively remodels nature' (Eisenstein 1949, p. 5), cVR montage somehow facilitates nature approaching the essential cinema's montage which keeps a 'straightforward photographic respect for the unity of space' (Bazin, 2004, p. 46). In Eisenstein's words, in cVR the creator can approach montage as a 'Tonal Montage' (Eisenstein, 1949, p. 75), a montage that takes into consideration the tone of the whole narrative event, the set of dynamics that come together in the emotional sound of the scene.

Before working on the actual montage of ZENA, the two 180° video files of each shot were stitched with the Kodak PixPro 360° Stitch software[5] to create an equirectangular monoscopic video file. These shots were later edited with the video editing software Final Cut Pro X[6], in which I made colour correction and audio editing, with the Surround Sound pre-set, that allows me to re-create surround sound fields from stereo source. During the postproduction of ZENA, I had to edit NUs formed by single scenes, one-shot and multi-shot, as well as NUs formed by a series of scenes. Below, each type of NU is described and exemplified by means of ZENA's realisation.

One single shot Narrative Unit

In total, there are seven One-shot Scenes NUs in ZENA. I am taking as example NU 7, that corresponds to the first encounter

---

5   The stitch software specific for the Kodak PixPro 360°camera.
6   I did not choose FCPX for any specific reason, but simply because it is the video editing software that I have been using on my pc. When I started this study, neither FCPX nor Adobe Premiere CC had the immersive video setting, only the last updates of both tools allow immersive video and immersive audio.

with the contagonist of the film, Sercan. This character livens up the plot by threatening to steal the magic clepsydra, but later in the story he will try to help Lorenzo save the precious object. This NU is reached as one of Lorenzo's three possible choices when he arrives at the new world, the present ZENA: (a) I feel lost (b) I know my city, and (c) Somebody is waiting for me (this NU comes after option c).

I chose this NU to exemplify the process because it has a camera movement at the beginning of the scene, and afterwards there is an internal movement of the characters that forces the interactor to look around following Sercan. The camera is in Interactor Role 3, that is, the interactor is the eye of the magic cane that Lorenzo holds in his hand. As a one-shot scene NU, at the end of the scene interactors will face again a decision-making moment. Technically, the editing of this scene was very simple, it consisted in setting the start and the end of the scene, synchronising the audio tracks (binaural microphones, ambient audio from recorder and the audio of the camera) and spatializing the final audio track in the editing software.

This NU has two outputs or choices; in it, I did not use any text to help the interactor since Lorenzo must escape from the hands of Sercan who threatens him with a knife pointed at his throat. Lorenzo, and therefore the interactor, must only choose which of the two narrow streets he wants to escape; labels on the links would just take extra-time to read, breaking the suspense created by the scene. At the end of this NU, 30 seconds were allowed, to give the interactor the time to decide. Additionally, two annexes of the scene were recorded, with Lorenzo escaping through the alley that has been chosen by the interactor. These scenes, that were used after several NUs, were added with an automatic transition after the decision making and an automatic transition to connect the completion with the following NU.

Multi-shot Scene Narrative Unit

In ZENA, the interactor will find four NUs of this type, which are formed by several shots that are part of the same narrative moment. The different shots help to give the interactors a better understanding of the space in which they are, different points of view of the same element, and contextualises the completion of the event, either in the same space, or a space related to the same location.

To exemplify this type of NU, I will use ZENA's NU 9, which corresponds to the moment of the Revelation, in which Lorenzo and the interactor meet the magic helper Chronos who gives him more information about his mission together with some mystical messages; for this reason, this scene was written in a magical way: Chronos talks to him as a voice over and, in general, the scene has a very unhurried rhythm that slows down the experience. The scene was shot in a very suggestive location of Genoa's old city, the old gate *Porta Soprana*. Upon entering one of the towers of the gate, Chronos calls Lorenzo inviting him to climb to the top of the tower. The interactor is in NT3, meaning that Lorenzo is carrying the magic stick.

This multi-shot scene, and therefore this NU, is formed by five shots that add suspense to the scene before he meets Chronos:

- Shot 1. Natural Eye Line - Wide Shot of Porta Soprana: Lorenzo is in front of the gate. People walk around, some of them look incredulous at Lorenzo.

- Shot 2. Natural Eye Line - Close up of Lorenzo's face: Lorenzo is inside one of the towers with the spiral staircase around him. A voice calls him: 'Lorenzo'.

- Shot 3. Natural Eye Line - Close up of Lorenzo's face: Lorenzo is climbing the stairs; he is in the middle of his way up. He is so close to the railing that if the interactors look down, they can see the bottom of the stairs, if looking up they can see the ceiling of the tower. The voice keeps calling him.

- Shot 4. Above Lorenzo's Eye Line - Close up of Lorenzo's face: Lorenzo is about to get to the top, but he is scared. The interactor can see him from a high angle shot. The voice tells him not to be scared.

- Shot 5. Natural Eye Line - Close up of Lorenzo's face: Lorenzo is at the top of the tower; around him he can see the new ZENA. Chronos reveals herself to him and gives him some hints to accomplish his mission.

The transitions between these shots were simple cuts, passing from one shot to the other. However, while shooting I was very careful to always keep the front camera towards the front of Lorenzo, and the back camera towards his body. By doing this, the interactor could always find Lorenzo in the same position, maintaining the spatial orientation. Regarding the sound design, the audio was also cut with each image cut, so passing from one place to the other also meant to change the sound landscape. On top of the tower, the voice of Chronos speaking to Lorenzo was spatialized, while Lorenzo's breathing (recorded with the binaural microphones) was intensified.

Sequence Narrative Unit

In cinema, a sequence edits together a group of related scenes that share the same event, time, space or thematic. In IFcVR, the sequence NU puts together different scenes until a decision-making moment is reached. The need to unite several scenes arises from two possible cases: a decision is not presented to the interactor until that moment, or the output of a previous sequence is connected to the successive sequence before the interactor returns to decide. However, it is important to keep in mind that the IFcVR sequence puts together different time-spaces with different events. Unlike the transition occurring between different shots that belong to the same scene, the type of cut between scenes obeys the tone of each of those small worlds and the narrative or artistic need of the creator.

Although most of the time I simply used a cut to make the transition between one shot and another, especially within the same scene, sometimes I used other types of transition to give an aesthetic and narrative value to the experience. For instance, a slow dip into black when Lorenzo is falling asleep in NU1/Sce1; a fast dip to black when the Master shoots Lorenzo with a gun; a slow dip to white accompanied by a sound effect to simulate the time travel that takes Lorenzo into the current day ZENA, or a fade out between a NU and the other to create an ellipsis.

5.3.2 The Interactive Montage

Once all NUs are crafted for both video and sound, it is time to create the interactive structure, the labyrinth that will allow interactors to trace their own experience. This phase is not only about connecting the pieces but about making them work in interaction, running the experience along with the HCI through which the interactor will have agency within the storyworld. In the case of ZENA, I used the software WondaVR[7] to perform the interactive montage. WondaVR allows the creation of experiences that can be downloaded on a device or played in streaming. Beyond the technicalities, I will expose some insights from my experience with ZENA about the creation of a filmic interactive experience that is fluid and pleasing for both eyes and ears. At this point, the work is quite simple if an accurate screenwriting has been done; if the shooting considered the positioning of the camera as well as the moments of interaction, and if the editing of the NUs was done in a meticulous way, both in the treatment of the image and in the treatment of sound.

In this phase of the IFcVR production, most of the work must be done by trial and error. The trials test whether the hotspots and the multimedia materials visually adapt to the space; whether the interactions work and tackle what could happen if the interactor fails to decide on time. In this section, I am describing two processes within the interactive montage: the construction of the mind map and the location of the hotspots in space.

Setting the Mind Map

The construction of the mind map is a process that was previously done during the development of the narrative design. From the development to the final structure, this blueprint should change very little during the creation of the experience. Significant changes put forward new NUs that have been added, as well as connections or alternative paths that were not initially contemplated, that were created in successive phases or that were even eliminated. Changing the interactive structure implies that the narrative itself has been changed.

Within the interactive montage software, the process consists of:

1. Uploading all the assets that the experience needs: 360° video files, audio files (music, sound effects or the spatial audio file), graphic elements (hotspots, multimedia materials) that can be

---

7   https://www.wondavr.com/

texts, images, sounds, 3D objects and flat videos to overlay upon the spherical video.

2. Locating in the storyboard space each NU in the order that has been given by the narrative design and configuring the settings of each.

3. Working individually on each NU. At this point, each NU can be edited in the timeline, very similar to the video editing timeline, in which we can locate when the multimedia assets should appear or disappear. This includes the insertion of Internal Links or objects that appear within that specific NU.

Connecting the Narrative Units

External Links are the ones that connect a single NU with one or multiple NUs. This process follows the narrative design and at this point the work is mostly technical. However, there is an important difference if the IFcVR is based on cognitive interaction or biofeedback interaction. If it is an IFcVR experience where the interactor consciously chooses its way forward, the project presents a UI through which the filmic experience offers the interactor the ludic component. If, on the other hand, the IFcVR experience is based on the interactor's biofeedback and therefore interactors do not have a conscious control of their choices, the interface disappears and the cVR experience flows as a symbiosis between the narrative and the interactor's emotions. In this work, I am referring to a IFcVR experience with cognitive interactions, as it is the case of ZENA.

In cognitive interaction, the connections between NUs are made through a hotspot, a target in space that displays different alternatives to the interactor at the decision-making moment. The hotspots can be part of the story (i.e., two characters that present two different alternatives) or can be some graphic elements not belonging to the storyworld. These targets, that can be visual or also be auditory if working with spatial audio, appear in sync with the narrative event, so as the interactor is ready to decide. The hotspots work as channels through which the narrative event is decompressed. However, when we give the interactors the power to choose between several options, they must know what those options are. This knowledge of the different possibilities should be a result of what the interactor has seen during the scene, therefore they are an output of the preceding narrative event. It is, however, possible to offer some hints about what can happen if one option or the other is taken, or about the feelings and thoughts of the avatar character. Hotspots, therefore, may contain a bit of text that explains the option; can trigger off the interactor's wayfinding sense if they must choose which way to go; can be explained verbally by the characters, or they can simply activate objects and characters from the storyworld.

Locating the Hotspots

The narrative design together with the interactive screenplay indicates how the narrative units are connected between them: what type of hotspot will be used, if it is diegetic or extradiegetic, if it is visual or auditory. Thus, at this part of the interactive montage, the hotspots as a visual or audio file will be added within each NU at the decision-making moment, locating it within the scene/space and setting its behaviour. Below I propose some suggestions for interactive editing, arising from my experience creating ZENA.

Location in Space. I recommend setting the hotspots at this time of assembly, and not on the assembly of the cVR, so that the visual target is not a flat object of the equirectangular video, but an object with a body inside the VR environment. Interactive montage software allows to give depth and body to the placement of objects in 360º space.

Type of Interaction. This setting establishes how the hotspot is activated and what type of behavior it has, if it is an internal link that displays extra multimedia material, or if it is an external link that changes to the next NU. This setting is related to the type of HCI through which interactors activate the hotspot if it is a joystick, a vocal command, or the head movement.

Once the task of connecting all the NUs is completed, the interactive narrative structure will be complete and the debugging phase will start, to verify that all the hotspots work and that the decision-making moments are narratively effective in terms of timing, sound, and graphic design.

5.3.3 *Subtitles*

The dialogues of ZENA were written and recorded in Italian, hence, when the project was chosen to participate in the Art Exhibition ICIDS (International Conference on Interactive Digital Storytelling) in 2017, English subtitles in ZENA were added for an international audience. Until that moment I had never seen a subtitled cVR project, and even today there are very few projects of this kind with subtitles. Although, this aspect of production was not included for the UX evaluation, more than 50 non-Italian speakers have been able to enjoy ZENA from start to finish, without problems to follow the course of the events. A sign that the subtitles worked correctly.

Subtitles are a useful tool to reach a wider audience, not only for translations but also for people with hearing problems. In this section, I will share some lessons that were learnt from subtitling ZENA.

The issue to tackle when subtitling in VR is 'How to insert the captions in a spherical space while interactors are looking in different directions and can easily miss the subtitles?' To accomplish this mission, once again I relied fully on the interactor's interest in the narrative events. My intuition was that the interactor would have closely followed the movements and actions of the characters in space. This kind of faith in the interactor is fundamental in VR and cVR in general, as we are using this specific medium to give visual freedom.

The subtitling work is recommended to be done during the interactive montage, and not during the editing of each linear NU. If the caption is treated as a separate asset from the 360º video file, it can be overlaid upon the video and set with characteristics such as location in space, depth, and volume, so that it can be read with a better clarity. What made ZENA's subtitles clear and efficient, regardless of the movements of the actors in the space were three key aspects: simple text, speech balloons and timing.

Simple text. A good subtitle is, above all, a good translation, and second, a good translation that fits into the screen. In immersive environments it is important that the caption does not occupy too much space with too many words to read. We must remember that interactors are constantly exploring space and we do not want to spend a lot of time reading a text.

Speech balloons. The most natural thing for me to do, was to write the subtitles in speech balloons that can be located near to the character that is speaking, just as comics do. By doing this, each single speech balloon will always follow the position of the character within the space, and therefore is always related to the character that is speaking. The styling of the speech balloons can differ to identify different speakers or sound sources.

Timing. Unlike the cinema technique where the new caption replaces the other, in VR we can give each speech balloon a longer time. This extra time allows the interactors to catch up if they were looking somewhere else.

6.
EVALUATION

6.1. *Is IFcVR an Entertainment Artefact?*

Contemporary debates on cyberculture and the impacts of technology on society have shifted from the 90's widespread scepticism about scientific and technological development (Schroeder, 1994), to a more open and aware mindset that recognizes how a certain technology can appear and alter our lifestyle in the blink of an eye. But even with this new worldview, VR still encounters great difficulties in being understood and adopted, as evidenced by Gartner's *Hype Cycle of Emerging Technologies of 2018*[1] report (Panetta, 2018). Taking a step back, we are still wondering who the VR audience(s) are and how the concept of spectatorship is being addressed by the companies that produce VR hardware and content. Until now, the strategy that companies such as Facebook Oculus and Google Daydream have taken, to mention the most famous ones, can be compared to the strategies that movie makers and movie merchants of the Nickelodeon era used, as Burst writes in *The Imagined Audience in the Nickelodeon Era*:

> "What was important to shaping the decisions of moviemakers, in the short run, as they shaped the movies, was not who the audiences were and what they wanted, but instead how the makers imagined their audience and its desires [...] In the immediate process of moviemaking, it was most likely the short-run speculation that directly shaped any given film and its style." (Burst, 2011)

---

[1] https://www.gartner.com/smarterwithgartner/5-trends-emerge-in-gartner-hype-cycle-for-emerging-technologies-2018/

This short-run speculation can also be perceived by VR independent creators that are producing experiences without knowing precisely how and by whom their products will be experienced. VR as a medium will be able to define its audiences to create for them, as well as it will understand its utilities for society itself and its place in the world market. Take the feature film for example, it took several years before it became the main product of the film industry, and when that happened it started to be promoted as narrative art. This legitimization, as Burst notices, had, therefore, a profound impact on its diffusions, "ending its definition as lower-class amusement, and establishing its legitimacy among middle and upper classes" (Burst, 2011). Along this line, we wonder who the audience of VR is. Is it the working class? the tired businessman? the *Matinee Ladies*?

Since the genesis of this research work, I focused on the study of a mediatic and narrative hybrid, especially from the creator's point of view; therefore, I approached the IFcVR purely as an entertainment product, which can also be a media for narrative learning (Dettori, 2016) or for promotional, touristic, or informative purposes, but with the main goal of offering a pleasant and entertaining experience. Research on entertainment psychology has shown how effective is entertainment to encode and store media messages as it is, in the first place, an intrinsic human activity (Bryant & Vorderer, 2013). Thanks to the developments on the psychology of entertainment, we know that "entertainment can provide individuals with both pleasure and meaning" (Oliver et al., 2014); that entertainment is not just a purely joyful and fun activity, but as Mary Beth Oliver writes "an entertainment that is poignant, meaningful, or even tragic may be gratifying for some people [...] because it allows individuals the opportunity to contemplate and experience questions such as purpose-in-life or the human condition or to fulfil higher order needs such as the need for relatedness" (Oliver et al., 2014). In the same way, we now acknowledge that meaningful entertainment experiences "can remind viewers of elements of shared humanity.

I am highlighting the importance of entertainment in this chapter because a relevant, and not yet answered, question I have often asked myself, and people have asked me during this study, is *why would someone want to have an IFcVR experience*? Referring specifi-cally to IFcVR and the possible elements that can motivate an indi-vidual to consume this kind of content, I find that the convergence of perceptive immersion, narrative, and interactivity results in a powerful mix to generate emotions in the audience, and emotions as said by Bartsch (2012) are at the heart of entertainment media. Game studies have shown that, beyond mere interaction, video-games with a compelling and engaging story "may be particularly able to be meaningful", while "autonomy and competence are as-sociated with enjoyment, and feelings of relatedness and particu-larly insight are strongly associated with appreciation" (Oliver et al, 2016).

My approach to undertake the study of the user experience (UX) of IFcVR is very much in line with the thought of Zillmann and Bryant (2013) presented in their book *Selective Exposure to Com-munication*. They claim that mass media research has mostly fo-cused on the societal impact of the media, in how media influence people and affect their behaviour, documenting broadly undesir-able effects. In contrast, only a few desirable effects have received similar attention. Although Zillmann and Bryant understand mass media as entertainment media, such a conception allows us to create a bridge toward the study of new media audiences. The study of the VR impact on society is crucial as we are dealing with a technology that has emerged from deep human desires to fulfil (Schroeder, 1994). Nonetheless, at this moment of its history, it may be advantageous to pay attention to "questions such as why people enjoy whatever they elect to watch or hear, and why they elect to watch or hear, in the first place, whatever it is that they elect to watch or hear" (Zillmann & Bryant, 2011).

Audience research has shifted from the idea of an uncritical and submissive mass, to fully recognizing the active role of the audi-ences and the role of their contexts and backgrounds when using a certain media or interpreting a certain text. This acknowledg-ment of audience (as both a group and individuals) translates into several fields of media and cultural studies, including audience studies within their scope, as well as research on media or text production incorporating an audience study (Livingstone, 1998). It is worthwhile to question how to use the term "audience(s)", es-pecially within the VR studies, as VR has the capability to be a *one-*

to-one, one-to-many, and *many-to-many* medium. Even less is our knowledge about IDN's audiences, as well as their uses and gratifications, which have failed to address the production of content towards their needs and purposes. Since the bases for the formation of a new discipline for the study of interactive digital narratives are now being set (Koenitz, 2018), legacy media audiences' historiography can be edifying for the field.

For the scope of this study, independently of the potential applications or developments of VR and IFcVR, I am handling the IFcVR text in the same way as a novel or a film can be treated, with that intimate one-to-one relationship that arises between creator and interactor. After having presented the theoretical bases to approach the IFcVR hybrid, and then having detailed the production of an IFcVR prototype, it was important for the completion of this work to understand if IFcVR could be, in the first instance, an entertaining experience. With this goal in mind, entertainment is understood as a twofold element: the enjoyment provided by the interactor's agency, together with narrative and perceptive immersion.

6.2. *Protocol Proposal for IFcVR UX Evaluation*

The current scarcity of IFcVR experiences has a direct consequence on the lack of research on the production workflow (from development to post-production), potential applications, and assessment tools for measuring user experience (UX) in terms of enjoyment and engagement. This lack of user feedback hinders the creation of a medium-conscious narratology (Wolf, 2011) for IFcVR as a hybrid genre, as well as the detection of IFcVR audience. The study of the UX is the basis of the design and improvement of successful systems and interfaces, as UX measures user's satisfaction, from a pragmatic and hedonic point of view (Bevan, 2008). Human-Computer Interfaces (HCI) evaluation standards, protocols and techniques (Bevan, 2016; Issa & Isaias, 2015) can partially help to evaluate the usability aspects (effectiveness, efficiency, satisfaction, learnability, accessibility and safety) (Bevan, 2008) of the IFcVR system, but they leave out aspects related to the degree of entertainment of a given IFcVR experience, as they do not take into consideration narrative aspects that are peculiar to cVR and IDN. The protocol proposal presented in this chapter aims to contribute to fill this gap.

An evaluation protocol for IFcVR needs to tackle aspects related to the VR system by including its usability, the sense of presence and the degree of sickness that certain cVR experiences may cause, as well as to evaluate aspects related to the IDN, the degree of user agency, the narrative immersion as the perceptive immersion, and the degree of enjoyment, affect, transformation and continuation desire (Schoenau-Fog, 2014). To achieve such a comprehensive view, the protocol needs to gather both qualitative and quantitative data, so as to analyse non-filtered and spontaneous data as well as structured and cognitively processed information about the UX. To this end, the proposed evaluation protocol joins three *ad hoc* instruments: an observation grid, a questionnaire, and a semi-structured interview.

The protocol will be illustrated through a pilot application on the IFcVR fully functional prototype ZENA.

6.2.1. *IFcVR Analysis Toolbox*

The IDN User Experience Dimensions toolbox proposed by Cristian Roth and Hartmut Koenitz (Roth & Koenitz, 2016) offers an interdisciplinary approach that can be applied to the evaluation of a wide range of technologies and narratives. This is a flexible analytical framework that "connects research in psychology, based on Entertainment Theory, with a humanities-based perspective" and allows us to get an overview of what should be evaluated in an IDN. However, for the purposes of this study, I needed some other categories to focus on very specific technical aspects related to the possibilities offered by IFcVR, and in some cases these categories did not belong directly to the micro categories presented in the initial framework. Table 1 presents a breakdown of the categories proposed by Roth and Koenitz with the adaptation and the addition of some specific categories[2] related to both IF and cVR.

---

2   The categories added are marked with an asterisk, while the adapted categories are listed in the right column.

Agency	System's Usability	
	Autonomy	Intuitive use of HCI to Activate the Hotspots
		Use of Text as a Guide for the Decision-making
		Length of the Decision-making moments
		Type of Hotspot if Visual or Auditory
		Use of Diegetic and Extradiegetic Hotspots
	Effectance	
Perceptual Immersion	Realism of the cVE*	
	Presence	
	Flow (Audiovisual and Interactive)	Awareness of the Camera Position
		Awareness of Editing Cuts between shots and NUs
		Use of Interaction Feedback
	Use of Spatial Audio	
Narrative Immersion	Cinematic Continuity*	
	Understanding and remembering the story*	
	Believability	
	Role Identification	
	Curiosity	
	Visual exploration of the Space Vs Interest on the Scene Events*	
	Diegetic and Extradiegetic Sound	Use of the Voice Over
		Use of Music
Transformation	Sense of "Living" the Film Vs Video Game Feeling*	
	Aesthetic Pleasantness / Eudaimonic Appreciation	
	Positive or Negative Affect able	
	Continuation Desire*	
	Enjoyment	

Table 1. IFcVR User Experience Measurement Categories of Analysis.
*: *Specific IFcVR categories*

Even though linear cVR is considered itself as an IDN, IFcVR adds an upper level of interactive creation and reception. While the first level refers to what happens inside each immersive narrative unit, the second level is related to the navigation path that the user creates through the whole experience. These levels will determine the methods to be used to measure the enjoyment of the experience. Following the definition of *local and global affectance* proposed by Roth and Koenitz (2017), I identified the levels of IFcVR as follows:

1.   Local - cVR assessment: aspects related to what happens inside each NU.

2.   Global - IDN assessment: aspects related to how users navigate between nodes that lead to the final IDN outcome.

Local Assessment - Aspects related to Cinematic Virtual Reality. As a place-based experience, the effects on emotion, enjoyment and narrative flow regarding IFcVR rely on what happens within each NU. On a first level, UX is based on what occurs within the *scene-space*; the interaction consists in what the user chooses to see. Data collection instruments such as head tracking (Rothe & Hußmann, 2018; Bala et al., 2016), body movements and biometrics (Bian et al., 2016; Cipresso et al., 2014) software has been used to measure the behaviour and emotional involvement of the user during the immersive experience in correlation to what they are seeing-living within the *scene-space*.

Since IFcVR is mostly based on 360° video, aspects related to the level of realism offered by the video, image, and cinematic techniques, such as the position of the camera or the internal and external cuts, the use of the spatial audio (Aspöck et al, 2018) and the diegetic or extradiegetic sound (voice over, music, effects) can be used to evaluate the quality of the cinematic VR experience and of its audiovisual language.

Global Assessment - Aspects related to Interactive Digital Narrative. In IFcVR, during each *scene-space,* users face decision-making moments that represent the agency level offered by IFcVR. Users make their choices based on the information given by the NU and the level of engagement they are experiencing. Agency in IFcVR, where the VE cannot be modified by the users, can be measured by the intuitive use that the users can make of the proposed HCI to make choices that will change the course of the story, or to activate the hotspots that offer extra-information. Hence, HCI measurements that regard usability parameters (such as time on task, time to learn, number of errors, etc.), help to reflect the level of effectance and autonomy that influence the enjoyment of the overall interactive experience.

6.2.2. *Procedure Design*

The design of the evaluation procedure follows the division between the Local and the Global level. Being that the local enjoyment of the experience happens while each NU is being lived, this aspect needs to be measured during the experience, with specific instruments to analyse what the interactors are seeing in space, what they are thinking or feeling during that narrative unit and how their bodies respond by being present in that scene/space. The global enjoyment of the experience, on the other hand, can be measured once the interactors have travelled all the way to the end, and can retrospectively analyze what decisions they made and what their consequences were. Summarizing, the procedure design was divided into two moments, in each of which different methods and intrusions were used. Table 2 illustrates the procedure design:

	Analysis	Methods
User Characteristics	Participant Tendencies	Consensus Demographic Data Expertise level in Film, Videogames and VR
During the Experience	Local Assessment (cVR): Scene-Space	User's Journey System Recording Observation of Body Movements Think-aloud Protocol
After the Experience	Global Assessment (IDN): Final Journey	Questionnaire Semi-structured Short Interview

Table 2. Procedure Design IFcVR User Evaluation Protocol

During the Experience
The *During-the-Experience* phase corresponds to the local assessment and analyses aspects related to the cVR quality of each NU, and consequently to the *decision-making* moments. This moment of the evaluation is very important because we will be analysing how the interactors relate physically and emotionally with

the IFcVR experience. It is a crucial moment because while they are immersed, we can observe them without any kind of filter. This behavioural evaluation will allow us to know, in real time, to which elements of the scene or space the interactors devote more visual attention, how active they are in the cVE, what are their thoughts or natural reactions during the reception of the story. The aim of this data choice is to correlate body movements, feelings, and thoughts, together with what interactors were observed at a specific time inside the *scene-space* or NU. This correlation allows us to analyse the construction of the scene from the cVR point of view, to analyse how much a user follows a scene or prefers to observe the space, and to understand the mental and emotional process of each interactor when choosing one way or the other.

Lacking technological tools such as motion sensors, biometric sensors, or VR analytics software, for the evaluation of the prototype three types of qualitative data were collected simultaneously and correlated through an Observation Grid Table 3 while the users were experiencing the film: User's Journey System Recording, Observation of Body Movements, and the Think-aloud Protocol (Nielsen et al., 2002). *During-the-Experience,* interactors and the system's mirror view can be recorded in video. This option allows us to review and correlate, in a second moment, aspects of the evaluation.

N.U	Time	System Recording	User Observation	Think-aloud
		Scene Space	Move in place Walk around Touch attempts Head movement Others	Attitude About the Story About the Space About the Movie Discomfort System Usability

Table 3. During-the-Experience Observation Grid

After the Experience

The *After-the-Experience* phase corresponds to the global assessment, evaluating the user's final journey, that is, the output resulting from the instantiation process. This part of the evaluation will allow us to know in depth the reflections of the users on various aspects of the IFcVR experience. Two instruments were proposed for this phase: a questionnaire and a short semi-structured interview. User's characteristics and tendencies questions were included in the initial part of the *After-the-Experience* questionnaire.

The aim of this part of the evaluation is to gather user's retrospective quantitative and qualitative data regarding the overall journey in relation to agency, perceptive and narrative immersion, transformation aspects (enjoyment, aesthetic pleasantness, affect) and the level of physical discomfort. This mixed method allows a better comprehension of UX aspects related to their cognitive remembrance and understanding of the story, their feeling of presence within the cVE, their level of enjoyment, and their feelings in determining if the IFcVR experience was perceived as watching a film or playing a video game.

Questionnaire. The questionnaire considers aspects related to the immersive experience and to the interactive narrative. Table 4 presents the structure of the proposed questionnaire, which is based on the ITC-SOPI questionnaire: Sense of Presence in Cross-media Experiences (Kennedy et al., 1993), using as main structure the toolbox for the evaluation of User Experience of Interactive Digital Narrative (Roth and Koenitz, 2016). Finally, some questions were added from the Simulator Sickness Questionnaire (SSQ) (Lessiter et al., 2001) to spot the physical discomfort caused by the IFcVR artefact.

The final questionnaire contained a set of 73 questions: 6 questions on demographic data, 6 questions on User's knowledge and consumption of films, videogames and VR; 57 questions had a response option on a five-point Likert scale (1 = strongly disagree; 5 = strongly agree), 1 was a multiple choice question with constructed answer and 3 open questions explored users' appreciation of story features (scenes, places and characters); finally, an open comment about the experience was requested.

User Dimensions	Categories	N°Q
User Information	Demographic data	4
	Knowledge (Expertise) and Use of: Films, Videogames and VR	6
	Nausea tendency and use of glasses	2
Agency	System Usability	3
	Autonomy	4
	Effectance	3
Perceptive Immersion	Realism of the cVE	6
	Presence	5
	Flow	2
Narrative Immersion	Curiosity and Suspense	4
	Believability	5
	Role Identification	5
	Sound (Voice Over, Music)	2
	Scene Vs Space	4
Transformation	Enjoyment	4
	Film Vs Video Game Feeling	3
	Affect	4
Physical Discomfort	General Discomfort	2
	Visual Discomfort	2
	Nausea	3

Table 4. Structure of the IFcVR Questionnaire

Semi-structured Short Interview. The interview consisted of a short dialogue in which users were invited to share their thoughts and feelings about the experience in a retrospective way. The questions covered several topics that allowed us to understand the Transformation aspect from different points of view: Understanding of the story and the journey, Enjoyment and Affective aspects of the IFcVR experience.

IQ1, Can you tell us what the story was about?

IQ2, Can you relate your journey? (Remembrance of the navigation path and the choices that lead them to   the specific ending)

IQ3 What aspects of the story caught your attention? (Characters, places, sounds, etc.)

IQ4 How did you feel during the Virtual Experience? (Impressions about the experience)

IQ5, Do you have any suggestions for future improvements or projects?

6.3. *Evaluating ZENA's User Experience*

ZENA was created with the aim of investigating the realisation of an IFcVR artefact, but above all, to test if this hybrid format could be capable of transmitting different types of messages and give rise to entertaining and meaningful experiences. A positive evaluation would stimulate and guide the creation of interesting IFcVR products.

6.3.1. *Participants*

The prototype was tested by a total of 62 participants, within the age range 12 - 64 years (M = 30.46, SD = 15.02), 64.5% female. The test was developed in three different sessions, one user at a time. Each session corresponded to a different group:

G1 = Genoa's middle and high school students (24 participants)

G2 = adults non-residents in Genoa (19 participants)

G3 = videomakers and/or researchers residents in Genoa (19 participants)

Participants were asked if they were residents of Genoa or if they have visited the city in the past to differentiate the sensation of *being* in the city of residents and non-residents. 56% of the participants were residents. 95% of them had been in Genoa at least once. G3 group was differentiated to highlight expert views on cinematic language, VR development and new media applications.

Among the participants, 33.3% were enrolled in high school, 10% in middle school, 6.7% already had a bachelor's degree, 25% had a master's degree and 15% were enrolled or had already finished their PhD program and 10% had a technical diploma. Concerning the physical discomfort of participants, such as nausea or use of glasses, 51.7% of the participants wore glasses while 36.7% often suffered from motion sickness.

Participants were asked about their knowledge, expertise and frequency of use of video games, cinema, and VR. 3.3% play video games every day, 5% play weekly, 36.7% play occasionally and 55% never play. This 55% corresponds to the participants older than 40 years. Regarding film consumption: 51.7% watch more than one film a week, 26.7% at least one film a week, 18.3% a few times a month and only 3.3% a few times a year. Regarding knowledge about film production, 41.7% reported intermediate, 38.3% basic, 11.7% none and 8.3% expert. 63.3% had never used a VR HMD. 43.3% did not have any knowledge about VR production, 46.7% had a basic knowledge, an 8.3% an intermediate knowledge, while 1.7% were VR experts.

Therefore, the test included a group of people who were used to watching films very often but not to playing video games, and neither knowing nor using VR HMDs. Hence, for them the cinematographic language was natural, allowing us to evaluate if the cinematic narrative in the 360° environment was perceived as fluid, despite the multiple possibilities of navigation paths. On the other hand, their little use of video games and VR systems allowed us to have a clearer idea of how intuitive and easy to use the interactive system for the non-expert user was.

In 68.3% of the cases, the experience ran in a fluid way and without technical errors; 25.8% experienced an error due to the expiration of the decision-making time, while 5.9% experienced system errors or freezing that were corrected immediately.

6.3.2. Procedure

The evaluation protocol in total took between 20 and 30 minutes for each participant, depending on the navigation path they took in ZENA. Below I will briefly explain how the protocol was applied.

The first phase of the evaluation process started from the moment in which the opportunity to live the experience was offered to the user. This was the first decision that the user must make, if they accepted or not to be isolated in a neo-reality that will disconnect them, for some minutes, from their own reality. Some instructions were given to the participants before putting the HMD on:

- Participants were not asked to express their thoughts, but only encouraged to talk about their feelings and impressions when they wanted, so as the think-aloud process would not interfere with the enjoyment of the experience.
- Very few explanations about the use of the artefact were given, since at the beginning of ZENA the mechanism of interaction was illustrated. This also provided information on how intuitive the interaction was.
- All the participants were told that the experience could be suspended at any time if they felt discomfort or boredom.

A video recording was carried out with G3 participants: the user's navigation path was recorded by mirroring the HDM vision on a computer, while the user's body movements and think-aloud were recorded with a video camera. The video recording allowed the observation grid to be completed later on.

Once the experience was over, a questionnaire and a short semi-structured interview were submitted to all participants. After allowing a prudent time to rest their eyes and return to reality, the participants were asked to answer a Google Forms questionnaire on a laptop. Once the questionnaire was completed, the short semi-structured interview was carried out.

6.4. *Results*

6.4.1. *During the Experience*

The observation grid provided data to evaluate the overall appreciation of the story in relation with space. In this part of the evaluation, three components were taken into consideration: (1) The system mirroring, (2) Participant's body movements, and (3)

The thinking-aloud. Below I will present the insights gained from this data that can be useful for the creators when designing their IFcVR experiences is presented.

The System Mirroring: First the Story, then the Space.

Mirroring the system allowed us to see what the participants were looking at on the HMD. By combining the system mirroring with users' body movements, I could notice some behaviours related with their way to approach the immersive storytelling. In the first place, most of the participants looked for the protagonist every time they found themselves in a new space, and only after this character was spotted, they felt free to visually explore the space and the elements around. It was noticed in all the participant's body movements that they followed the movements and actions of the characters in the scene, especially in those scenes that were designed to make them turn around while following the characters, or to look for the hotspots. This corresponds to a high level of narrative immersion, to role identification, curiosity and suspense. Interactors wanted to know what was going to happen to the characters, how the story was going to unfold; based on this insight, I strongly believe that creators need to rely on their story and adequate the space around it, instead of adapting the story to the space, forcing the eye and the attention of the interactor.

Body Movements: Interactors Are Present.

Observing how people move in physical space while their minds are in a different, virtual space gives us precious information about their level of immersion. They disconnect their cognition from the real space and the more time they spend in the cVE, the more comfortable they feel exploring that other space. Unlike a computer-generated VE, a quality of cVE is that it looks like reality, even though we easily realise that we cannot interact with the environment as we do in real life. We recognize CGVE as unreal, and this unreality reaffirms its truth.

From the participant's body movements, it was noticed their wish of interacting with the cVE. Some participants moved around in the room, others simulated walking during moving-camera scenes (avoiding nausea), while others tried to touch characters and objects during the experience, still others tried to go closer to objects that they wanted to see better. Participants who tried to touch the VE or changed position in space felt a higher level of VE realism, some even reported feeling the smell of the sea or of the streets, and those that they felt were real were their favourite locations. All these body movements were attempts to interact with the cVE, and at the same time they indicated the level of presence and realism that they felt in the cVE. This active body attitude mostly characterised people without previous experience with VR, which was more than half of the partcicpants.

With the type of interaction that was used in ZENA, the physical attitude of the participants was very relevant when it comes to the *decision-making* moments. Participants that were bodily passive mostly focused on the narrative events rather than exploring the spaces; they also delayed in making decisions at branching points while those who were physically active were able to spot the hotspots and make their decisions in a shorter time.

When designing VR experiences in general, we must remember that interactors are aware of entering a different reality. During the user evaluation of ZENA, two participants took off the HMD, one of them was afraid and refused to continue the experience, while the other one needed some time to accept the isolation with the HMD and then he restarted the experience. As creators, we need to be sensitive and respectful of the presence of the interactor, but, on the other hand, also ingenious, and playful to coordinate interactor's body movements with what is happening within the immersive interactive film.

Thinking-aloud: Living the Film.
To take a record of the thoughts that the participants expressed out loud provided some insights about their narrative immersion. Most of the participants, when they needed to express some feeling or thought about the experience, used the verb *To Be* in the present tense to indicate where they were, who they were with or to refer their choices (e.g. "I am at the tower", "I am Lorenzo!", "I am going this way"), in the same way, they always used the first person to describe situations (e.g. "I don't trust the master"). However, each group had different thoughts when talking during the experience, and those thoughts were in line with their ages and expertise with videogames, VR, or films.

Participants from G1, middle and high school students, expressed feelings regarding the story. They talked to characters to give them instructions, or they spoke to themselves about the choices to make. G2 participants, being non-resident adults, shared comments about the novelty of the VR experience and the places that they remembered. They were trying to recognize the streets and squares of the city. G3, formed by video makers and researchers, shared thoughts about the quality of the audiovisual experience (e.g.: "I can feel the different heights of the camera", "the cuts between scenes are practically imperceptible") and about the system usability by asking questions about the technical development of the experience (e.g., "How did you do this?", "This camera position/movement works").

6.4.2. *After the Experience*

Questionnaire. The average outcomes divided into macro categories are presented below. The first macro category is *Agency*. Participants felt that the interactive system was intuitive and easy to use. Regarding effectance, participants felt that their choices were influencing the story, even though they did not feel totally autonomous during the experience.

The second macro category was *Perceptual Immersion*. This category takes into consideration the factors supporting a sense of presence within the cVE. The data shows a similar level of Presence and Realism; the high values obtained for both aspects confirms that cinematic VR can indeed generate a good level of presence. Flow shows a high score, and this is interesting because ZENA involves a large variety of types of camera positions, transitions, points of view, and spaces. The fact that participants felt that the audiovisual content flowed naturally motivates further audiovisual experimentation with 360º video and spatial audio.

Narrative Immersion is the third macro category; it shows data regarding narrative elements and the role they played during the experience. The lower level was Story Participation, which concerns how much the participants felt they were participating in the story. I consider that the low score obtained does not represent a negative aspect, because it is consistent with the type of interactivity and medium used. The cVE is not modifiable as a CGVE and, at the same time, interacting only with the head to choose between a range of options does not represent a real participation if it is unfolding in each scene. Curiosity and Role Identification reach a fair score, while items as Voice Over and Music had a determining role in enhancing the narrative immersion; this suggests that VR is an effective medium for visualising oral stories and sound landscapes, and that voice-over and music are powerful instruments for audiovisual storytelling. The highest score was obtained by the Visual Exploration of the Spaces; within this category, it was interesting to know the level of curiosity of the participants in exploring the spaces, if the film allowed them enough time to do so, and if the choice of the locations contributed to the narrative immersion. An interesting result emerges from comparing the answers to the open questions *"What was your favourite scene?"* and *"What was your favourite place and Why?"*; usually the favourite scene matched with the favourite place, and the preferences were due to the level of presence that the users felt in those places, the particularities of the spaces, and to the narrative event that took place in them.

The *Transformation* category contains four micro-categories: Enjoyment and Affect; Continuation Desire; and the Video game vs. Film feeling. Regarding the desire to continue using the film, 58% of the participants wished the experience to continue; this is a high result if we consider that ZENA is very long if compared with usual VR and cVR experiences. 15% of the participants restarted the experience immediately after it was over, to explore other possible narrative paths.

In the *Transformation* category, two questions were included to check if using the artefact raised a feeling like watching a film or playing a video game. The results show a very close balance between both feelings: 54% for film, while the feeling of being playing a video game resulted in 46%. This information contributes to address a relevant question often debated among the IDN community if an interactive experience should be considered a movie or a videogame. The data collected suggest that this IFcVR was perceived as neither a video game nor a film; it represents a new kind of experience of its own. The filmic feeling, however, slightly prevails upon the videogame, as IFcVR is a video-based narrative.

The last part of the questionnaire, dedicated to Physical *Discomfort*, reported rather low scores; Visual Discomfort resulted in the most problematic aspect with $M = 2.65$. These results are likely influenced by the fact that several scenes contain camera movements which can cause discomfort to people who suffer from motion-sickness. Another possible cause is the use of cellphone VR headsets whose visual quality is usually not excellent.

Even though the data provided by the questionnaire presented low scores related to Narrative Immersion, the open questions complemented the information related to the narrative immersion showing very positive results that also allowed interesting correlations. For example: the favourite place also corresponds to the favourite scene; during the scenes shot in the labyrinth of narrow streets of the historical centre, participants felt high levels of suspense and curiosity, and some of them felt them so real to remember the characteristic smells of the historical centre. Among the eight characters, the favourite one was Lorenzo, protagonist, and avatar-character, with a 35% of the appreciation.

Semi-Structured Short Interview.
The short interview, 5 minutes average, contributed to evaluating the level of understanding of the story and how participants remembered it.

IQ1, Can you tell us what the story was about?

IQ2, Can you relate your journey? (Remembrance of the navigation path and the choices lead them to the specific ending)

IQ3 What aspects of the story caught your attention? (Characters, places, sounds, etc.)

IQ4 How did you feel during the Virtual Experience? (Impressions about the experience)

IQ5, Do you have any suggestions for future improvements or projects?

All participants could elaborate a recap of the main plot of the story (IQ1), and relate the decisions they made during the experience, clearly reconstructing their navigation path (IQ2). Some of the participants reported their feelings when choosing a path:

"I started again after completing the route. I wanted to continue, as if it was not enough. Probably in large part I was guided by my intuition. I had little way of "consciously choosing". I felt guided, rather than capable of deciding my destiny".

"I felt that the final goal was not very clear, I asked myself "what should I look for physically?", So I made my choices based on my knowledge and my relationship in the city (example: I went to the sea because I like the sea more than the mountain and not because I understood that my goal was to look for a certain thing that was more likely to be on the sea than towards the mountain). However, it was very enjoyable and there is a lot of potential in this field.":

"The story is fun for different reasons. 1) The possibility of deciding the course of events kept me focused. 2) The plot is compelling. 3) The possibility to explore the spaces of all the scenes generates a lot of fun in the "spectator". 4) The "redefinition" of the places that I explored also in reality impressed me a lot!"

They could also elaborate on the aspects that caught their attention (IQ3). Some frequent comments were about the ability to see the city:

"I think I saw more of the city in this experience than in my 15 years of life".

"The places that I liked the most were the alleys. I frequent them often and had the impression to really find myself there.".

"The Ancient Port of Genoa because I was in my city virtually".

The story and the characters were considered interesting, with comments on the personality of the characters, the acting quality, and how the turn of events surprised them. Another aspect highlighted was the soundtrack:

"I liked the sound effects (the ambient; the sea; when I went back to the past the music was from the Middle Ages; the sound of people talking)."

"The joint death of Sercan and the Master. Very well structured, but above all interesting from the point of view of the turns of the story."

A representative comment regards the coherence of the story:
"Being able to choose the paths of the character is fun as it has a logical consequence. (e.g.: the choice I'm lost leads Lorenzo to the church which in my eyes makes a lot of sense)".

"My favourite scene was the one in which Lorenzo had to choose whether to give the hourglass or not to the Master. Because it was the only time I chose based on the scene (the tone of voice with which the Master spoke) and not based on my emotions towards the city."

The impressions of experiencing a virtual experience in general (IQ4) were quite positive, especially if we consider that 63.3% of the participants had never worn an HMD before. Some of the participants commented:
"Good experience to escape from the stress of daily life."
"Nice but tiring"
"At first I was a bit fearful, then I had fun".

Some comments concerned technical aspects of the cVR experience:
"It is very strange not to see my own body."
"The graphic quality is still low and can be improved."
"It is possible to optimise the times in which we have to make choices".

Finally, their suggestions for future improvements or projects (IQ5) highlighted the value of the experience regardless of the genre of film they experienced and imagined applications for tourism or education.

6.4.3. *Overall conclusions on ZENA*

One of the answers to the question: *What was your favourite scene?* was "when Sercan pointed the knife at me in the alleys of Genoa[3]" while another answer was "When I had to decide whether to trust the Master or not[4]". These two answers suggest a discreet

---

3   "Quando Sercan mi ha puntato il coltello addosso nei vicoli di Genova".
4   "Quando ho dovuto decidere se fidarmi del maestro oppure no".

success of ZENA, but also highlight the potential of IFcVR. The first one shows the level of immersion, perceptive and narrative, of cinematic VR: the participant uses the pronoun *me* to describe the situation, although the one who is threatened with a knife is Lorenzo. It also refers to a scene of suspense, where there are movements of the camera requiring the interactor to have an active physical state. Next, the participant names the location in which the scene takes place, Genoa's old alleys, demonstrating interest both in the narrative event and in the place where it took place. The second claim shows an interactor who enjoyed having decision-making power over the development of events, they are also spotting the ordeal scene or the maxi-climax of ZENA. In this scene, the decision of the interactor is crucial for the positive or negative end of the experience, therefore it carries with it an important dramatic load that generates suspense and emotion in the interactor. This scene appears after three quarters of the total duration of the experience, and after that the interactor must make several decisions. What makes this scene special is precisely the narrative path that leads to that decision. It confirms not only a solid narrative design of the interactive story, but also a conception of *climax* that can be useful and perhaps necessary for all interactive narratives: a narrative moment that leads to *that* important decision.

The Interactive Fiction (IF) aspect was pretty much appreciated. The interface showed to be intuitive and easy to use at the decision-making moments, however a serious flaw was faced by a quarter of the experimenters involved. The flaw is related to the time allowed for decision making. While interactors were deciding, the video continued to play until its duration allowed it. Once the video was finished, interactors found themself in a black space. This is a subject that must be considered during preproduction and postproduction, because if the decision-making must be made in the current video, enough time must be granted to allow the user to interact. Otherwise, a mechanism must be generated (e.g., loop of video) to give the user a prudent time to choose. In ZENA many decisions were of rapid action and were based on spatial decisions: which street to take, or to go to the sea or to the mountain. Others were more intuitive, in which the interactors had to trust one or another of the characters. Therefore, not all decisions were based entirely on events, some of them were random decisions (one street or the other). When I asked the participants what their favourite scene was, many answered the scene in which they had to decide whether to trust the Master or not, and the justification was precisely that in this scene they should choose based on the events. Therefore, another important output of this evaluation is that, in ZENA's case, interactors preferred decisions based on narrative events, in opposition to some decisions that did not have a direct relationship to the narrative (i.e., selecting one street or another).

6.5. *Final Remarks on the IFcVR Evaluation*

As a narrative hybrid, it was necessary to evaluate the main components of the artefact as well as the whole. This led to a complex protocol that included different types of information, as well as a long questionnaire that should be validated as a consistent evaluation tool. Likewise, the dataset obtained from this protocol can be interpreted in very different ways as it gives very specific information about ZENA, which can be helpful for future improvements of ZENA itself. Nonetheless, evaluating ZENA only as an IFcVR product, and understanding from this example whether this hybrid genre can be successful or not, is double-edged. On the one hand, if an artefact such as ZENA, with a simple story and limited means of production, can result in an entertaining experience, it surely opens up a promising path for future IFcVR experiences. On the other hand, the proposed protocol might focus too much on ZENA's features, missing to achieve a wide-angle look on IFcVR.

Regarding the cinematic VR aspect, the results confirm that a VE created through 360º video can convey a fully immersive experience that is perceived as real and generates high levels of presence in the interactor. Interactors also reacted very well with several audiovisual experiments, such as changes of camera position, colour changes, cuts, and transitions, showing that 360º video can deliver an audiovisual experience in a fluid way, and it does not necessarily need to be a static experience. Nonetheless, the most important aspect regarding the cVR component is a solid contribution to address the dilemma "how do I make interactors look where I want them to look?". This is an issue I have been addressing throughout this work, and one of the main contributions of this experience is the fact that users first get in touch with the narrative and afterwards they feel free to explore and identify the space. When they are already following the discourse, they are constantly putting the story bits together. Therefore, one of the main lessons for the creators that this study has achieved can be summarised in "Trust your story and trust the interactor".

Regarding the whole IFcVR, during this first evaluation and during the reproductions of ZENA in other environments outside of the evaluation, interactors movements and expressions during and after the IFcVR experience were positive. They moved, screamed, laughed, and talked. These results confirm that interactors enjoy being able to change the course of the narrative events and that they remember their experience as one who remembers a trip, also remembering their favourite places and people, as well as their decisions. The idea of thinking of the IFcVR as a journey also responds to the mixed sensation of perceiving this experience as an intersection between the videogame and the film. These two components intermingle particularly well in VR. Finally, we can refer to the IFcVR as an entertaining interactive experience. Due to its ability to entertain, the IFcVR can transmit different types of stories and messages, being able to create a meaningful experience for the interactor.

7.
CONCLUSION

A hundred years ago, cinema as a medium arose from a high number of inventions and media forms, some of which subsequently disappeared, but nevertheless contributed to give birth to a new, relevant medium. Cinema, as an industry, has been continuously evolving by proposing new formats, new narratives, and new spaces, until it achieved its place in society. Cinema, as an art form, was designed by experimenting with techniques, stories and *mise-en-scene* from earlier media and could be formally defined through comparative studies with its predecessors. This was carried out not with the intention of readapting old media in a new, emerging medium, but with the legitimate intention to learn from and exploit what had already been written, elaborated, and told in other ways and with other supports. Cinema was also involved in experiments with spherical screens, multiple screens and even with the audience pushing buttons to select the end of the movie.

Today, we can see a similar path in the development of Virtual Reality. But, unlike cinema, VR has a history of encounters and disagreements with the public and is still far from becoming what its pioneers dreamed: a medium able to transmit perceptions of the world, through a post-symbolic communication. Instead, what we have today is an audiovisual medium whose screen frees the image from the frame, but constrains human vision and hearing and, by doing this, it encapsulates human cognition. The VR screen reproduces audiovisual contents that constitute our main interface with a virtual environment (VE). The VE is an *image-event* that looks to create in its users the feeling of presence, realism, and immersion, while several types of human-computer interfaces allow us to explore and interact with the VE in different ways: through vocal, gestural, haptic and biofeedback interfaces, among others. It is not surprising that storytellers, especially from film and video making, are attracted to VR to tell their stories, especially when they have the power to lock the interactor in it.

Capturing reality in 360° is one of the possibilities to create VR narratives. The recording of real scenarios has been directly related to cinematography, under the term Cinematic VR (cVR). cVR has a unique characteristic that differentiates it from cinema and brings it closer to theatre. Interactors are immersed in space, they understand the storyworld as a real space and can see people in real dimensions as if they were in the middle of a theatre stage, surrounded by the actors. But they are not actually there, they are invisible for the actors, so cinema's *spectatorial voyeurism* (that intriguing feeling of being watching someone else's life) is intensified by the feeling of being present. In my opinion, this is the point of strength of cVR fictional narratives. However, the mere fact of being surrounded by a moving image is presented as a somehow cruel confinement, because who is in *there* has no way to interact with the environment, being just able to observe and listen to it. This contrast between the perceptive immersion and the scarce or missing level of agency of the interactor pushed the development of the proposed IFcVR: not only to offer interactors some possibilities of interaction with the VE, but to intensify the immersion - this time leveraging on narrative- by empowering the interactors to influence the narrative development and by giving them the possibility to create their own unique final journey. If interactors can live the *spectatorial voyeurism* and at the same time intervene in what happens to the characters in the storyworld, they (partially) become the directors of those characters' storylines. VR gives interactors a kind of *safe place* from which to control others' lives. This is the core of the IFcVR experience.

This research does not present the IFcVR as an existing product, but investigates the definition of this hybrid as an interactive digital form of narrative, by dissecting and analysing each of its roots. This research, both in theory and practice, was carried out from the point of view of the creators, to give them some conceptual tools and methodologies to create IFcVR products, or similar formats, as *experiences* rather than simply as *artefacts*. From their artistic pole, creators must master the materiality of the medium that will convey their messages. To deeply master the roots of what can be achieved by merging cinematic virtual reality and interactive fiction, I propose an epistemological approach that inter-weaves aesthetics, narratology, and interactivity. Throughout this theoretical path, a brief archaeology of the panoramic vision was made, pointing out how it evolved into VR, a medium that locates the human perception at the centre of the (story)world. This aes-thetic shift invites us to re-think the communicative act and the reception of the VR text, that is experience itself.

As the IFcVR content is transmitted through its cVR compo-nent, from it we can analyse issues regarding the discourse time and story time, as the problem of the point of view in VR, the nar-rative density, and the discourse speed, from narratology and cine-matic point of view, achieving an understanding of the filmic form of the IFcVR. Going up one reading level, the IFcVR text opens a kind of matryoshka-like narrative artefact in which each of its different components has a specific role within the story and in the discourse, its form, substance, expression and manifestation. Being able to separate IFcVR content from its expression, creators can choose through which kinds of human-computer interfaces will deliver and shape the IFcVR discourse. With this theoretical background, the creation labour starts: the development of the interactive digital narrative experience, the production on set or location of the cinematic VR narrative units and the postproduc-tion, that comprises both cVR montage as the interactive mon-tage. The IFcVR creation was put into practice through the reali-sation of ZENA, which was finally submitted to user evaluation. IFcVR assessment constitutes the last part of this research work.

During the development of this study, some issues of the IDN and VR fields were tackled in relation to IFcVR. The most recur-rent issues are (1) the concern of directors to control the attention of the user without the support of the cinematic shot, which im-plies a side issue regarding the disappearance of the director's role, and (2) the use of the so called *dramatic arc* for the narrative de-sign of the interactive experience. The first aspect arises especially from creators that come from a cinematic or video background. For them, not having the framing in shots reduces their power to indi-cate the viewer what they have to see. This is a problem depending on the choice of the medium and therefore on the knowledge we have of it. When a creator chooses VR, as a spatial medium, to tell an audiovisual story, it is because space has a predominant value in experience, it is intrinsically related to the narrative immersion of the interactor. Otherwise, if the intention is to give the interactor audiovisual frames, it may be useful to reconsider the choice of the medium and opt for a framed moving-image. However, it is possible to accentuate objects and characters within the *scene-space*, giving different semantic meanings to the interactor's view. This multiplicity of semantic shots in cVR can be achieved according to: the positioning of the camera in space; the Interactor type; and the height of the camera with respect to the points of interest. It is also possible to play with the movement either of the camera or, even better, of the characters and objects within the *scene-space*. In the same way, spatial audio plays an important role not only for the perceptive immersion, but also as an agent for narrative immersion, as it can guide the interactor in space, as well as stress or relax certain situations. Through these methods, creators are impressing their artistic intentions, without mentioning other types of interfaces different to the audiovisual.

Results from the evaluation of ZENA suggest that interactors are interested in following the story; they look for the characters and, even when they are exploring the space, they are constantly building relationships between the space and the scene. The concerns of video makers can be summarized in: "trust the interactor and trust your story". This takes us to the implicit concern of this issue: what is the role of the director if interactors are free to look at what they want? "Trust your story" does not mean to prepare the space/scene, on the contrary, it means re-inventing the role of the director. In IFcVR, and cVR, directors are *experience directors*, they must manage the stage and the actors as a theater director would, but at the same time they need to locate themselves in the place of the *all-feeling eye*, to transmit the interactors their own perceptions of the world. The potentiality of VR relies on the illusion of being free in another reality. This means having autonomy, agency, and power to act, to be. A controlling attitude over the interactor's experience goes against the essence of VR. As creators our role is to create a rich and wide storyworld, and a solid system, but in the end we must keep in mind that the experience belongs only to the interactor.

The second issue regards the use of a *dramatic arc* or *story arc,* or a known narrative structure such as the Hero's Journey to support the interactive structure. To address this issue, we can take into consideration the distinction between IFcVR content (story) and discourse. The IFcVR content can relate a hero's journey, while the discourse can use a dramatic arc to support the interactive structure. The use of these paradigms or structures is related, on the one hand, to the authors' need of creating identification with the characters through already known archetypes and patterns, and, on the other hand, to assure a constant dramatic progression that is independent of the interactor's decisions. Both needs are subject to the storytelling dynamics of creating tension up to reach a final resolution that satisfies and rewards the receiver. In IFcVR, and in general, in IDN, each story beat or narrative unit is a step of progression. Each of them adds information to the story and pushes the storyline forward. The dramatic arc therefore is not an interactive structure by itself; it can be considered as an imaginary line that must go through each of the possible paths taken by the interactors, so that at one point of their journeys they can reach an epiphany, a climax, or several climaxes (for example, several mini climaxes with one main maxi climax). In other words, a narrative reward to the users for their time and emotional involvement.

In Interactive Fiction, interactivity represents a creative challenge for storytellers. It does not create emergent narratives, but rather performs within a pre-scripted structure. This means that each narrative unit has an independent and irreducible identity, and what interactors do is only to jump between one and the other, making conscious or unconscious decisions. A second level of interactivity regards extra information, perceptive or narrative, that interactors can access or feel. IFcVR's kind of interactivity makes the Fiction (in IF) have a greater weight than interactivity itself, in the whole construction of the experience. The cVR narrative units carry all the narrative weight of the experience, placing the main role of interactivity on the decision-making time. Serious and complex decisions that require introspection and attention, as well as decisions that seem banal but that can change forever the story development. This is the reason why IFcVR is not a videogame. Although the ludic spirit is in its DNA, interactivity does not trigger the narrative, it is the narrative that leads to interactivity. IFcVR is not a film in the traditional sense, either, but its cinematographic soul is undeniable, as reality is *mise-en-scene*, and the scene guides the whole journey. With these premises, we have a greater power, to be present within the film and affect its core.

The development of this study, both in theory and in practice, highlights the potential of the Interactive Fiction in Cinematic Virtual Reality as a narrative artefact. The understanding of the aesthetic, narrative, and interactive notions of a possible genre, has the same importance as the impulse of creating it. The production of ZENA, therefore, remains one of the biggest contributions of this work, as it is the first VR fiction film shot in Genoa, and probably one of the first ones of Italy. Perhaps, in a future historiography of VR films, ZENA will be nominated, and creators may look to the insights learnt from its production process. Virtual reality (VR) is at the forefront of demonstrating its relevance to a broad audience. Amid the pervasive influence of artificial intelligence in our technological landscape, the increasing integration of the Internet of Things into our daily lives, and the expansion of human-computer interfaces into the realm of biological data, the world of immersive and interactive narratives stands before a vast array of possibilities.

Metz previously described cinema as a phenomenological art by nature, but immersive experiences outperform cinema by creating experiences that interactors perceive as real. As we move closer to this horizon and continue to explore the limitless potential of immersive technologies, it is almost inevitable that soon we will access an alternate reality and live it in narrative form. In the verge of a massive consumption of XR devices and experiences, Interactive Fiction in Cinematic Virtual Reality (IFcVR) should be viewed as a flexible framework rather than a fixed artefact or genre. It has the potential to enable the creation of cinematic experiences that blur the distinction between genuine and artificial experiences. The combination of conscious and subconscious decision-making, the structure of interactive fiction, AI's real-time generative capabilities, and the profound power of immersion can result in customized alternate realities, which we can simply refer to as immersive interactive movies.

REFERENCES

5 Lessons Learned While Making Lost. 2017. Oculus.com. https://www.ocu-lus.com/story-studio/blog/5-lessons-learned-while-making-lost/

Aarseth, Espen. (2012). 'A narrative theory of games', *Proceedings of the International Conference on the Foundations of Digital Games, FDG '12:* 109-33. *doi:10.1145/2282338.2282365*

Aarseth, Espen. J. (1997). *Cybertext perspectives on ergodic literature* (Baltimore: Johns Hopkins University Press)

Afra, Kia. 2015."'Vertical Montage" and Synaesthesia', *Music, Sound, and the Moving Image,* 9(1): 33-61. doi:10.3828/msmi.2015.2

Agamben, Giorgio. 2016. *Che cos'è un dispositivo?* (Milan: Nottetempo)

Alexander, F. Matthias. 1974. *Resurrection of the body* (New York: Dell Publishing Co., Inc)

Allen, Richard. 2007. 'Psychoanalytic Film Theory', In *Miller, T. A companion to film theory* (Hoboken: Blackwell) pp. 64 - 83

Amores, J., Benavides, X., & Maes, P. (2016). 'PsychicVR', *Proceedings of the 2016 CHI Conference Extended Abstracts on Human Factors in Computing Systems, CHI EA '16.* doi:10.1145/2851581.2889442

Apple. *Final Cut Pro X: Pan audio.* 2018. Retrieved from https://support.apple.com/kb/PH12578?locale=en_US&viewlocale=en_US

Aranyi, G., Pecune, F., Charles, F., Pelachaud, C., & Cavazza, M. 2016. 'Affective Interaction with a Virtual Character Through an fNIRS Brain-Computer Interface', *Frontiers in Computational Neuroscience,* 10. doi:10.3389/fncom.2016.00070

Aristotle. The Poetics. (n.d.). Retrieved from https://www.gutenberg.org/files/1974/1974-h/1974-h.htm

Arnheim, Rudolf. 1957. *Film as art* (Oakland: University of California Press.

Aspöck, L., Kohnen, M., & Vorlaender, M. 2018. 'Evaluating immersion of spatial audio systems for virtual reality', *The Journal of the Acoustical Society of America,* 143(3): 1829-1829. doi:10.1121/1.5036003

Ayala, A., Martinez, P., Loredo, A., Rosas, R., & Reyes, P. 2018. 'Virtual Reality for Social Phobia Treatment', In S*mart Technology: First International Conference, MTYMEX 2017, Monterrey, Mexico, May 24-26, 2017, Proceedings,* 213: p. 165

Aylett, R., & Louchart, S. 2003. 'Towards a narrative theory of virtual reality', *Virtual Reality, 7*(1): 2-9. doi:10.1007/s10055-003-0114-9

Baker, Geroge. 2006. *Dramatic technique* (Elibron.

Bala, P., Dionisio, M., Nisi, V., & Nunes, N. 2016. 'IVRUX: A Tool for Analyzing Immersive Narratives in Virtual Reality', *Interactive Storytelling Lecture Notes in Computer Science,* 10045: 3-11. doi:10.1007/978-3-319-48279-8_1

Bala, P., Nisi, V., & Nunes, N. 2017. 'Evaluating User Experience in 360º Storytelling Through Analytics', *Interactive Storytelling Lecture Notes in Computer Science,* 10690: 270-273. doi:10.1007/978-3-319-71027-3_23

Barfield, W., & Furness, T. A. 1995. *Virtual environments and advanced interface design* (Oxford: Oxford University Press)

Barthes, R., & Duisit, L. 1975. 'An Introduction to the Structural Analysis of Narrative', *New Literary History, 6*(2): 237. doi:10.2307/468419

Bartsch, Anne. 2012. 'Emotional Gratification in Entertainment Experience. Why Viewers of Movies and Television Series Find it Rewarding to Experience Emotions', *Media Psychology,* 15(3): 267-302. doi:10.1080/1521 3269.2012.693811

Bateman, Chris (ed). 2008. Game writing: Narrative skills for videogames. Course Technology

Baudrillard, J., & Glaser, S. F. 2014. *Simulacra and simulation* (Ann Arbor: The University of Michigan Press)

Bazin, André. 2004. *What Is Cinema? Vol. I.* (Oakland: University of California Press)

Beck, J., & Egger, R. 2017. 'Emotionalise Me: Self-reporting and Arousal Measurements in Virtual Tourism Environments', *Information and Communication Technologies in Tourism 2018,* pp. 3-15. doi:10.1007/978-3-319-72923-7_1

Bell, A. 2010. *The possible worlds of hypertext fiction* (London: Palgrave Macmillan)

Bellassai, J., Gordon, A. S., Roemmele, M., Cychosz, M., Odimegwu, O., & Connolly, O. 2017. 'Unsupervised text classification for natural language interactive narratives', in *Proceedings of the 10th International Workshop on Intelligent Narrative Technologies,* 13: 162-68. Snowbird, Utah, October.

Ben-Shaul, Nitzan. 2008. *Hyper-narrative interactive cinema: Problems and solutions.* (Amsterdam and New York: Rodopi)

Bender, Stuart. 2018. 'Headset attentional synchrony: Tracking the gaze of viewers watching narrative virtual reality', *Media Practice and Education,* 20(3): 1-20. doi:10.1080/25741136.2018.1464743

Bevan, Nigel. 2008. *Classifying and selecting UX and usability measures*

Bevan, N., Carter, J., Earthy, J., Geis, T., & Harker, S. 2016. 'New ISO Standards for Usability, Usability Reports and Usability Measures', *Lecture Notes in Computer Science Human-Computer Interaction. Theory, Design,*

Development and Practice, 9731: 268-78. doi:10.1007/978-3-319-39510-4_25

Bian, Y., Yang, C., Gao, F., Li, H., Zhou, S., Li, H., Meng, X. 2016. 'A framework for physiological indicators of flow in VR games: Construction and preliminary evaluation', *Personal and Ubiquitous Computing*, 20(5): 821-832. doi:10.1007/s00779-016-0953-5

Blades Mark. 1991. 'Wayfinding Theory and Research: The Need for a New Approach'. In: Mark D.M., Frank A.U. (eds) *Cognitive and Linguistic Aspects of Geographic Space. NATO ASI Series (Series D: Behavioural and Social Sciences), vol 63.* Springer, Dordrecht

Blank, M. & Lebling, D. 1980. *Zork I. [Interactive fiction]* (Cambridge, MA: Infocom)

Blankendaal, R. A., & Bosse, T. 2018. 'Using Run-Time Biofeedback During Virtual Agent-Based Aggression De-escalation Training', *Advances in Practical Applications of Agents, Multi-Agent Systems, and Complexity: The PAAMS Collection Lecture Notes in Computer Science*, 10978: 97-109. doi:10.1007/978-3-319-94580-4_8

Blascovich, J., Loomis, J., Beall, A. C., Swinth, K. R., Hoyt, C. L., & Bailenson, J. N. 2002. 'Immersive Virtual Environment Technology as a Methodological Tool for Social Psychology', *Psychological Inquiry, 13*(2): 103-124. doi:10.1207/s15327965pli1302_01

Bødker, Susanne. 2006. 'When second wave HCI meets third wave challenges', *Proceedings of the 4th Nordic Conference on Human-computer Interaction Changing Roles*, NordiCHI '06: 1-8. doi:10.1145/1182475.1182476

Bogart, Anne. 2008. *And then, you act: Making art in an unpredictable world* (London: Routledge)

Bolzoni, Lina. 1984. *Il teatro della memoria: studi su Giulio Camillo* (Liviana)

Borah, Porismita. 2016. 'Media Effects Theory', *The International Encyclopedia of Political Communication*, pp, 1-12. doi:10.1002/9781118541555.wbiepc156

Bordwell, D., & Thompson, K. 2010. *El arte cinematográfico: Una introducción* (Barcelona: Paidós)

Borges, Jorge. 2009. *El Hacedor.* (Madrid: Alianza Editorial)

Bottino, R., Freina, L., & Tavella, M. 2016. 'From e-learning to VR-learning: An example of learning in an immersive virtual world', *Journal of E-Learning and Knowledge Society.* 12: 101-13.

Bowman, D. A., Koller, D., & Hodges, L. F. 1998. 'A methodology for the evaluation of travel techniques for immersive virtual environments', *Virtual reality*, 3(2): 120-31.

Brooks, C. & Warren, R.P. 1943. Focus della Storia, Focus della Narrazione, Distanza. In

Meneghelli, Donata. 1998. *Teorie del punto di vista* (Scandicci: La nuova Italia editrice)

Bruner, Jerome. 2003. Making stories: Law, literature, life. (Cambridge: Harvard University Press)

Bryant, J., & Vorderer, P. (Eds.). 2013. *Psychology of entertainment* (London: Routledge)

Bryant, J., & Miron, D. 2004. 'Theory and research in mass communication', *Journal of Communication, 54*(4): 662–704. https://doi.org/10.1111/j.1460-2466.2004.tb02650.x

Bullinger, A. H., Hemmeter, U. M., Stefani, O., Angehrn, I., Mueller-Spahn, F., Bekiaris, E., ... & Mager, R. 2005. 'Stimulation of cortisol during mental task performance in a provocative virtual environment', *Applied psychophysiology and biofeedback, 30*(3): 205-216.

Butsch, Richard. 1994. 'Bowery B'hoys and Matinee Ladies: The Re-Gendering of Nineteenth-Century American Theater Audiences', *American Quarterly*, 46(3): 374 - 405. https://doi.org/10.2307/2713270

—— 2011. 'The Imagined Audience in the Nickelodeon Era', *The Wiley-Blackwell History of American Film*. doi:10.1002/9780470671153.wbhafoo4

Campbell, Joseph. 2008. *The hero with a thousand faces* (Novato, CA: New World Library)

Carlson, Marvin. 1993. *Places of performance - the semiotics of theatre architecture*. (Ithaca, NY: Cornell University Press)

Carmona, Carlos. 2017. 'The Role and Purpose of Film Narration', *Journal of Science and Technology of the Arts*, 9(2): 7-16.

Carolina Cruz-Neira, Daniel J. Sandin, and Thomas A. DeFanti. 1993. Surround-screen projection-based virtual reality: the design and implementation of the CAVE. *In Proceedings of the 20th annual conference on Computer graphics and interactive techniques*, SIGGRAPH '93: 135-142. DOI: https://doi.org/10.1145/166117.166134 ACM, New York, NY, USA

Caughie, John. 1981. *Theories of authorship: British film institute readers in film studies* (East Sussex: Psychology Press)

Cavazza, M., & Pizzi, D. 2006. 'Narratology for Interactive Storytelling: A Critical Introduction', *Technologies for Interactive Digital Storytelling and Entertainment Lecture Notes in Computer Science*, 4326: 72-83. doi:10.1007/11944577_7

Cipresso, P., Serino, S., Giglioli, I. A., Giuliano, I., Borra, D., Farina, A., & Riva, G. 2014. 'Low-Cost Motion-Tracking for Computational Psychometrics Based on Virtual Reality', *Lecture Notes in Computer Science Augmented and Virtual Reality*, 8853: 137-148. doi:10.1007/978-3-319-13969-2_11

Cowley, S. & Vallée-Tourangeau, F. (Eds). 2013 *Cognition Beyond the Brain.* (London: Springer)

Crary, J., & Acquarelli, L. 2013. *Le tecniche dell'osservatore: Visione e modernità nel XIX secolo* (Torino: Einaudi)

Crawford, Chris. 2005. *Chris Crawford on interactive storytelling* (Berkeley: New Riders Games)

Crifaci, G., Tartarisco, G., Billeci, L., Pioggia, G., & Gaggioli, A. 2012.' Innovative technologies and methodologies based on integration of virtual reality and wearable systems for psychological stress treatment. *International Journal of Psychophysiology'*, 85(3): 402. doi: 10.1016/j.ijpsycho.2012.07.105

Chatman, Seymour., 1978. *Story and discourse: narrative structure in fiction and film.* (Ithaca and London: Cornell University Press.)

—— 1989. *Story and discourse: Narrative structure in fiction and film.* (Ithaca, NY: Cornell University Press)

Chen, H., Dey, A., Billinghurst, M., & Lindeman, R. W. 2017. 'Exploring the design space for multi-sensory heart rate feedback in immersive virtual reality', *Proceedings of the 29th Australian Conference on Computer-Human Interaction, OZCHI '17.* doi:10.1145/3152771.3152783

Chen, K.H. (Ed.) & Morley, D. (Ed.). 1996. *Stuart Hall* (London: Routledge)

Chen, S. Y., Gao, L., Lai, Y. K., Rosin, P. L., & Xia, S. 2018. 'Real-time 3D Face Reconstruction and Gaze Tracking for Virtual Reality', *In 2018 IEEE Conference on Virtual Reality and 3D User Interfaces (VR)*, pp. 525-526. (IEEE)

Chen, Z., Peng, W., Peiris, R., & Minamizawa, K. 2017. 'ThermoReality: thermally enriched head mounted displays for virtual reality', *In ACM SIGGRAPH 2017 Posters* p. 32

Cho, D., Ham, J., Oh, J., Park, J., Kim, S., Lee, N., & Lee, B. 2017. 'Detection of Stress Levels from Biosignals Measured in Virtual Reality Environments Using a Kernel-Based Extreme Learning Machine', *Sensors,* 17(10): 2435. doi:10.3390/s17102435

David, E. J., Gutiérrez, J., Coutrot, A., Silva, M. P., & Callet, P. L. 2018. 'A dataset of head and eye movements for 360° videos', *Proceedings of the 9th ACM Multimedia Systems Conference on, MMSys '18.* doi:10.1145/3204949.3208139

De Kerckhove, Derrick. 2016. *La rete ci renderà stupidi?.* Vol. 4. LIT EDIZIONI (Rome: Castelvecchi)

Dettori, Giuliana. 2016. 'Learning through the design of interactive stories: Exploring the concept of storyworld', *In Proceedings of the 6th International Workshop on Adaptive Learning via Interactive, Collaborative and Emotional approaches (ALICE 2016)*, Ostrava (CZ), 7-9 Sept. 2016, pp. 370-374

Diodato, Roberto. 2005. *Estetica del virtuale.* (Milan: Bruno Mondadori)

—— 2012. *Aesthetics of the Virtual*, SUNY Series in Contemporary Italian Philosophy (Albany: State University of New York Press)

Dooley, Kath. 2017. 'Storytelling with virtual reality in 360-degrees: A new screen grammar', *Studies in Australasian Cinema,* 11(3): 161-171. doi:10.1080/17503175.2017.1387357

Dorozhkin, D. V., & Vance, J. M. 2002. 'Implementing Speech Recognition in Virtual Reality', *Volume 1: 22nd Computers and Information in Engineering Conference.* pp. 61-5. *doi.org/10.1115/DETC2002/CIE-34390*

Douglas, J. Yellowlees. 2003. *The end of books-or books without end? Reading interactive narratives.* (Ann Arbor: The Univ. of Michigan Press)

eevo Features (2018). Retrieved from https://eevo.com/features

Eisenstein, S., & Leyda, J. 1949. *Film form; essays in film theory.* edited and translated by *Jay Leyda* (New York: Harcourt, Brace & World)

Ellenshaw, H., Kushner, D., Miller, R. (producers) and Steven Lisberger (director). 1982. TRON [Motion Picture] (EU.: Disney)

Fearghail, C. O., Ozcinar, C., Knorr, S., & Smolic, A. 2018. 'Director's Cut - Analysis of Aspects of Interactive Storytelling for VR Films', *Interactive Storytelling Lecture Notes in Computer Science*, pp. 308-322. doi:10.1007/978-3-030-04028-4_34

Feliciati, Pierluigi. 2010. Il nuovo teatro della memoria. Informatica e beni culturali in Italia, tra strumentalità e sinergie. Retrieved from https://www.academia.edu/771134/Il_nuovo_teatro_della_memoria._Informatica_e_beni_culturali_in_Italia_tra_strumentalit%C3%A0o_e_sinergie

Field, Syd. 2005. *Screenplay the foundations of screenwriting.* (New York: Delta Trade Paperbacks)

Fischer, Lucy. 2007. 'Film Editing', in *Miller, T. A companion to film theory* (Oxford: Blackwell), p. 64 - 83

Fludernik, Monika. 1996. *Natural Narratology* (London: Routreledge)

Frasca, Gonzalo. 1999. 'Ludologia kohtaa narratologian', *Parnasso, 3.* English translation Ludology meets narratology: Similitudes and differences between (video) games and narrative. Available at: http://www.ludology.org

Freytag, Gustav. 1895. *Technique of the drama: an exposition of dramatic composition and art.* S. Griggs.

Fusi, G. 2017. *Video interattivi: studio di un caso con video a 360°* (Unpublished bachelor dissertation). (Genoa: Università degli Studi di Genova)

Gaudreault, A. & Jost, F. 2007. 'Enunciation and Narration', In Miller, T. *A companion to film theory* (Oxford: Blackwell) p. 45 - 63

Geiselhart, F., Rietzler, M., & Rukzio, E. 2016. 'EyeVR', *Proceedings of the 2016 ACM International Joint Conference on Pervasive and Ubiquitous Computing Adjunct, UbiComp '16.* doi:10.1145/2968219.2971384

Genette, Gérard. 1972. *Figures III* (Paris: Seuil)

——— 1976. 'Focalizzazioni', in *Meneghelli, D., Teorie del punto di vista* (Scandicci: La nuova Italia editrice)

——— 1980. *Narrative discourse: An Essay in Method* (Ithaca, N.Y.: Cornell University Press)

——— 2001. *Paratexts: Thresholds of interpretation.* (Cambridge: Cambridge University Press.)

Gibson, William. 1986. *Neuromancer* (New York: Ace Books)

Gödde, M., Gabler, F., Siegmund, D., & Braun, A. 2018. 'Cinematic Narration in VR – Rethinking Film Conventions for 360 Degrees' *Virtual, Augmented and Mixed Reality: Applications in Health, Cultural Heritage, and Industry Lecture Notes in Computer Science*, pp. 184-201. doi:10.1007/978-3-319-91584-5_15

Google Spotlight Stories. 2017. Atap.google.com. https://atap.google.com/spotlight-stories/

Gorini, A., Pallavicini, F., Algeri, D., Repetto, C., Gaggioli, A., & Riva, G. 2010. 'Virtual reality in the treatment of generalized anxiety disorders', *Stud Health Technol Inform*, 154: 39-43

Gradl, S., Wirth, M., Zillig, T., & Eskofier, B. M. 2018. 'Visualization of heart activity in virtual reality: A biofeedback application using wearable sensors', *2018 IEEE 15th International Conference on Wearable and Implantable Body Sensor Networks (BSN)*. doi:10.1109/bsn.2018.8329681

Grau, Oliver. 2003. *Virtual Art: From Illusion to Immersion* (Cambridge: MIT Press)

Green, Max. 2016. *How the Brain Reacts to Scrambled Stories*. The Atlantic. Retrieved from https://www.theatlantic.com/health/archive/2016/01/linear-storytelling-psychology/431529/

Gruenefeld, U., Löcken, A., Brueck, Y., Boll, S., & Heuten, W. 2018. 'Where to Look', *Proceedings of the 10th International Conference on Automotive User Interfaces and Interactive Vehicular Applications, AutomotiveUI '18*. doi:10.1145/3239060.3239080

Guger, C., Groenegress, C., Holzner, C., Edlinger, G., Slater, M., & Sánchez-Vives, M. V. 2009. 'Brain computer interface for virtual reality control', *Cyberpsychology & Behavior,* 12(1): 84-84.

Hales, Chris (ed). 2014. *Expanding practices in audiovisual narrative* (Newcastle upon Tyne: Cambridge Scholars Publishing)

Hall, Stuart. 2006. *The meaning of new times* (London: Routledge), pp. 233-247

—— 1986. 'On Postmodernism and Articulation. An Interview with Stuart Hall. Edited by Lawrence Grossberg', *Journal of Communication Inquiry,* 10: 45 - 60

—— 1980. 'Codificar y Decodificar', In *Culture, Media & Lenguaje* (London: Hutchinson), pp. 129-139

—— (Ed.). 1997. *Representation: Cultural representations and signifying practices Vol. 2*. (Thousand: Sage)

Halligan, Fionnuala. 2015. *The art of movie storyboards: Visualising the action of the world's greatest films* (London: Ilex)

Ham, J., Cho, D., Oh, J., & Lee, B. 2017. 'Discrimination of multiple stress levels in virtual reality environments using heart rate variability? *2017 39th Annual International Conference of the IEEE Engineering in Medicine and Biology Society (EMBC)*. doi:10.1109/embc.2017.8037730

Hammoud, Riad. 2006. *Interactive Video* (New York: Springer-Verlag Berlin Heidelberg)

Hatavara, M., Hyvärinen, M., Mäkelä, M., & Mäyrä, F. (Eds.). 2015. *Narrative theory, literature, and New media: narrative minds and virtual worlds.* (London: Routledge)

Hayles, N. Katherin. 2012. *How we think: Digital media and contemporary technogenesis. Ill.* (Chicago: The University of Chicago Press)

Heim, Michael. 1990. Heidegger and Computers. Retrieved 29 June 2018, from http://www.mheim.com/wp-content/uploads/2014/05/Heidegger-and-Computers-1990.txt

—— 1993. The metaphysics of virtual reality. (New York: Oxford University Press)

—— 2012. Cyberspace. Retrieved from http://www.mheim.com/wp-content/uploads/2014/05/Cyberspace.e0147-revised-2012-copy.pdf

Henrikson, R., Araujo, B., Chevalier, F., Singh, K., & Balakrishnan, R. 2016. 'Multi-Device Storyboards for Cinematic Narratives in VR', *Proceedings of the 29th Annual Symposium on User Interface Software and Technology,* UIST '16. doi:10.1145/2984511.2984539

Herman, D., Jahn, M., & Ryan, M. 2008. *Routledge encyclopedia of narrative theory.* (London: Routledge)

Hickson, S., Dufour, N., Sud, A., Kwatra, V., & Essa, I. 2017. *Eyemotion: Classifying facial expressions in VR using eye-tracking cameras,* arXiv preprint arXiv:1707.07204. https://arxiv.org/abs/1707.07204

Hiwiller, Zack. 2016. *Players making decisions: Game design essentials and the art of understanding your players* (New York: New Riders)

Hoffman, D. D., Singh, M., & Prakash, C. 2015. 'The Interface Theory of Perception', *Psychonomic Bulletin & Review, 22*(6): 1480-1506. doi:10.3758/s13423-015-0890-8

Holton, Richard. 2006. 'The act of choice', in *Philosophers' Imprint 6:* p.1-15.

Hopkins, Marcelle. 2017. Pioneering Virtual Reality and New Video Technologies in Journalism. Retrieved from https://www.nytimes.com/2017/10/18/technology/personaltech/virtual-reality-video.html

Hou, G., Dong, H., & Yang, Y. 2017. 'Developing a Virtual Reality Game User Experience Test Method Based on EEG Signals', *2017 5th International Conference on Enterprise Systems (ES).* doi:10.1109/es.2017.45

Howard, I. P., & Rogers, B. J. 1996. *Binocular Vision and Stereopsis.* (Oxford: Oxford University Press)

Hoyos, V. G., & Vargas, G. G. 1996. La Teoría de la Acción Comunicativa. p. 47-64

Hühn, P., Schmid, W., & Schönert, J. 2009. *Point of view, perspective, and focalization: Modeling mediation in narrative* (Berlin: Walter de Gruyter)

Huhtamo, Erkki. 2013. *Illusions in motion: Media archaeology of the moving panorama and related spectacles* (Cambridge: The MIT Press)

——— 2014. Push the Button, Kinoautomat will do the rest! Media Archaeological Reflections on Audience Interactivity. In Kelomees, R., & Hales, C. (eds) *Expanding practices in audiovisual narrative* (Newcastle upon Tyne: Cambridge Scholars Publishing)

Huxley, Aldous. 1954. *The doors of perception and Heaven and hell* (New York: Harper & Row Publishers)

Iser, Wolfgang. 1997. *The act of reading: A theory of aesthetic response.* (Baltimore: Johns Hopkins University Press)

Issa, T., & Isaias, P. 2015. 'Usability and Human Computer Interaction (HCI)', *Sustainable Design*, pp. 19-36. doi:10.1007/978-1-4471-6753-2_2

Jenkins, H. 2004. Game design as narrative architecture, in *N. Wardrip-Fruin & P. Harrigan (Eds.), First Person: New Media as Story, Performance, and Game* (Cambridge: MIT Press), pp. 118-130)

Jiang, L., Stocco, A., Losey, D. M., Abernethy, J. A., Prat, C. S., & Rao, R. P. 2018. *BrainNet: A Multi-Person Brain-to-Brain Interface for Direct Collaboration Between Brains.* arXiv preprint arXiv:1809.08632.

Jost, F. 2004. "The Look: From Film to Novel: An Essay in Comparative Narratology." In *A Companion to Literature and Film* (Malden, MA: Blackwell), pp. 71-78.

Joyce, Michael. 2001. *Afternoon, a story* (Watertown: Eastgate Systems)

Kallmann, M., & Thalmann, D. 1999. 'Direct 3d interaction with smart objects', *In Proceedings of the ACM symposium on Virtual reality software and technology*, pp. 124-130. ACM.

Kamath, R. S., & Kamat, R. K. 2013. 'Development of an Intelligent Virtual Environment for Augmenting Natural Language Processing in Virtual Reality Systems', *International Journal of Emerging Trends & Technology in Computer Science (IJETTCS), 2*: 198-203

Kamppari-Miller, Saara. 2017. *VR Paper Prototyping* – Prototypr. Retrieved from https://blog.prototypr.io/vr-paper-prototyping-9e1cab6a75f3

Kelomees, R., & Hales, C. 2014. *Expanding practices in audiovisual narrative* (Newcastle upon Tyne: Cambridge Scholars Publishing)

Kennedy, R. S., Lane, N. E., Berbaum, K. S., & Lilienthal, M. G. 1993. 'Simulator Sickness Questionnaire: An Enhanced Method for Quantifying Simulator Sickness', *The International Journal of Aviation Psychology*, 3(39: 203-220. doi:10.1207/s15327108ijap0303_3

Kerckhove, D. D., & Dewdney, C. 1995. *The skin of culture: Investigating the new electronic reality* (Toronto: Somerville House Publishing)

Kjær, T., Lillelund, C. B., Moth-Poulsen, M., Nilsson, N. C., Nordahl, R., & Serafin, S. 2017. 'Can you cut it?', *Proceedings of the 23rd ACM Symposium on Virtual Reality Software and Technology, VRST '17.* doi:10.1145/3139131.3139166

Knoller, Noam. 2012. 'The Expressive Space of IDS-as-Art', *Lecture Notes in Computer Science*, 7648: 30–41. https://doi.org/10.1007/978-3-642-34851-8_3

Knoller N., Ben Arie U. 2009. 'Turbulence – A User Study of a Hypernarrative Interactive Movie', in *Iurgel I.A., Zagalo N., Petta P. (eds) Interactive Storytelling. ICIDS 2009. Lecture Notes in Computer Science*, 5915. (Berlin: Springer)

Koenderink, Jan. 2014. 'The All Seeing Eye?', *Perception, 43*(1): 1-6. doi:10.1068/p4301ed

Koenitz, H.: Understanding Interactive Digital Narrative: Immersive Expressions for a Complex Time. Routledge, London and New York (2023). https://doi.org/10.4324/9781003106425.

Koenitz, Hartmut (2010). 'Towards a Theoretical Framework for Interactive Digital Narrative', *Interactive Storytelling Lecture Notes in Computer Science*, 6432: 176-185. doi:10.1007/978-3-642-16638-9_22

—— 2014. 'An Iterative Approach towards Interactive Digital Narrative – Early Results with the Advanced Stories Authoring and Presentation System', *Lecture Notes in Computer Science New Horizons in Web Based Learning*, 7697: 59-68. doi:10.1007/978-3-662-43454-3_7

—— 2016. *Interactive Storytelling Paradigms and Representations: A Humanities-Based Perspective*. In Nakatsu, R et al. (eds.) Handbook of Digital Games and Entertainment. (Singapore: Springer)

—— 2016. 'Design Strategies for Interactive Digital Narratives. Proceedings of the *ACM' International Conference on Interactive Experiences for TV and Online Video, TVX '16*. doi:10.1145/2932206.2932428

—— 2018). 'Narrative in Video Games', *Encyclopedia of Computer Graphics and Games*, pp. 1-9. doi:10.1007/978-3-319-08234-9_154-1

—— 2018. 'Thoughts on a Discipline for the Study of Interactive Digital Narratives', *Interactive Storytelling Lecture Notes in Computer Science*, 11318: 36-49. doi:10.1007/978-3-030-04028-4_3

Koenitz, H., Ferri, G., Haahr, M., Sezen, D., & Sezen, T. İ. 2015. *Interactive digital narrative history, theory and practice* (London: Routledge, Taylor & Francis Group)

Koenitz, H., Haahr, M., Ferri, G., & Sezen, T. I. 2013. 'First Steps towards a Unified Theory for Interactive Digital Narrative', *Transactions on Edutainment X Lecture Notes in Computer Science*, 7775: 20-35. doi:10.1007/978-3-642-37919-2_2

Krishna, Golden. 2015. *The best interface is no interface: The simple path to brilliant technology* (New York: New Riders)

Kurosawa, Akira. 1983. *Something like an autobiography* (New York: Vintage Books)

Laarni, J., Ravaja, N., Saari, T., Böcking, S., Hartmann, T., & Schramm, H. 2015. 'Ways to Measure Spatial Presence: Review and Future Directions', *Immersed in Media*, pp. 139-185. doi:10.1007/978-3-319-10190-3_8

Landow, George. 1994. *Hyper - Text - Theory.* (Baltimore: Johns Hopkins University Press)

Lanier, Jaron. 2018. *How we need to remake the internet.* Ted Talk 2018. Retrieved April 14, 2018 from Jaron Lanier: How we need to remake the internet | TED Talk

Lavalle, S. M., Yershova, A., Katsev, M., & Antonov, M. 2014. 'Head tracking for the Oculus Rift', *2014 IEEE International Conference on Robotics and Automation (ICRA).* doi:10.1109/icra.2014.6906608

Lecuyer, A., Lotte, F., Reilly, R., Leeb, R., Hirose, M., & Slater, M. 2008. 'Brain-Computer Interfaces, Virtual Reality, and Videogames', *Computer,* 41(10): 66-72. doi:10.1109/mc.2008.410

Lee, S., Ha, G., Cha, J., Kim, J., Lee, H., & Kim, S. 2015. 'CyberTouch - Touch and Cursor Interface for VR HMD', *Communications in Computer and Information Science HCI International 2015 - Posters' Extended Abstracts,* 528: 503-507. doi:10.1007/978-3-319-21380-4_85

Legrand, Dorothee. 2007. 'Pre-reflective self-consciousness: On being bodily in the world', *Janus Head,* 9: 493-519. https://doi.org/10.5840/jh20069214

Lele, Ajey. 2013. 'Virtual reality and its military utility', *Journal of Ambient Intelligence and Humanized Computing,* 4(1): 17-26.

Lessiter, J., Freeman, J., Keogh, E., & Davidoff, J. 2001. 'A Cross-Media Presence Questionnaire: The ITC-Sense of Presence Inventory', *Presence: Teleoperators and Virtual Environments,* 10(3): 282-297. doi:10.1162/105474601300343612

Lewis, B. Roland. 1918. *The Technique of the One-act Play: A Study in Dramatic Construction* (Boston: JW Luce and Company)

Lin, J., Duh, H., Parker, D., Abi-Rached, H., & Furness, T. 2002. 'Effects of field of view on presence, enjoyment, memory, and simulator sickness in a virtual environment', *Proceedings IEEE Virtual Reality 2002,* 6(4) doi:10.1109/vr.2002.996519

Lin, Y., Chang, Y., Hu, H., Cheng, H., Huang, C., & Sun, M. 2017. 'Tell Me Where to Look', *Proceedings of the 2017 CHI Conference on Human Factors in Computing Systems,* CHI '17. doi:10.1145/3025453.3025757

Livingstone, Sonia. 1998. 'Relationships between media and audiences: Prospects for future audience reception studies', in Liebes, T., and Curran, J. (Eds.), Media, *Ritual and Identity: Essays in Honor of Elihu Katz.* (London: Routledge)

—— 2013. 'The Participation Paradigm in Audience Research', *The Communication Review,* 16(1-2): 21-30. doi:10.1080/10714421.2013.757174

Lok, B. & Hodges, L. 2004. 'Human Computer Interaction in Virtual Reality', in Ross, M. (Ed) *Encyclopedia of Human Computer Interaction.* (Barrington, MA: Berkshire)

Lombardi, M., Biocca, F., Freeman, J., IJsselsteijn, W. A., & Schaevitz, R. J. 2015. Immersed in media: Telepresence theory, measurement & technology (Luxembourg: Springer)

Louchart, S., & Aylett, R. 2004. 'The emergent narrative theoretical investigation', In *the 2004 Conference on Narrative and Interactive Learning Environments*, pp. 21-28.

Löwe, T., Stengel, M., Förster, E., Grogorick, S., & Magnor, M. 2017. 'Gaze Visualization for Immersive Video', *Eye Tracking and Visualization Mathematics and Visualization*, pp. 57-71. doi:10.1007/978-3-319-47024-5_4

Lumet, Sidney. 1996. *Making Movies*. (New York: Vintage Books)

Mackey-Kallis, Susan. 2001. *The hero and the perennial journey home in American film*. (Philadelphia: University of Pennsylvania Press)

Magliano, J. P., & Zacks, J. M. 2011. 'The Impact of Continuity Editing in Narrative Film on Event Segmentation', *Cognitive Science*, 35(8): 1489-1517. doi:10.1111/j.1551-6709.2011. 01202.x

Manovich, Lev. 1999. *Database as a Symbolic Form*. Retrieved from http://manovich.net/index.php/projects/database-as-a-symbolic-form

—— 2009. *Il linguaggio dei nuovi media* (Milan: Olivares)

Martin, J., & Ostwalt, C. E. 2018. *Screening the Sacred Religion, Myth, and Ideology in Popular American Film* (London: Routledge)

Mason Stacey. 2013. 'On Games and Links: Extending the Vocabulary of Agency and Immersion in Interactive Narratives', in: Koenitz H., Sezen T.I., Ferri G., Haahr M., Sezen D., Çatak G. (eds) *Interactive Storytelling. ICIDS 2013. Lecture Notes in Computer Science, 8230.* doi:10.1007/978-3-319-02756-2_3

Mateer, John. 2017. 'Directing for Cinematic Virtual Reality: How the traditional film director's craft applies to immersive environments and notions of presence', *Journal of Media Practice*, 18(1): 14-25. doi:10.1080/14682753.2017.130583

McCurley, Vincent. 2016. Storyboarding in Virtual Reality – Virtual Reality Pop. Retrieved from https://virtualrealitypop.com/storyboarding-in-virtual-reality-67d3438a2fb1

McGlashan, S., & Axling, T. 1996. 'A speech interface to virtual environments', *In Proc., International Workshop on Speech and Computers*.

McKee, Robert. 2010. *Story: Contenuti, struttura, stile, principi della sceneggiatura e per l'arte di scrivere storie* (Omero.

McLuhan, Eric. 2008. 'Marshall McLuhan's Theory of Communication: The Yegg'. *Global Media Journal -- Canadian Edition*, 1(1): 25–43.

McLuhan, Marshall. 1964. *Understanding media: The extensions of man*. (London: Routledge & Kegan Paul)

Meister, Jan Christoph, and Jörg Schönert. 2009. 'The DNS of mediacy', *Point of View, Perspective, and Focalization: Modeling Mediation in Narrative*, pp. 11-40.

Meskin, Aaron. 2008. 'Authorship', In *The Routledge companion to philosophy and film*, pp. 12-28. (London: Routledge)

Metz, C., & Taylor, M. 2007. *Film language: A semiotics of the cinema* (Chicago: University: of Chicago Press)

Milgram, Paul & Kishino, Fumio. 1994. 'A Taxonomy of Mixed Reality Visual Displays', *IEICE Trans. Information Systems*, vol. E77-D, no. 12: 1321-1329.

Miller, T., & Stam, R. 1999. *The Blackwell companion to film theory* (Oxford: Blackwell)

Mirandola, G. P., & Bausi, F. 2003. *Discorso sulla dignità dell'uomo.* (Parma: Fondazione P. Bembo)

Mitry, Jean. 2000. *The aesthetics and psychology of the cinema* (Bloomington: Indiana University Press)

Moghadam, K. R., & Ragan, E. D. 2017. 'Towards understanding scene transition techniques in immersive 360 movies and cinematic experiences', *2017 IEEE Virtual Reality (VR)*. doi:10.1109/vr.2017.7892333

Montfort, Nick. 2005. *Twisty little passages: An approach to interactive fiction.* (Cambridge: MIT Press)

Moulthrop, Stuart. 1992. *Victory garden.* (Watertown: Eastgate Systems)

Murray, Janet. 1997. *Hamlet on the holodeck: The future of narrative in cyberspace.* (Cambridge: MIT Press)

Nelson, Theodor. H. 1987. *Literary machines: The report on, and of, Project Xanadu concerning word processing, electronic publishing, hypertext, thinkertoys, tomorrow's intellectual revolution, and certain other topics including knowledge, education and freedom.* (Chicago: Mindful Press)

Nielsen, J., Clemmensen, T., & Yssing, C. 2002. 'Getting access to what goes on in people's heads?', *Proceedings of the Second Nordic Conference on Human-computer Interaction*, NordiCHI '02. doi:10.1145/572020.572033

Nielsen, L. T., Møller, M. B., Hartmeyer, S. D., Ljung, T. C., Nilsson, N. C., Nordahl, R., & Serafin, S. 2016. 'Missing the point', *Proceedings of the 22nd ACM Conference on Virtual Reality Software and Technology, VRST '16.* doi:10.1145/2993369.2993405

Nijholt, A., & Nam, C. S. 2015. Arts and Brain-Computer Interfaces (BCIs). *Brain-Computer Interfaces, 2(2-3)*, 57-59. doi:10.1080/232626 3x.2015.1100514

Nite, SKY. 2015. *Virtual reality insider: Guidebook for the VR industry* [Kindle Version] (Berkeley: :New Dimension Entertainment)

Oculus Connect 3 Opening Keynote. 2017. *YouTube*. Retrieved 18 April 2017, from https://www.youtube.com/watch?v=hgzohFokkVw

Oettermann, Stephan. 1997. *The panorama: History of a mass medium* (New York: Zone Books)

Oliver, M. B., & Raney, A. A. 2011. 'Entertainment as Pleasurable and Meaningful: Identifying Hedonic and Eudaimonic Motivations for Entertainment Consumption', *Journal of Communication, 61*(5): 984-1004. doi:10.1111/j.1460-2466.2011. 01585.x

Oliver, M. B., Ash, E., Woolley, J. K., Shade, D. D., & Kim, K. 2014. 'Entertainment We Watch and Entertainment We Appreciate: Patterns of

Motion Picture Consumption and Acclaim Over Three Decades' *Mass Communication and Society*, 17(6): 853-873. doi:10.1080/15205436.2013. 872277

Oliver, M. B., Bowman, N. D., Woolley, J. K., Rogers, R., Sherrick, B. I., & Chung, M. 2016. 'Video games as meaningful entertainment experiences', *Psychology of Popular Media Culture*, 5(4): 390-405. doi:10.1037/ ppm0000066

Olmedo, H., Escudero, D., & Cardeñoso, V. 2015. 'Multimodal interaction with virtual worlds XMMVR: eXtensible language for MultiModal interaction with virtual reality worlds', *Journal on Multimodal User Interfaces*, 9(3): 153-172.

Paez, S., & Jew, A. 2013. *Professional storyboarding: Rules of thumb* (Waltham: Focal Press)

Panetta, Kasey. 2018. 5 *Trends Emerge in the Gartner Hype Cycle for Emerging Technologies*, 2018. Gartner.com. Retrieved 29 December 2018, from https://www.gartner.com/smarterwithgartner/5-trends-emerge-in-gartner-hype-cycle-for-emerging-technologies-2018/

Phelan, J., & Rabinowitz, P. J. 2008. *A companion to narrative theory*. (Hoboken: Blackwell Publishing)

Piaget, Jean. 1997. *The language and thought of the child*. (London: Routledge)

Porteous, J., Teutenberg, J., Charles, F. & Cavazza, M. 2011. 'Controlling Narrative Time in Interactive Storytelling', *Proceedings of the 10th International Conference on Autonomous Agents and Multiagent Systems (AAMAS)*, pp. 449-456

Price, William. 1908. *The analysis of play construction and dramatic principle*. (New York: WT Price)

Propp, Vladimir. 2003. *Morfologia della fiaba; Le radici storiche dei racconti di magia*. (Rome: Grandi tascabili economici Newton Compton)

Ramchurn, R., Wilson, M., Martindale, S., & Benford, S. 2018. '#Scanners 2 - The MOMENT', *Extended Abstracts Of The 2018 CHI Conference On Human Factors In Computing Systems, CHI '18*. doi:10.1145/3170427.3186481

Reed, Aaron. 2012. *Creating interactive fiction with Inform 7* (Boston: Course Technology)

Renard, Y., Lotte, F., Gibert, G., Congedo, M., Maby, E., Delannoy, V., Lécuyer, A. 2010. 'OpenViBE: An Open-Source Software Platform to Design, Test, and Use Brain–Computer Interfaces in Real and Virtual Environments', *Presence: Teleoperators and Virtual Environments*, 19(1): 35-53. doi:10.1162/pres.19.1.35

Rettberg, Scott. 2017. 'The American Hypertext Novel, and Whatever Became of It?', In Koenitz, H.(ed) *Interactive digital narrative: History, theory and practice*. (London: Routledge)

Reyes, María. (2022). 'From screenwriting to space-writing'. *DISEGNO: A DESIGNKULTÚRA FOLYÓIRATA*, 6(1): 86-103.

—— 2017. 'Screenwriting Framework for an Interactive Virtual Reality Film'. Paper presented at the 3rd Immersive Research Network Conference iLRN. http://castor.tugraz.at/doku/iLRN2017/iLRN2017OnlineProceedings.pdf

Ridout, S. J., Spofford, C. M., Wout-Frank, M. V., Philip, N. S., Unger, W. S., Carpenter, L. L., & Shea, M. T. 2017. 'Heart Rate Variability Responses to a Standardized Virtual Reality Exposure in Veterans with PTSD', *Current Treatment Options in Psychiatry,* 4(3): 271-280. doi:10.1007/s40501-017-0118-9

Riedl, M. O., & Bulitko, V. 2012. 'Interactive Narrative: An Intelligent Systems Approach', AI Magazine, 34(1): 67. doi:10.1609/aimag.v34i1.2449

Riegler, A., Peschl, M., & Stein, A. 2000. *Understanding Representation in the Cognitive Sciences: Does Representation Need Reality?* (Boston: Springer US)

Rizzo, A., Morie, J. F., Williams, J., Pair, J., & Buckwalter, J. G. 2005. *Human emotional state and its relevance for military VR training.* (California: University of Southern California Marina Del Rey Ca Inst for Creative Technologies)

Rogers, Everett M. 2010. *Diffusion of innovations.* (New York: Simon and Schuster)

Ron-Angevin, R., & Díaz-Estrella, A. 2009. 'Brain–computer interface: Changes in performance using virtual reality techniques', *Neuroscience Letters,* 449(2): 123-127. doi:10.1016/j.neulet.2008.10.099

Roncallo-Dow, Sergio. 2014. 'Marshall McLuhan. El medio (aún) es el mensaje 50 años después de comprender los medios'. *Palabra Clave - Revista de Comunicación,* 17(3): 582–588. https://doi.org/10.5294/pacla.2014.17.3.1

Rooij, M. V., Lobel, A., Harris, O., Smit, N., & Granic, I. 2016. 'Deep', *18szszof the 2016 CHI Conference Extended Abstracts on Human Factors in Computing Systems,* CHI EA '16. doi:10.1145/2851581.2892452

Roth, C., & Koenitz, H. 2016. 'Evaluating the User Experience of Interactive Digital Narrative', Proceedings *of the 1st International Workshop on Multimedia Alternate Realities,* AltMM '16. doi:10.1145/2983298.2983302

Rothbaum, B. O., Hodges, L. F., Ready, D., Graap, K., & Alarcon, R. D. 2001. 'Virtual reality exposure therapy for Vietnam veterans with posttraumatic stress disorder', *The Journal of clinical psychiatry,* 62(8): 617-22

Rothe, S., & Hußmann, H. 2018. 'Guiding the Viewer in Cinematic Virtual Reality by Diegetic Cues', *Lecture Notes in Computer Science Augmented Reality, Virtual Reality, and Computer Graphics,* pp. 101-117. doi:10.1007/978-3-319-95270-3_7

Rothe, S., Hußmann, H., & Allary, M. 2017. 'Diegetic cues for guiding the viewer in cinematic virtual reality', *Proceedings of the 23rd ACM Symposium on Virtual Reality Software and Technology,* VRST '17. doi:10.1145/3139131.3143421

Rouse, Rebecca. 2016. Media of Attraction: A Media Archeology Approach to Panoramas, Kinematography, Mixed Reality and Beyond, In: *9th International Conference on Interactive Digital Storytelling, ICIDS 2016,* pp.97-107

Ruthrof, Horst. 1997. *Semantics and the Body: Meaning from Frege to the Postmodern* (Toronto: University of Toronto Press)

Ryan, Marie. 1999. 'Immersion vs. Interactivity: Virtual Reality and Literary Theory', *SubStance* 28(2): 110-137. (Baltimore: Johns Hopkins University Press) Retrieved April 16, 2018, from Project MUSE database

Ryan, M. (2009). From Narrative Games to Playable Stories: Toward a Poetics of Interactive Narrative. Storyworlds: A Journal of Narrative Studies 1(1), 43-59. University of Nebraska Press. Retrieved April 17, 2017, from Project MUSE database.

—— 2013a. Possible Worlds | the living handbook of narratology. Lhn.uni-hamburg.de. Retrieved 31 July 2018, from http://www.lhn.uni-hamburg.de/article/possible-worlds

—— 2014. Story/Worlds/Media: Tuning the Instruments of a Media- Conscious Narratology. In Ryan, M., & Thon, J. Storyworlds across media: Toward a media-conscious narratology. (Lincoln: University of Nebraska Press)

—— 2015a. *Narrative as virtual reality 2: Revisiting immersion and interactivity in literature and electronic media.* (Baltimore: Johns Hopkins University Press)

—— 2011. Fiction, Cognition, and Non-Verbal Media. In Grishakova, M. & Ryan, M (eds) *Intermediality and Storytelling.* (Berlin: De Gruyter, series Narratologia)

—— 2013b. Impossible Worlds and Aesthetic Illusion. In Bernhard, W. & Wofl, W. (eds) *Aesthetic Illusion in Literature and Other Media.* (Amsterdam/New York: Rodopi), pp. 131-48.

—— 2015b. *Narrative as virtual reality 2: Revisiting immersion and interactivity in literature and electronic media.* (Baltimore: John Hopkins University)

—— 2014. *Story/Worlds/Media: Tuning the Instruments of a Media- Conscious Narratology.* In

Ryan, M., & Thon, J. Storyworlds across media: Toward a media-conscious narratology. (Lincoln: University of Nebraska Press)

Ryan, M., & Thon, J. 2014. *Storyworlds across media: Toward a media-conscious narratology* (Omaha: University of Nebraska Press)

Ryan, Marie-Laure. 1991. *Possible Worlds, Artificial Intelligence, and Narrative Theory.* (Bloomington: Indiana University Press)

Sassatelli, L., Pinna-Déry, A., Winckler, M., Dambra, S., Samela, G., Pighetti, R., & Aparicio-Pardo, R. 2018. Snap-changes. *Proceedings of the 2018 International Conference on Advanced Visual Interfaces,* AVI '18. doi:10.1145/3206505.3206553

Schank, Roger. 2000. *Tell me a story: Narrative and intelligence* (Evanston-Northwestern University Press)

Schlickers in Hühn, P., Schmid, W., & Schönert, J. 2009. *Point of view, perspective, and focalization: Modeling mediation in narrative* (Berlin: Walter de Gruyter)

Schoenau-Fog, Hentik. 2014. 'At the Core of Player Experience: Continuation Desire in Digital Games', *Handbook of Digital Games*, pp 388-410. doi:10.1002/9781118796443.ch14

―― 2015. 'Adaptive Storyworlds', in *Interactive Storytelling Lecture Notes in Computer Science*, 9445: 58-65. doi:10.1007/978-3-319-27036-4_6

Schreer, Oliver. 2005. *3D Video Communication: Algorithms, concepts and real-time systems in human centred communication.* Wiley.

Schroeder, R. 1994. 'Cyberculture, cyborg post-modernism and the sociology of virtual reality technologies', *Futures*, 26(5): 519-528. doi:10.1016/0016-3287(94)90133-3

Sheikh, A., Brown, A., Evans, M., & Watson, Z. 2016. 'Directing attention in 360-degree video', *IBC 2016 Conference.* doi:10.1049/ibc.2016.0029

Singer, M.J. & Witmer, B.G. 1998. 'Measuring Presence in Virtual Environments: A Presence Questionnaire', *In Presence: Teleoperators and Virtual Environments*, 7(3): 225-240

Skakov, Nariman. 2013. *The cinema of Tarkovsky: Labyrinths of space and time* (London: I. B. Tauris)

Spierling, U., Grasbon, D., Braun, N., & Iurgel, I. 2002, 02. 'Setting the scene: Playing digital director in interactive storytelling and creation', *Computers & Graphics*, 26(1): 31-44. doi:10.1016/s0097-8493(01)00176-5

Sra, Misha, Xuhai Xu, and Pattie Maes. 2018. 'Breathvr: Leveraging breathing as a directly controlled interface for virtual reality games', *Proceedings of the 2018 CIII Conference on Human Factors in Computing Systems*

Strate, Lance. 2008. 'Studying Media as Media: McLuhan and the media ecology approach', *Media Tropes*, 1(1): 127-142

Sutcliffe, A. G., Poullis, C., Gregoriades, A., Katsouri, I., Tzanavari, A., & Herakleous, K. 2018, 03. 'Reflecting on the Design Process for Virtual Reality Applications', *International Journal of Human–Computer Interaction*, 35(2): 168-179. doi:10.1080/10447318.2018.1443898

Syrett, H., Calvi, L., & Gisbergen, M. V. 2016. 'The Oculus Rift Film Experience: A Case Study on Understanding Films in a Head Mounted Display', *Lecture Notes of the Institute for Computer Sciences, Social Informatics and Telecommunications Engineering Intelligent Technologies for Interactive Entertainment*, pp. 197-208. doi:10.1007/978-3-319-49616-0_19

Szilas, Nicolas. 1999. 'Interactive drama on computer: beyond linear narrative', *In AAAI Fall symposium on narrative intelligence*, 144: 150-156

—— 2002. 'Structural models for interactive drama', In *2nd Conference on Computational Semiotics for Games and New Media 02–04 September 2002 Universität Augsburg*, p. 22

Tarkovski, A., & Hunter-Blair, K. 1987. *Sculpting In Time Reflections on the Cinema*. (Austin: University of Texas Press)

Tatarkiewicz, W., & Jaworska, K. 1993. *Storia di sei idee: L'arte il bello la forma la creatività l'imitazione l'esperienza estetica* (Palermo: Aesthetica edizioni)

The Raycast. 2018. *Interaction in VR - Unity*. Retrieved September 17, 2018, from https://unity3d.com/learn/tutorials/topics/virtual-reality/interaction-vr

Tieri, G., Gioia, A., Scandola, M., Pavone, E. F., & Aglioti, S. M. 2017. 'Visual appearance of a virtual upper limb modulates the temperature of the real hand: A thermal imaging study in Immersive Virtual Reality', *European Journal of Neuroscience, 45*(9): 1141-1151. doi:10.1111/ejn.13545

Tikka, Pia. 2008. *Enactive cinema: Simulatorium Eisensteinense* (Helsinki: University of Art and Design Helsinki)

Tornitore, Tonino. 2013. *Della Narratologia* [Versione per Kindle] (Genova: Genova University Press)

Tricart, C., & Mendiburu, B. 2017. *Virtual Reality Filmmaking Techniques & Best Practices for VR Filmmakers* (Abingdon-on- Thames: Taylor and Francis)

van't Wout, M., Spofford, C. M., Unger, W. S., Sevin, E. B., & Shea, M. T. 2017. 'Skin conductance reactivity to standardized virtual reality combat scenes in veterans with PTSD', *Applied psychophysiology and biofeedback, 42*(3): 209-221.

Vertov, Dziga. 2004 *Lines of Resistance: Dziga Vertov and the Twenties*. Edited by Yuri Tsivian, translated by Julian Graffy. (Pordenone: La Giornate del Cinema Muto) p. 318-9

Vidali, Paolo. 1998. 'Esperienze e comunicazione nei nuovi media', in G. Bettetini, F. Colombo, *Le nuove tecnologie della comunicazione*. (Milan: Bompiani). p 306

Virtual reality: Lessons from the past for Oculus Rift - BBC News. 2013. BBC News. Retrieved from http://www.bbc.com/news/technology-2387769

Vogler, Christopher. 2008. *The writer's journey: Mythic structure for storytellers and screenwriter's* (Studio City: Michael Wiese Productions)

Vosmeer, M. & Schouten, B. 2017. 'Project Orpheus A Research Study into 360° Cinematic VR', In *Proceedings of the 2017 ACM International Conference on Interactive Experiences for TV and Online Video*, TVX '17. doi:10.1145/3077548.3077559

Vosmeer, M., & Schouten, B. 2014. 'Interactive Cinema: Engagement and Interaction', *Interactive Storytelling Lecture Notes in Computer Science*, 8832: 140-147. doi:10.1007/978-3-319-12337-0_14

Vosmeer, M., Roth, C., & Koenitz, H. 2017. 'Who Are You? Voice-Over Perspective in Surround Video', *Interactive Storytelling Lecture Notes in Computer Science*, 10690: 221-232. doi:10.1007/978-3-319-71027-3_18

Vredenburg, K., Isensee, S., & Righi, C. 2002. *User-centered design: An integrated approach* (Upper Saddle River: Prentice Hall PTR)

Wardrip-Fruin, N., & Montfort, N. 2003. *The new media reader* (Cambridge: MIT Press)

Weerdmeester, J., Rooij, M. V., Harris, O., Smit, N., Engels, R. C., & Granic, I. 2017. 'Exploring the Role of Self-efficacy in Biofeedback Video Games', *Extended Abstracts Publication of the Annual Symposium on Computer-Human Interaction in Play*, CHI PLAY '17 *Extended Abstracts*. doi:10.1145/3130859.3131299

Wolf, Werner. 2011. 'Narratology and Media(lity): The Transmedial Expansion of a Literary Discipline and Possible Consequences', *Current Trends in Narratology*, pp. 145-180 doi:10.1515/9783110255003.145

—— 2009. 'Illusion (aesthetic)', *Handbook of narratology*, pp. 144-160.

Wyrwoll Claudia. 2014. *User-Generated Content. In: Social Media*. Springer Vieweg (Wiesbaden: Springer Vieweg)

Xavier, Ismail. 2007. 'Historical Allegories', in Miller, T. *A companion to film theory* (Hoboken: Blackwell), p. 45 – 63

Zillmann, D., and Jennings, B. 2013. *Selective exposure to communication.* (London: Routledge)

Zhang, T., Tian, F., Hou, X., Xie, Q., & Yi, F. 2018. 'Evaluating the Effect of Transitions on the Viewing Experience for VR Video', In *2018 International Conference on Audio, Language and Image Processing (ICALIP)*, pp. 273-277. IEEE.

Zhao, W., & Madhavan, V. 2005. 'Integration of voice commands into a virtual reality environment for assembly design', In *Proceedings of the 10th Annual International Conference on Industrial Engineering Theory, Applications & Practice*.

MIMESIS GROUP
www.mimesis-group.com

MIMESIS INTERNATIONAL
www.mimesisinternational.com
info@mimesisinternational.com

MIMESIS EDIZIONI
www.mimesisedizioni.it
mimesis@mimesisedizioni.it

ÉDITIONS MIMÉSIS
www.editionsmimesis.fr
info@editionsmimesis.fr

MIMESIS COMMUNICATION
www.mim-c.net

MIMESIS EU
www.mim-eu.com

Printed by
Rotomail Italia S.p.A.
December 2023

www.ingramcontent.com/pod-product-compliance
Lightning Source LLC
LaVergne TN
LVHW032255060326
832902LV00024B/4599